D0765765

CHRONICLE OF THE

QUEENS
OF
EGYPT

Joyce Tyldesley

CHRONICLE OF THE
QUEENS
OF
EGYPT

FROM EARLY DYNASTIC TIMES
TO THE DEATH OF CLEOPATRA

with 273 illustrations, 173 in color

Thames & Hudson

CONTENTS

pages 6–7
Preface

pages 8–23
Introduction:
Royal Consorts and Female Kings

DYNASTIES 0–2   pages 24–35

THE FIRST QUEENS
The Early Dynastic Period
3100–2650 BC

Meritneith proves a woman capable of taking power

Special Features
The Women of Abydos • The Goddess Neith

DYNASTIES 3–8   pages 36–63

QUEENS OF THE PYRAMID AGE
The Old Kingdom
2650–2125 BC

From Hetepheres' tomb treasures to Khamerernebty and Khentkawes,
wives of the great pyramid builders

Special Features
Personal Hygiene • Fit for a Queen: The Treasures of Hetepheres I •
The Vulture Headdress and Uraeus

DYNASTIES 9–17   pages 64–85

CHAOS AND REBIRTH
The First Intermediate Period, Middle Kingdom and
Second Intermediate Period
2125–1539 BC

Two dominant dynasties emerge: Herakleopolis and Thebes;
Prosperity returns and a female pharaoh reigns: Sobeknefru;
Invasion of the Hyksos: Asiatic rule from Avaris in the Delta

Special Features
Wigs and Hairdressing • Women's Health and Childbirth •
The Lahun and Dahshur Treasures • Women in Literature •
The Double-Plumed Headdress

(Half-title) Found in western Thebes, this armlet in the form of a vulture is thought to have belonged to Queen Ahhotep I, mother of the New Kingdom king Ahmose.

(Frontispiece) 'The White Queen'. Meritamun, daughter and wife of Ramesses II. Found in the Ramesseum, this piece is now in Cairo Museum.

© 2006 Thames & Hudson Ltd, London

Text © 2006 Joyce Tyldesley

All Rights Reserved. No part of this publication may be reproduced or transmitted in any form or by any means, electronic or mechanical, including photocopy, recording or any other information storage and retrieval system, without prior permission in writing from the publisher.

First published in 2006 in hardcover in the United States of America by Thames & Hudson Inc., 500 Fifth Avenue, New York, New York 10110

thamesandhudsonusa.com

Library of Congress Catalog Card Number 2005911288

ISBN-13: 978-0-500-05145-0
ISBN-10: 0-500-05145-3

Printed and bound in China by Everbest Printing Co Ltd

Khamerernebty II

Nefret

Meritamun

Cleopatra VII

PREFACE

This book sets out to explore the developing role of the queen of Egypt from Predynastic times until the death of Cleopatra VII in 30 BC. It draws upon a combination of archaeological and textual evidence to tell a fascinating story: a story of political and religious power, of bloody battles, eternal beauty, divinity and death. And it encompasses a wide range of women – queen consorts, queen mothers, shadowy harem queens, and the few queens who managed to overcome centuries of tradition and prejudice to rule their land as female kings. But, when we strip away the glamour and the personalities, is this a story worth telling? Can it ever be valid to tell a 'women's history', focusing on just one aspect of a mechanism as complicated as the Egyptian royal family?

I firmly believe that it can. Egyptologists have always understood that the king or pharaoh, the living link between the mortal and the divine, was considered vital to the survival of Egypt. Now there is increasing evidence to confirm that the consort, as the feminine element of the semi-divine monarchy, was vital to the survival of the king. No king ever ruled Egypt unmarried. Just as Egypt would always need a king, so that king would always need a wife by his side. And, like all of Egypt's women, that queen had to be able to support her husband whenever and however necessary. By learning more about the religious and political duties assigned to the queen consort we can gain an increased understanding not only of Egyptian ideas of kingship, but of the subtleties and complexities of dynastic history, dynastic religion and, indeed, dynastic life. Although there have been some excellent books published on particular aspects of queenship – most notably Lana Troy's groundbreaking *Patterns of Queenship in Ancient Egyptian Myth and History* – plus many books published about individual queens, there has until now been no volume dedicated to the wider aspects of Egyptian queenship. This book aims to fill that gap; I hope that it will appeal to anyone, from student to general reader, with an interest in ancient Egypt.

The book is divided into two sections. As it would be impossible to discuss the queens of Egypt without some understanding of the role of women in the wider community the first section, the introduction, begins with a consideration of the rights and responsibilities of the wife and mother in the traditional dynastic family, then proceeds to examine the specific example of the royal family. The king's role is explored in some detail, as the queen's relationship with her husband and/or son defined her status. Finally the introduction considers the vital question of how we define a queen of Egypt.

The second part of the book documents the lives of individual queens on a dynasty-by-dynasty basis and follows the development of their increasingly complex titles, regalia and funerary provisions. This is not an unbroken history; as the chronological tables clearly demonstrate, there are gaps in our knowledge, particularly during the earlier dynasties. Nor is it an even history. Some queens are well represented while others, who may have been equally important, are known by name only. Nevertheless, it is an absorbing story.

Yellow jasper fragment of a head of an Amarna-period queen, which has been identified as both Tiy (consort of Amenhotep III) and Nefertiti (consort of Akhenaten). The provenance of the piece is unknown, although it is likely to have come from Amarna. Metropolitan Museum of Art, New York.

Nefertari, wife of Ramesses II, illustrates the increasingly complex role of the queen consort as she appears on the façade of the Lesser Temple of Abu Simbel bearing the regalia of the goddess Hathor. Nefertari is perhaps the best example of a queen whose name and image are today well known, but whose life remains a tantalizing blank.

The better documented of Egypt's queens have been provided with datafiles summarizing the most important aspects of their lives. The majority of the queens have also been provided with names written in hieroglyphs or cartouches generously made available by Wolfram Grajetzki, whose *Ancient Egyptian Queens: a Hieroglyphic Dictionary* (2005) has proved an invaluable research tool for those interested in royal names and titles. Where a name or cartouche is missing it is because it is not known from hieroglyphic inscriptions.

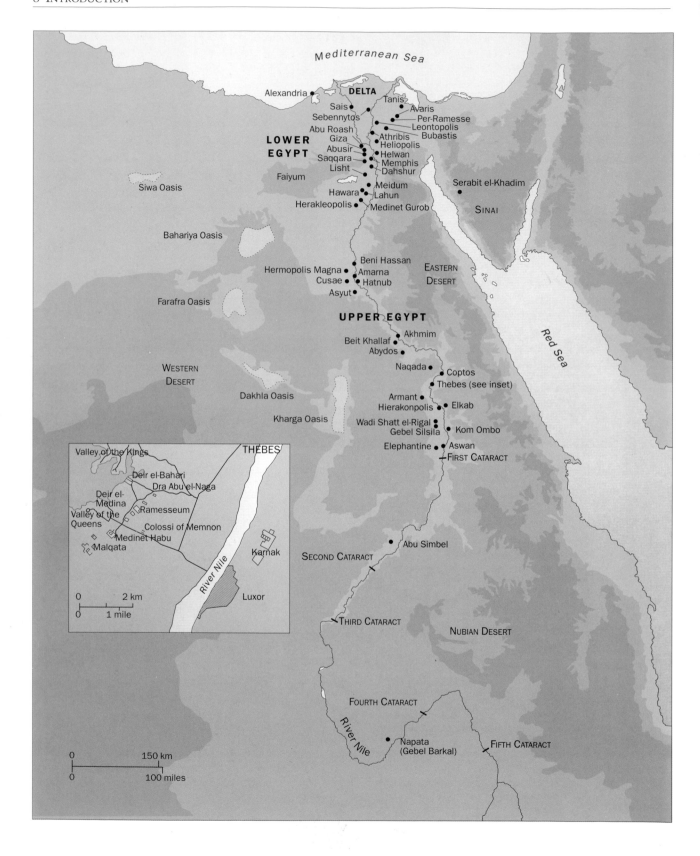

Mediterranean Sea

DELTA

Alexandria

LOWER
EGYPT

Sais
Sebennytos
Abu Roash
Giza
Abusir
Saqqara
Lisht

Tanis
Avaris
Per-Ramesse
Leontopolis
Bubastis
Athribis
Heliopolis
Helwan
Memphis
Dahshur

Siwa Oasis

Faiyum

Hawara
Herakleopolis

Meidum
Lahun
Medinet Gurob

Serabit el-Khadim

SINAI

Bahariya Oasis

Beni Hassan
Hermopolis Magna
Cusae
Asyut

Amarna
Hatnub

EASTERN
DESERT

Farafra Oasis

UPPER EGYPT

Red Sea

WESTERN
DESERT

Dakhla Oasis

Akhmim
Beit Khallaf
Abydos

Naqada
Coptos
Thebes (see inset)

Kharga Oasis

Armant
Hierakonpolis

Elkab

Wadi Shatt el-Rigal
Gebel Silsila

Kom Ombo

Elephantine
Aswan
FIRST CATARACT

THEBES

Valley of the Kings

Deir el-Bahari
Dra Abu el-Naga

Deir el-
Medina
Ramesseum
Valley of the
Queens
Colossi of Memnon
Medinet Habu
Malqata

Karnak

River Nile

Luxor

0   2 km
0   1 mile

SECOND CATARACT

Abu Simbel

THIRD CATARACT

NUBIAN DESERT

FOURTH CATARACT

River Nile

Napata
(Gebel Barkal)

FIFTH CATARACT

0   150 km
0   100 miles

INTRODUCTION: ROYAL CONSORTS AND FEMALE KINGS

When the jealous god Seth murdered his brother, King Osiris, he sealed his body into a lead-coated coffin and cast it into the river Nile. Seth had hoped that everyone would forget Osiris so that he might rule Egypt in his brother's place, but he had reckoned without the courage and determination of Osiris' sister-wife, Queen Isis. Isis sought out the coffin that still held the dead Osiris and brought it back to Egypt for burial. Later, when Seth had hacked his dead brother into many pieces, she transformed into a giant bird to search for his remains. Isis used her magical powers to bring the mutilated Osiris back to a semblance of life. Nine months later she gave birth to his son, Horus. As Osiris retreated to rule the land of the dead, Isis protected her son until he was old enough to claim his rightful crown.

The ancient story of Isis and Osiris is an important and informative myth. Not only does it explain the crucial relationship between the living king of Egypt (the Horus King) and his dead father (the Osiris King), it introduces us to Isis, the blueprint for the perfect Egyptian queen. Nowhere else do we get such a clear explanation of the queen's role. By analysing Isis' actions we can see that the ideal queen of Egypt is a wife capable of bearing the son who will one day take his father's place. In good times the queen will remain very much in the background, supporting her husband and attending to her domestic duties in an unobtrusive way. But, should bad times arise, she must be capable of independent action, of using her wits to deputize for her husband and protect her child. These are in fact the responsibilities and rights of all Egyptian wives; it is the semi-divine nature of her husband's position that sets the queen of Egypt apart from other women. And so, before we can understand the role of the queen, we need some understanding of the role of the Egyptian wife.

As the dynastic age progressed, Isis' role as the mother and protector of the infant king Horus grew in popularity. Art historians have speculated that images of Isis nursing Horus may have inspired the early Christian artists who depicted Mary with the infant Jesus in a similar fashion.

The 19th Dynasty craftsman Sennedjem and his wife Iyneferti expected to enjoy an afterlife that mirrored life in Egypt. Here on the walls of their Deir el-Medina tomb chapel we may see them working in the fertile fields. Sennedjem, as the tomb owner, takes the lead. Iyneferti follows behind, supporting her husband.

Family life

Egypt, blessed with a broad river and fertile green fields, was the wealthiest country in the ancient world. She had warehouses packed full of grain, abundant fish, fowl, game and livestock, and plentiful supplies of mud, stone and gold. While the Nile functioned correctly, flooding the fields once a year and bringing much-needed moisture to the sun-baked soil, no one need go hungry. Foreigners, condemned to till dry and stony ground, could only marvel at this good fortune, while the Egyptians themselves felt nothing but pity and contempt for those who lived outside their borders.

And yet, even in Egypt, things were far from perfect. Inexplicable illnesses, workplace accidents and the perils of childbirth combined to make life an uncertain, temporary affair. With no proper medical care, no real understanding of hygiene or the human body, illnesses as seemingly innocuous as toothache or diarrhoea could herald death. Those who survived childhood could expect to live for maybe 40 years; anything beyond this was a bonus.

The affluent – those whose sheltered lives allowed them to live longer than their poorer neighbours – had a moral duty to provide for the orphaned and the disadvantaged, but there was no official welfare programme guaranteed to protect the unfortunate, the feckless and the poor. In times of trouble the family provided the one and only reliable support mechanism, with children not only an insurance against a poverty-stricken old age, but a guarantee (if such things can ever be guaranteed) that dead parents would receive the correct funerary offerings for at least the immediate future.

Naturally, the family was considered an institution of immense importance. Everyone – commoner, king and god alike – was expected to marry. Girls were raised to be, first and foremost, good wives and mothers. A man without a wife was seen as immature and incomplete, and callow schoolboys were advised to wed early and father as many children as possible: 'Take a wife when you are still young, so that she may give you a son; she should bear for you while you are still young, it is good to make people,' argued the persuasive New Kingdom scribe Ani. Homosexuality must have existed, as it exists in all societies, but it was rarely mentioned.

The Old Kingdom dwarf Seneb, his wife, son and daughter. The children stand where, in a more conventional pairing, Seneb's legs would be. Seneb's children, less important than their parents, are naked. His wife and daughter are both pale, an artistic convention intended to stress the 'indoor' nature of women's lives. Cairo Museum.

In this respect, Egypt was not so very different from any other pre-industrial society. Marriage was a practical bond designed to create a viable economic unit; children were an investment, the blessings who would support their parents in old age. Destined to follow in their parents' footsteps, boys were trained in the trades and professions by their fathers and uncles, while girls stayed at home learning domestic skills. In their early teens they would marry – cousin-cousin and uncle-niece marriages being common – and the whole cycle would begin again.

Where Egypt did differ to a remarkable degree from other societies was in the rights allowed to her women, both married and single. In most ancient and many modern cultures including, until relatively recently, the 'advanced' western world, women were not considered to be full members of society. In Egypt, men and women of equivalent social status were treated as equals in the eyes of the law. This meant that women could own, buy, sell, earn and inherit property. They could live unprotected by male guardians and, if widowed or divorced, could care for their children alone. They could bring cases before, and be punished by, the law courts. And they could deputize for their husbands in matters of business. This freedom, this contradiction of what many societies have seen as the natural order, fascinated the classical tourists who visited Egypt towards the end of the dynastic age. Herodotus entertained his Greek readers with his description of this most unusual country:

...the people, in most of their manners and customs, exactly reverse the common practice of mankind. For example women attend the markets and trade, while the men sit at home at the loom.... The women carry burdens upon their shoulders while men carry them upon their heads. Women urinate standing up, men sitting down....[1]

We can only speculate why Egypt should have allowed her women such generous rights; indeed, the better question would surely be to ask why other societies felt it necessary to take the opposite approach. There is no obvious answer – it may simply be that in Egypt the sheer abundance of food, the lack of pressure on land and resources, and the strict social hierarchy that proclaimed the king ultimate owner of everything, made any restriction unnecessary.

Mistress of the house

It is hard for modern readers to gain any real understanding of the subtle nuances and practicalities of ancient Egyptian family life. However, it would certainly be naive to assume that their legal equality allowed married couples to lead identical or even similar lives. Husbands and wives had complementary but opposite roles, and this well-understood allocation of duties according to gender was made explicit in the artistic convention that, in marked contrast to Herodotus' observations, saw women depicted as white-skinned 'indoor' people, while men appeared as brown-skinned 'outdoor' workers. In dynastic Egyptian sculpture the

Women were free to work outside the home, although their domestic duties and lack of formal education restricted their employment opportunities. (*Opposite above*) Wooden model of male and female servants recovered from the Deir el-Bahari tomb of Meket-Re. Metropolitan Museum of Art. (*Opposite below*) Wooden model of a winged *djeryt*, one of the two women who, acting the part of the goddesses Isis and Nephthys, accompanied funeral processions to the tomb. Liverpool University Museum.

men almost invariably stride forward to meet the world, while their wives stand immobile and sheltered beside, and slightly behind, them.

In the perfect family the wife, the 'Mistress of the House', was responsible for all internal, domestic matters. She raised the children and ran the household. With this work done she was free, if she wished and had the time, to work outside the home either in a paid or voluntary capacity. Many poor women contributed to the family income either by working alongside their husbands, or by establishing their own small businesses, selling surpluses (bread, beer or food) to their neighbours. Many wealthy women, freed by their servants from the domestic tasks burdening their less fortunate sisters, 'worked' unpaid as priestesses, serving the gods through music, dance and song in the local temple. Meanwhile, Egypt's husbands, assuming responsibility for external matters, worked outside the house and officially liaised with the wider world. Married couples supported each other but, while the man, the dominant partner, played the more obvious wage-earning role, it was the woman who, in 3,000 years of dynastic sculpture, was consistently shown physically supporting her husband with an arm placed firmly around his waist or shoulder.

Childcare, cooking and cleaning are important duties, but they have little impact on the archaeological or written record. Consequently Egypt's women tend to be hidden behind the men whose prestigious appointments allowed their achievements to be preserved on papyrus and on stone tomb walls. This bias in the evidence is apparent even in the royal family where the king, in approving the wording of official texts and the subjects of formal artworks, effectively chooses how much or how little of the queen's role is revealed to us. It is made worse by the shortage of domestic sites that might have helped us to understand more of women's lives. The Egyptians built their towns and cities from mud-brick, reserving stone for the temples and tombs that they hoped would last for eternity. Over the centuries the mud-brick palaces and houses have crumbled away, flattened to form a base for later buildings or dissolved into a rich mud which, until relatively recently, was routinely spread over the fields as fertilizer. Only a few domestic sites have survived, either because they were built in atypical locations, or because they were built from stone. It is a curious irony that the humble houses of the remote New Kingdom workmen's village of Deir el-Medina have

survived more or less intact, while the contemporary mud-brick palaces – magnificent, extensive buildings which we know were plastered, painted and tiled so that they sparkled in the bright sunlight and dazzled those fortunate enough to see them – survive only as ground plans if they survive at all.

The royal family

The royal family was a family superficially like any other. The king dealt with external affairs while his wife, primarily occupied with domestic matters, supported him in his work wherever necessary. Their children were brought up to fulfil their destinies, the boys as potential future kings, and the girls as potential future queens. However, several important differences set the royal family apart from all others. And all those differences stemmed directly from the status of the husband.

The king of Egypt was a demi-god living, temporarily, amongst mortals. Born a mortal, to a mortal mother, he acquired at the moment of his coronation a patina of divinity that allowed him to stand part way between his subjects and their deities. This made him the only living Egyptian who could communicate with the gods and, in theory, the only one who could make offerings in the temples. Death would transform him into a full god; fused with the king of the underworld Osiris, he could then take his place alongside the other immortals. But, for the time being, he was charged with serving the gods on earth, and this meant supplying them with *maat*.

Maat is a concept that has no literal translation into English, although it is often defined as a combination of 'rightness', justice, truth, order, 'unchangedness' and the status quo. Its opposite, chaos or *isfet*, is far easier for us to appreciate. *Maat* was personified in the form of a goddess, the beautiful, eternally young daughter of the sun god, who can be distinguished by the prominent feather of truth worn on her head. Scenes from many dynasties show various rulers standing with Maat beside them, or offering a miniature, squatting image of Maat to the gods. And, as both Maat and the queen are the constant female companions of the king, it is not surprising that their roles, duties and even appearance came to be somewhat confused.

In order to maintain *maat*, the king stuck to the formulae that had proven effective from prehistoric times. His was a combination of practical and ritual roles which the Egyptians saw as one and the same responsibility, but which we today see as three distinct duties: head of the judiciary, head of the bureaucracy and head of the priesthood. Following well-established precedent the king officiated in the temples, presided over the law courts and defended his country against the enemies – both external (foreigners) and internal (criminals) who represented the forces of chaos. In so doing he ensured that Egypt functioned correctly, that *maat* was preserved and that the gods remained happy.

This overwhelming need to preserve *maat* was responsible for the innate conservatism of the Egyptians. Any deviation from tradition was

(*Opposite*) Isis, wife of Thutmose II and mother of Thutmose III. A harem queen of little importance during her husband's reign, when she was completely overshadowed by the queen consort Hatshepsut, she rose to sudden, and maybe posthumous prominence following her son's accession to the throne. Cairo Museum.

(*Below*) Maat, goddess of truth and personification of the concept *maat*, opens her wings to embrace and protect the cartouche of the 19th Dynasty queen Nefertari. On her head Maat wears the feather of truth. Tomb of Nerfertari, Valley of the Queens.

potentially dangerous – who knew what seemingly innocuous difference might upset its balance? In consequence, perceptions of kingship, and of queenship, changed but slowly over time. This conservatism is particularly apparent in the artistic repertoire, where words (hieroglyphic writings) are represented by pictures, and where pictures can often be read as words or sentences. Change in official art – the art that decorated the tomb and temple walls – was not undertaken lightly. For this reason, and somewhat misleadingly, the queens of the Old Kingdom do not at first sight appear very different from their Ptolemaic counterparts.

Every crown tells a story. Here the two tall plumes, cow horns, solar disk, modius, vulture headdress and double uraeus are clear iconographic links with the cults of Hathor, Amun and Mut.

The queen consort

How do we define a queen? In our modern world a queen can be either the wife of a king, or a ruling monarch. In ancient Egypt, where all royal titles stressed the relationship of the individual to the king, the queen's title defined itself. A queen – *hemet-nesu* literally translates as 'King's Wife' – was a woman who was, or had been, married to a king. But, as all Egypt's kings were polygamous, this definition encompassed a broad spectrum of women with different duties and expectations, while excluding some women whom we today would definitely class as queens.

First and foremost amongst Egypt's queens were those ladies who, as consorts, played an official role in political and religious matters. These women were distinguished from their fellow wives by an increasingly wide variety of titles (only the most relevant titles are included in this book), the most ubiquitous being 'King's Great Wife', a title used from the 12th Dynasty onwards, and by an increasingly complex series of crowns. As the essential female element in the monarchy, the spouse of a semi-divine being, the consort was herself a source of religious and political power. She was the mother of the nuclear royal family, the queen who was represented in all official writings and artwork. If all went well, she would eventually become the next 'King's Mother' (or rather, the next 'King's Wife, King's Mother' as all titles were cumulative, with increasing numbers of titles conferring increasing status), a position of great honour and divinity. She might even be called upon to rule Egypt on behalf of an absent husband or an infant son. If things went badly, however, she would be forced into early retirement as another woman's child was selected as Egypt's next king.

The king usually, but not always, inherited his position. His consort was always chosen by or for him. Just how, when or by whom she was chosen we do not know but, given the extent and importance of her duties, the choice was not one to be undertaken lightly. The ideal queen was surely a member of the royal family, a woman who had been raised from birth to understand her role. And so we find brother-sister, or half brother-half sister unions a regular feature of royal family life. These incestuous marriages, which so shocked the early Egyptologists, made perfect sense to the ancients. They ensured that the queen was both well trained and loyal to her husband and their children. They provided appropriately royal husbands for princesses who might otherwise remain unmarried (while Old and Middle Kingdom princesses were allowed to marry outside the immediate royal family, this tradition had ended by the New Kingdom), and they effectively restricted the number of legal claimants to the throne by reducing the number of royal grandchildren. They even provided a satisfying link with the gods. Isis and Osiris, Seth and Nephthys, Geb and Nut, and Shu and Tefnut had all enjoyed incestuous unions although their marriages, made at the beginning of time, were at least in part due to the shortage of non-related marriage partners.

However, brother-sister marriages were by no means compulsory, and the commoner-born 18th Dynasty queens Tiy and Nefertiti prove that

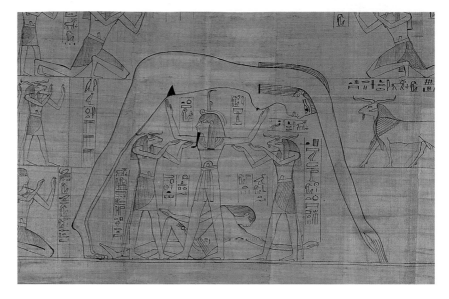

(*Right*) The sky goddess Nut stretches over her brother-husband, the fertile earth god Geb. The two have quarrelled, and are being held apart by their father, the air god Shu. Nut will soon give birth to Osiris, Isis, Seth and Nephthys.

(*Below*) Queen Tiy, consort of Amenhotep III, was born a commoner yet her sons were acknowledged as heirs to the Egyptian throne. In this Theban relief she wears a complicated crown decorated with multiple uraei which link the queen both with the kingship and with the goddess Hathor, daughter and Eye of Re. The double snakes on her brow wear the crowns of Upper and Lower Egypt, but the tall feathers that once completed Tiy's crown have been lost. Royal Museums of Art and History, Brussels.

non-royal queens were entirely acceptable. Nor were incestuous marriages found outside the royal family until the very end of the dynastic age. The paucity of Egyptian kinship terminology (father, mother, brother, sister, son, daughter being the only terms used), and the tendency to apply these terms rather loosely so that 'sister' could be used to describe a sibling, a wife or a lover, confused many early Egyptologists.

Less common, and far more complex than the brother-sister marriages, are the father-daughter unions that characterize the lengthy reigns of Amenhotep III and Ramesses II. Only one of these marriages produced any suspicion of a child (a daughter, born to Bintanath, daughter of Ramesses II). We must therefore question the extent to which these are 'true' marriages in all senses of the word. Is a King's Great Wife literally all that her name suggests? Or can it sometimes be a ceremonial title, perhaps used to endow an otherwise unmarriageable princess with position and independent wealth? It is important that we do not allow our modern moral prejudices to interfere with our judgment, but could these marriages simply be a device to allow an ageing king to utilize an adult daughter's services as deputy to her equally ageing mother? Maybe even a device used to allow the senior queen to advance to an even more respected role? Certainly, in the few parallel occasions where a mother acts as her son's consort (during the later part of the reign of Amenhotep I, for example), no one has suggested that incest is involved.

A reconstructed ebony and ivory veneered cosmetic box recovered from the 12th Dynasty burial of Sithathoriunet at Lahun. Included amongst the queen's treasures were a polished silver mirror, gold-handled copper razors, whetstones, a small silver dish and four obsidian cosmetics jars decorated in gold. Metropolitan Museum of Art, New York.

The harem queens

A considerable distance behind the queen consort stood the other King's Wives, the ladies housed in the royal harem palaces who might, at a time of dynastic crisis, be summoned from relative obscurity to become the next King's Mother. Egypt's harem palaces were remarkable institutions: economically independent female-based communities built to house all the king's dependants – his sisters, aunts, wives and the women inherited from his dead father – plus their children, servants and attendants. Modern attention has, however, focused on the king's many wives.

From earliest times Egypt's kings had been polygamous, and in this respect they differed both from their gods and from their people. Polygamy offered certain advantages. It allowed the king to emphasize his wealth – only a rich man could afford to keep many wives and children unless, of course, he sent them out to work. It stressed his differentness to his people and allowed him to make a series of simultaneous diplomatic alliances. It also ensured that, if by some misfortune the Great Wife should fail to produce an heir, there was a plentiful supply of highborn and well-trained boys available to take their father's place. However, the system had its disadvantages. Too many sons born to different wives of equal rank could confuse rather than protect the succession, while too many ambitious wives with time on their hands could spell danger for the king.

Although all the harem wives were queens, they were by no means queens of equal status. Some were the daughters or sisters of Egyptian kings, some were important foreign-born princesses sent to Egypt to make diplomatic marriages, and some – often described in modern texts as concubines or mistresses, terms which carry unfortunate cultural connotations – were ladies of less exalted birth who were unlikely ever to play any part in state affairs. The hidden life of the harem queen was very different from the public life of the queen consort, and we can only guess at the tensions that must have existed between the younger, more determined wives as they jostled to attract the king's attention. With no official duties to perform and no private estates to administer, the harem wives had little impact on political or religious life. They rarely feature in our story, and today their names and their graves are in almost all cases forgotten. But just occasionally, at times of national weakness, they were able to step out from the shadows to turn the tide of national events.

DATING THE QUEENS

Egypt's dynastic history stretches over 3,000 years from the unification of the country in *c.* 3150 BC (Dynasty 0) to the defeat of Cleopatra VII in 30 BC (Ptolemaic Dynasty). Before 3150 BC Egypt was prehistoric, a society without writing but a society which nevertheless already showed many of the characteristics which would define the dynastic age. After 30 BC Egypt, now queenless, was a province of the Roman empire.

The 31 numbered dynasties plus the final Ptolemaic Dynasty represent lines of kings who are connected, but who are not necessarily blood relatives. A significant number of pharaohs were adopted into their dynasties, while occasionally a dynasty cuts clean across a family line. The 18th Dynasty, for example, starts with Ahmose, son of the 17th Dynasty king Seqenenre Taa II, and includes Thutmose I, Ay and Horemheb, none of whom was born into the immediate royal family. Ideal for dating kings, the dynastic system – which essentially involves dating royal women by reference to their husbands – can become clumsy when used to date queens who generally feature as prominently, if not more so, in their son's reign. For example, we find that the King's Daughter, King's Sister, King's Wife, King's Mother Ahhotep was important both as wife to the 17th Dynasty Seqenenre Taa II, and as mother and regent to the 18th Dynasty Ahmose. Nevertheless the dynastic dating system is used here, as there is currently no acceptable alternative.

The dynasties are conventionally grouped into periods of strong rule (the Early Dynastic or Archaic Period, Old, Middle and New Kingdoms, Late and Ptolemaic Periods) interspersed with periods of weakened central authority (the First, Second and Third Intermediate Periods). Occasionally two competing dynasties rule Egypt at the same time: Dynasties 15 and 16, for example, are contemporary lines of kings. While kings belong to just one period, queens may belong to two. Straddling the junction between the 17th and 18th Dynasties, Ahhotep was both a Second Intermediate Period consort and a New Kingdom King's Mother.

For all periods we are lacking the personal records that would really make the queens come alive for modern readers. Monumental inscriptions can

Outside Egypt the Ptolemaic queen Arsinoe II was happy to be represented as a modern Greek woman. In Egypt, however, she appeared as an entirely typical Egyptian queen, complete with shift dress, heavy wig and double uraeus. So dressed, she becomes virtually indistinguishable from the many queens who have gone before. Vatican Museum.

be extremely informative, but also curiously stilted and unsatisfying. The powerful Early Dynastic queens are identified, more often than not, by the briefest of references: names on vessels, and wooden and ivory labels discarded by the thieves who robbed their tombs. The queens of the Old and, even more so, Middle Kingdom are remote creatures. We have fewer than two dozen Old Kingdom queens' statues, while the Middle Kingdom queens are primarily identified by their funerary monuments, sculptures and jewelry. The New Kingdom marks a turning point in our understanding of the royal family. The newly established empire paid for more stone buildings, more statues and more scribes than Egypt had ever seen before. With more texts, and more archaeological remains, we know far more about the later queens of Egypt than we do about their forbears. Cleopatra VII, a Ptolemaic queen who came into close contact with the literate classical world, enjoyed an inauspicious reign yet is the best documented of all. This unavoidable bias in the evidence is unfortunate, as it may lead us to underestimate the achievements of those queens whose history has to be reconstructed, piece-by-piece, from archaeological fragments glued together with educated guesswork.

A final problem arises when dynasties repeatedly give their daughters the same name. Here, to avoid any confusion either within this book or with other published texts, I have followed the convention of numbering some of the royal women using the accepted numbering system used in Dodson and Hilton's *The Complete Royal Families of Ancient Egypt* (2004). This can, however, lead to apparent gaps in the number sequence, as not all the royal women were queens. And so, to take an Old Kingdom example, we will meet Meresankh I, mother of King Snefru, and Meresankh III, wife of King Khafre. We will not, however, meet the insignificant Meresankh II who is a daughter of King Khufu, but who was neither a King's Wife nor a King's Mother and so does not feature in our history.

Female kings

Totally excluded from our definition of a queen as a king's wife or widow are those women whom we would today consider to be queens regnant – the women who, like Queens Elizabeth I and II of England, ruled Egypt in their own right. These women classified themselves as kings of Egypt, and used the full king's titulary. Although they themselves would have drawn a sharp distinction between female pharaohs and queen consorts, Sobeknefru, Hatshepsut and Tawosret each started their careers as a conventional King's Daughter or King's Wife, and all will be included in this study.

Studying the queens

The first historians to study the queens of Egypt approached their subject with a host of preconceptions. The classical writers who visited Egypt at the very end of the dynastic age had been happy to classify all Egyptian women – queens included – as louche, seductive temptresses, very exciting, and very different from their own (theoretically) chaste wives and sisters. This attitude still lingers in the public perception. Leaping forward hundreds of years, the late 19th- and early 20th-century Egyptologists were more or less uninterested in queens, seeing them as insignificant appendages to their kings.

(*Opposite*) There was no expectation that women would rule Egypt as female kings. On the few occasions that a woman did take the throne, the royal artists were faced with the problem of representing a woman in a man's role. Here on the wall of her Red Chapel at Karnak, the female pharaoh Hatshepsut appears with a male body and traditional male regalia to run a ceremonial race alongside the Apis bull.

(*Below*) The romantic, tragic story of Cleopatra VII, preserved by the classical authors and retold by Shakespeare, has influenced popular perceptions of Egyptian queenship. In this painting by Alexandre Cabanel (1823–89), although it depicts Cleopatra trying out her poison on her slaves, it is easy to understand how Caesar and Mark Antony may have been tempted by the queen's charms. Contemporary illustrations of Cleopatra, however, indicate that she was not a great beauty.

(*Opposite*) On this inlaid box lid Ankhesenamun, daughter of Akhenaten and Nefertiti, offers a bouquet of lotus blossoms to her husband and probable half-brother Tutankhamun. Found in Tutankhamun's tomb and now in Cairo Museum.

Much of our information concerning Egypt's queens comes from a funerary context, and is far less informative than we would like. This poorly made *shabti* figure was sculpted for the burial of one of the Queen Karomamas.

However, these early Egyptologists did develop one remarkable thesis. The 'heiress theory', heavily influenced by an ill-informed understanding of African matriarchies, decreed that Egyptian kingship was inherited through the female line, and that the king could only claim his throne by marrying the heiress, who was all too often his sister. This provided a neat, almost acceptable explanation for the otherwise inexplicable practice of incest. Like so many early theories about ancient Egypt, the heiress theory remained unexamined and unchallenged until the second half of the 20th century, when Egyptologists Barbara Mertz and Gay Robins, working independently, pointed out its most obvious flaw: that not all of Egypt's kings had married their sisters. Today it is realized that, although brother-sister marriages were in many ways ideal, they were by no means essential. The discredited heiress theory would not deserve a mention here, were it not for the fact that it remains in some of the older published literature.

More recently has come the realization that we have been guilty of seriously underestimating the complex multi-layered role played by the queen consort. Her most obvious responsibilities, the requirement to support her husband and raise his children, have always been understood, but even these most practical of duties are difficult to classify as – to the modern mind – they cross boundaries. Is the duty to bear children merely a practical requirement? Or is it a religious duty to allow the semi-divine king to be reborn as his own potentially divine son? The answer, of course, is that it is both. The Egyptians were happy to accept many explanations, many interpretations, for the same phenomenon or person, and if we are to gain any kind of understanding of their society we must suspend both our modern cynicism and our Greek-based tradition of either/or logic and follow their example.

It is the more hidden, 'religious' elements of the queen's role that are so difficult for us to pin down, although some of the explicit titles borne by later queens ('God's Wife'; 'God's Hand') hint at a duty to provide the necessary feminine element in rituals designed to arouse male gods. It is clear that the queen's religious responsibilities went far beyond her ability to observe or participate in routine ceremonies. Just as the king of Egypt stood as a representative for all mortal men before the gods, and could represent either all or one of the gods to his people, so his queen could stand for all women and represent either all or one of the goddesses.

The queen of Egypt quickly became an essential female element of the monarchy, with the king and queen together forming an unbeatable partnership – a perfect brother-sister balance of male and female – that would serve the gods, rule Egypt and confound chaos at the same time. Meanwhile the King's Wife and the King's Mother, both bearers and supporters of divine kingship, developed their own close bond. This is a theology that we will see developing as the dynastic age progresses, becoming most apparent during the New Kingdom Amarna Period. In the absence of any real scientific understanding, it is a theology that helped the Egyptians make sense of their world.

NAQADA III / DYNASTY 0
c. 3100

Various simultaneous local kings;
no recorded queens

DYNASTY 1
2950–2775

Narmer = ? = **Neithhotep**
Aha = ? = **Benerib, Khenthap**
Djer = ? = **Herneith**
Djet = ? = **Meritneith**
Den = ? = **Seshemetka, Semat,**
Serethor
Anedjib = ? = **Batirytes**
Semerkhet = ?
Qaa = ?

DYNASTY 2
2750–2650

Hotepsekhemwy = ?
Reneb/Nebre = ?
Nynetjer = ?
Weneg = ?
Sened = ?
Peribsen = ?
Khasekhemwy = = **Nimaathap**

Names of queens in **bold**
= = known marriage
= ? = possible marriage
= ? queen unknown

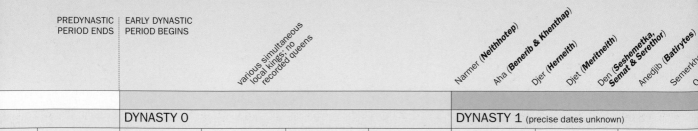

Naqada pot showing Early Dynastic female form

THE FIRST QUEENS
The Early Dynastic Period 3100–2650 BC

FOR EGYPTIAN WOMEN, the advent of agriculture in around 5500 BC and consequent village settlement had been a mixed blessing. The new diet raised female fertility so that women were now exposed to the perils of an annual pregnancy. More children made housework a full-time occupation, and it seems likely that this is the time when women's domestic duties became clearly defined in the Egyptian mind.

Legend has it that in the late 4th millennium BC the warrior Menes was crowned King of Upper and Lower Egypt. Archaeology indicates that the southern warrior Narmer united Egypt's city states to become the first king of the 1st Dynasty. His wife Neithhotep is the first of several Early Dynastic queens to bear a name associated with Neith, the ancient goddess of hunting and weaving. The queen's title 'Consort of the Two Ladies' is a precursor to the later 'King's Wife' and 'King's Mother' titles that emerged for royal ladies in the 2nd Dynasty.

The vast Abydos tomb complex of Djer, third king of the 1st Dynasty, included hundreds of subsidiary tombs for his harem women and servants. His wife Herneith had a separate tomb, which was far smaller than her successor Meritneith's king-sized tomb complex. Meritneith was to set an important precedent for royal women to deputize for their husbands or sons in times of crisis.

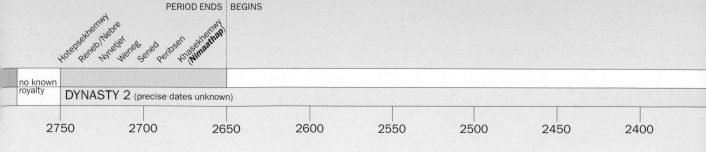

EARLY DYNASTIC | OLD KINGDOM
PERIOD ENDS | BEGINS

Hotepsekhemwy Reneb/Nebre Nynetjer Weneg Sened Peribsen Khasekhemwy *(Nimaathap)*

no known royalty

DYNASTY 2 (precise dates unknown)

2750   2700   2650   2600   2550   2500   2450   2400

DYNASTY 1
2950–2775

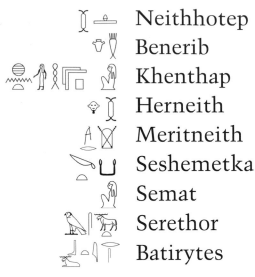

Neithhotep
Benerib
Khenthap
Herneith
Meritneith
Seshemetka
Semat
Serethor
Batirytes

DYNASTY 2
2750–2650

Nimaathap

FAMILY AND TITLES	

NEITHHOTEP
Husband
  Narmer
Parents
  Local Naqada
  royalty?
Son
  Aha
Titles
  Consort of the Two
  Ladies, Foremost of
  Women
Burial place
  Naqada 'Great
  Tomb'
	Unknown
	Son
	  Den?
	Titles
	  Consort of the Two
	  Ladies, Foremost of
	  Women
	Burial place
	  Saqqara (S3507)?

BENERIB
Husband
  Aha
Parents
  Unknown
Children
  Unknown
Burial place
  Abydos (Umm el
  Qa'ab Tomb B14)?
	MERITNEITH
	Husband
	  Djet
	Father
	  Djer?
	Mother
	  Unknown
	Son
	  Den
	Titles
	  Foremost of
	  Women, King's
	  Mother
	Burial pace
	  Abydos (Umm el
	  Qa'ab Tomb Y)

KHENTHAP
Husband
  Aha
Parents
  Unknown
Son
  Djer
Burial place
  Unknown
	NIMAATHAP
	Husband
	  Khasekhemwy
	Parents
	  Unknown
	Son
	  Djoser
	Titles
	  Great of Sceptre,
	  King's Wife, King's
	  Mother, Mother of
	  the King's Children
	Burial place
	  Beit Khallaf (K1)?

HERNEITH *Husband* Djer *Parents*	

NEITHHOTEP

A Naqada III ceremonial palette recovered from the ruins of the Early Dynastic temple of Horus at Hierakonpolis, southern Egypt (and now displayed in Cairo Museum), celebrates King Narmer at the moment of his triumph. On one side of the palette we see Narmer wearing the white crown of a southern Egyptian king as he raises a club to smash the head of the unfortunate enemy who grovels at his feet. On the reverse we see him wearing the red crown of a northern Egyptian king as he marches with his army to inspect the ranks of decapitated war dead. High in the sky above the king we see a woman with horns and cow ears observing events – she is Bat, an early form of the goddess Hathor. Even at this early stage in Egypt's history, it is obvious that Narmer rules a land whose kingly iconography is already well developed.

The meaning of a second ceremonial relic, also found in the Hierakonpolis temple, is less clear. The Narmer Macehead (today housed in the Ashmolean Museum, Oxford) shows the king, wrapped in a ceremonial cloak and wearing the red crown, seated in a raised pavilion or tent. Above the pavilion a large vulture hovers protectively. Around the pavilion there are disjointed images of captives, soldiers carrying standards, a sandal bearer, animals, a temple or shrine and a schematic representation of the sacred enclosure at Hierakonpolis. Approaching the pavilion in a carrying chair is a shrouded, featureless figure of indeterminate gender. Early Egyptologists leapt to the conclusion that they were observing a wedding. But the ancient Egyptians rarely mention their weddings. This marriage, then, must have been an occasion of above-average importance. Narmer, a southern warrior king, must have united his land by

(*Above*) The Narmer Palette reveals how, at the dawn of the dynastic age, the propaganda and regalia of kingship are already well developed. In a scene that will be repeated time and time again, the king is shown defeating the enemies who threaten to bring chaos to his land. Cairo Museum.

(*Below*) The limestone Narmer Macehead was one of a set of votive items known as the 'main deposit', discovered buried under the floor of the Old Kingdom temple of Hierakonpolis. The Macehead had been shattered, and only a tantalizing fragment of the original scene now survives.

force then sealed his position by marrying a daughter of his defeated northern enemy.

Confirmation of the wedding theory was sought from the name of the woman generally assumed to have been Narmer's wife. The name Neith-hotep translates as '[the goddess] Neith is satisfied'. The argument that only a northern woman would be named after the Delta goddess Neith, ingenious though it is, does not stand up to scrutiny. Neith had a powerful link with queenship and many of Egypt's Early Dynastic queens bore names compounded with 'Neith'. Indeed, the fact that she was buried at Naqada indicates that Neithhotep is more likely to have been a daughter of the long line of local Naqada chiefs or kings. An alternative, more acceptable interpretation of the macehead scene suggests that Narmer is celebrating his *heb-sed*, or jubilee, before a shrouded divinity.

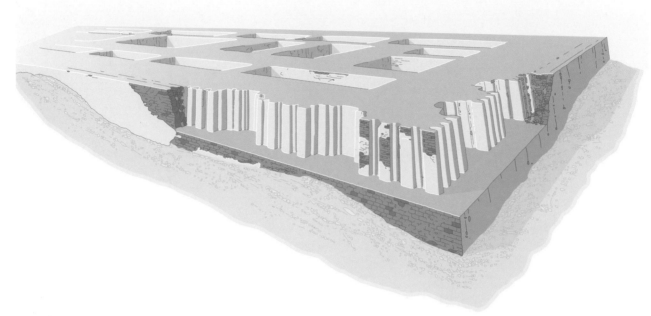

The Great Tomb

Excavating some 2 miles (3 km) outside the modern Naqada village in 1897, Jacques de Morgan uncovered a 1st Dynasty tomb so splendid it was immediately labelled the Great Tomb and assigned to the legendary King Menes. Seen from the outside the tomb was a typical mastaba (a rectangular mud-brick superstructure built above a burial pit and named after the Arabic word *mastaba*, meaning low bench). But this mastaba lacked a burial pit; instead, the superstructure had been converted into a ground-level burial chamber surrounded by storage chambers. The superstructure, measuring an impressive 177 by 88 ft (54 x 27 m), had recessed or niched 'palace façade'-style mud-brick walls, and the whole complex was protected by a thick enclosure wall. The tomb, already looted in antiquity, yielded a series of cosmetic items, stone vessels, ivory labels and clay sealings giving the names of Narmer, his son and successor Aha, and Neithhotep herself. The Naqada tomb was re-excavated by John Garstang in 1904. By then it was suffering badly from post-excavation erosion and it vanished soon after.

Additional references to Neithhotep have been found at Abydos and Helwan. Neithhotep is nowhere described as either a King's Wife or a King's Mother – these kinship titles are not found before the 2nd Dynasty. However, on an ivory lid recovered from the tomb of Djer at Abydos she is described as Consort of the Two Ladies, an epithet which may be the ancient equivalent of 'consort'. On just one seal (represented by several impressions) recovered from Naqada her name is presented in a *serekh*, the rectangular box representing the

(Opposite above) The Great Tomb at Naqada, first assigned to King Aha/Menes, is now believed to have belonged to either Aha's mother, Neithhotep, or to an anonymous local dignitary. The impressive size and sophisticated design of the mud-brick tomb reveal the skill of the Early Dynastic builders.

(Opposite middle and below) The Great Tomb yielded artifacts dating to the early 1st Dynasty. A series of carved ivory labels were originally attached to jewelry and other grave goods. This example in the British Museum displays the number forty. Neithhotep's bracelet (here re-threaded) is made from plaques of ivory and slate. Liverpool University Museum.

(Below and below right) Four beaded bracelets (now in Cairo Museum), and the earliest known example of an artificially mummified arm, recovered from the Abydos tomb of Djer. The subsequent, deliberate destruction of the arm serves as an important reminder of the vast amount of archaeological information that has been lost (deliberately or through ignorance) by those responsible for its recovery and preservation.

entrance to an Early Dynastic palace in which Egypt's earliest kings wrote their names. On top of the traditional king's *serekh* perched Horus the falcon, symbol of the living Horus kings. But on top of Neithhotep's *serekh* were the pair of crossed arrows that symbolized the goddess Neith. On the basis of this evidence it is generally agreed that Neithhotep was a queen who outlived her husband, Narmer, and was buried by her son Aha in the Great Tomb. Some scholars would take this further, citing the use of the *serekh* and the exceptionally large tomb as evidence that Neithhotep actually ruled Egypt on behalf of the infant Aha.

BENERIB AND KHENTHAP

Neithhotep has already been tentatively identified as the wife of Narmer and mother of Aha. An alternative interpretation of the evidence, that Neithhotep was the wife of Aha and regent for his successor Djer, is less convincing as the lady Benerib, whose name appears alongside Aha's on several occasions, has been cautiously identified as his consort. Benerib was not, however, Djer's mother. That honour goes to an otherwise unknown lady, Khenthap, whose name is recorded on the Old Kingdom Cairo Annals Stone. On the assumption that a king is more likely than not to be the son of the previous king, she too can be claimed as a wife of Aha.

HERNEITH

When, in 1900, Flinders Petrie investigated the Abydos tomb of King Djer, successor to Aha, he discovered a single, severed arm adorned, under its linen wrappings, with four gold bracelets bearing turquoise, amethyst, lapis lazuli and gold beads. It appeared that the arm had been hidden behind the tomb stairway by an ancient robber, and so saved from the looting which had wrecked the remainder of the burial. The bracelets led Petrie to assume that the arm

Saqqara mastaba S3507, tentatively identified as the tomb of Queen Herneith. Although the royal tombs at Abydos have yielded numerous female remains, there is no evidence to suggest that queen consorts of the Early Dynastic period were buried there alongside their husbands and sons.

belonged to one of Djer's queens rather than to the king himself, but unfortunately this theory cannot be tested. As Petrie himself records:

When Quibell [British archaeologist James Quibell, discoverer of the Narmer Palette] came over on behalf of the [Cairo] Museum, I sent the bracelets up by him. The arm – the oldest mummified piece known – and its marvellously fine tissue of linen were also delivered at the Museum. Brugsch [curator Émile Brugsch] only cared for display; so from one gold bracelet he cut away the half that was of plaited gold wire, and he also threw away the arm and linen. A museum is a dangerous place.[2]

Djer's tomb yielded female remains including a skull. However, circumstantial evidence suggests that this was not Djer's consort Herneith who, like the other Early Dynastic queen consorts, was apparently buried apart from her husband.

A large tomb (S3507) at northern Saqqara, the cemetery used by the elite who worked in the nearby administrative centre 'White Walls' (Memphis), has been tentatively assigned to Herneith. The Early Dynastic Saqqara tomb owners built mastabas which were effectively warehouses, designed to be filled with all the goods that the deceased, trapped for eternity in their tombs, might need. So impressive were these tombs that their excavators initially assumed that they belonged to kings. Only later was it realized that all the kings of the 1st Dynasty, and some of the kings of the 2nd, were buried in the Umm el-Qa'ab cemetery at Abydos. Djer's name was found inscribed on vases recovered from tomb S3507, which also yielded sealings naming Djer's successor Den (Herneith's son?) and the final king of the 1st Dynasty, Qaa.

Seen from the outside Saqqara tomb S3507 was a traditional mud-brick mastaba, but within the rectangular superstructure was hidden a pyramid-like mound of earth, itself faced with mud brick. Grave mounds

THE WOMEN OF ABYDOS

The 1st Dynasty Abydos royal tomb complexes included subsidiary burials: long, mud-brick lined trenches built around or even linked to the king's burial and subdivided into individual graves. In some cases the rows of graves were covered with one continuous roof or burial mound and so must have been sealed simultaneously. Inside their cells the dead, contracted and wrapped in natron-coated cloth, were buried in the short wooden coffins used by all of Egypt's elite at this time. Many had their own individual grave goods and their names and titles preserved on small limestone stelae. Crude though they appear by later standards, these stelae exhibit a uniformity that suggests they were carved in the royal workshops.

Djer's tomb complex, the largest, included 317 subsidiary graves, some of which were never occupied, and these have yielded 97 funerary stelae. While some are unreadable, 76 stelae bear women's determinatives indicating that they were carved to commemorate female burials. The surviving skeletal material shows that most of these women were young, although it has not been possible to determine exactly how they died. The status of the women is uncertain. Comparison with the impressive tombs provided for queens Neithhotep and Herneith would suggest that they are not members of the immediate royal family. Nevertheless, they are women considered important enough to merit burial beside their king. This was no insignificant honour, as it offered them the chance to share aspects of the king's divine afterlife.

Archaeologists are generally agreed that the women, and the few men, represent the king's personal servants, including women who may have been classed as harem wives. Other subsidiary graves included dwarves (a particular court favourite throughout the dynastic age) and favourite hunting dogs who were provided with their own funerary stelae.

The fact that the graves were simultaneously sealed suggests that they were meant for courtiers and members of the harem expected or even compelled to die with the king. They were, however, a short-lived, wasteful phenomenon that would be abandoned by the late 2nd Dynasty when the tomb complexes of kings Peribsen and Khasekhemwy were built without any form of subsidiary burial.

(Above) The small stone stelae that accompanied the satellite burials indicate that those chosen for burial alongside their king were considered worthy of respect.

(Below) Subsidiary burials around the Abydos tomb of King Den. Contemporary Saqqara mastaba tombs were also provided with subsidiary burials but these, far fewer in number and provided for artisans rather than courtiers, were not designed to be roofed simultaneously. There is no suggestion of mass murder, or mass suicide, at Saqqara.

or tumuli were a southern convention, mastabas a northern style. Does Herneith's combination of two tomb-types hint at an official link between Upper and Lower Egypt, or is it evidence for a rapidly developing funerary theology, one of the many tentative steps towards pyramid development?

(*Opposite top*) One of the pair of funerary stelae provided for the tomb of Meritneith (Tomb Y, Umm el-Qa'ab, Abydos).

(*Opposite centre*) Meritneith lived at a time when writing was just developing. This seal impression, recovered from her Abydos tomb, features wine jars, suggesting that it comes from a wine jar from one of the royal estates.

(*Opposite below*) Reconstruction of Meritneith's mud-brick Abydos tomb and its subsidiary graves. Meritneith is the only woman to have been accorded the honour of a royal tomb at Abydos.

THE GODDESS NEITH

Neith, one of Egypt's most ancient and complex goddesses, was the powerful and aggressive warrior-hunter deity of the Delta city of Sais. Warfare and hunting were considered male pursuits, yet Neith was famed for her archery skills, an aspect of her personality that was reflected in her epithet, 'Mistress of the Bow' and in her emblem of a shield and crossed bows or crossed arrows mounted on a pole. Famed for her wisdom, Neith would be asked to judge between the gods Horus and Seth when both claimed the Egyptian crown.

At the same time Neith was strongly associated with funerary rituals. Charged in the Old Kingdom Pyramid Texts with watching over the deceased, she would eventually become one of the four goddesses who protected the corners of New Kingdom coffins. As the goddess of weaving (the hieroglyphic name for her is a loom) it was Neith who supplied the dead with their wrappings.

Neith's mythology evolved as the dynastic age progressed. By the New Kingdom she was celebrated as the primeval goddess. She was the universal mother, the 'great cow' or 'great flood' who, in different mythologies, variously gave birth to the sun god Re and his arch-enemy Apophis, to mankind, or to the crocodile god Sobek. The Late Period Saite kings felt a particular devotion to Neith as the patron deity of their capital city.

Initially depicted in human form with two bows on her head, Neith was, from the 5th Dynasty onwards, customarily shown wearing the red crown of Northern Egypt. She could also appear as a cow, as a serpent or, when nursing Sobek, as a crocodile.

MERITNEITH

Unique amongst the otherwise exclusively male royal tombs of Abydos is the tomb complex built for Queen Meritneith. Meritneith's tomb (Tomb Y), complete with at least 40 subsidiary graves, was indistinguishable from the nearby kings' tombs, although the two stelae labelling her tomb lacked the *serekh* carved around the male royal names. Overlooking this aberration, Egyptologists accepted Meritneith as the male King Merneit, and it was only when it became obvious that she bore a female name ('beloved of Neith') that she was re-classified as an influential queen consort.

Meritneith has left a complicated archaeological trail with various seal impressions and inscribed bowls linking her with kings Djer, Djet and Den. The sealings from her own tomb were, as Petrie noted, unusual as none bore Meritneith's own name but many bore Den's. Just one sealing from the Saqqara cemetery (tomb 3503) shows her name written in a *serekh*. She is excluded from the King Lists (the roll of Egypt's rulers maintained by New Kingdom scholars) but is almost certainly included on a broken section of the Palermo Stone (a 5th Dynasty record of Egypt's earliest kings) where she is described as a King's Mother rather than a King.

How do we interpret this? It seems that Meritneith, perhaps the daughter of Djer, was married to the short-lived King Djet. Following the untimely death of her husband she was called upon to rule Egypt on behalf of her infant son Den. Indirect confirmation of this scenario is provided by Den's unusually long reign. Having inherited the throne as a child, he was able to celebrate two *heb-sed* jubilees while his mother, having served Egypt as a temporary king, was allowed the honour of burial amongst her fellow rulers.

Meritneith, and possibly Neithhotep before her, had set an important precedent. Already it was recognized that women were capable of taking power, albeit on a temporary basis. The ideal succession would remain a passing of the crown directly from father (Osiris) to son (Horus), but with death an ever-present threat for Egypt's hunt- and battle-loving kings, the queen might well be required to assist the young Horus in the first years of his reign. The choice of the queen as regent, a choice which more modern societies have hesitated to make, was the logical extension of the tradition that allowed wives, rather than fathers or brothers, to deputize for absent husbands. This made good sense. The queen was the person who would naturally be most loyal to the infant king and, as she was often a birth member of the royal family, was well trained for her responsibilities. In any case, there was a limited number of male guardians available to guide the infant king.

The royal sons

We have already seen how the royal family used brother-sister marriages as an effective means of reducing the number of royal grandchildren. The harem, perhaps, reduced the number of the consort's pregnancies. Even so, in an age lacking any reliable form of contraception, a consort was likely to produce several children. This was a desirable state of affairs; the high rate of infant and child mortality meant that no one could be certain who would eventually inherit the throne, and the idea of 'an heir and a spare' was a good one. But, once the succession had been decided and the new king crowned, there was no longer any need of the 'spares'. While the former King's Daughters automatically progressed to become either King's Sisters or, in many instances, King's Wives, the role of the King's Brother is unknown until the end of the Late Period when we find just one 'King's Brother, King's Father'. It seems that the accession of a brother to the throne automatically excluded his close male relatives from the nuclear royal family, which effectively consisted of the King and his mother, wife, sisters and children. Within this nuclear family, King's Daughters were at all times more conspicuous than their brothers.

SHESHEMETKA, SEMAT AND SERETHOR: QUEENS OF THE LATE 1ST DYNASTY

Meritneith is the last prominent 1st Dynasty queen consort. The four putative queens of King Den – Seshemetka, Semat, Serethor and an anonymous lady – have been identified from Abydos funerary stelae, and we know nothing about them beyond their names. Batirytes, mother of Semerkhet, is mentioned in the Cairo Annals Stone, but is otherwise an enigma.

Mastaba Tomb K1, Beit Khallaf, assigned to Queen Nimaathap. Later generations would revere Nimaathap, wife of Khasekhemwy (2nd Dynasty) and mother of Djoser (3rd Dynasty), as the ancestress of the 3rd Dynasty.

NIMAATHAP

The 2nd Dynasty is ill documented. It seems likely (but remains unproven) that the break between the 1st and 2nd Dynasties represents a change in ruling families, with power temporarily shifting to the north. This would explain why the first five kings abandoned the Abydos royal cemetery in favour of burial at Saqqara. Towards the end of the dynasty there are signs of civil unrest, maybe even a north-south civil war, which culminated in the emergence of the penultimate king, Peribsen – a king who was not ashamed to overturn a century of tradition by placing Seth rather than Horus on top of his *serekh*. Peribsen restored the custom of burial in the Abydos cemetery, a practice that was continued by his successor, the Horus king Khasekhemwy.

Given our uncertainty about the 2nd Dynasty succession, it is not surprising that we know very little about 2nd Dynasty queens. Only Nimaathap, mother of the pyramid-building King Djoser, is recorded in the tomb of her husband Khasekhemwy. She was probably buried by her son in a large mastaba tomb (K1) at Beit Khallaf, near Abydos; the smaller mastabas in the same graveyard may well have been built for members of her birth family. A cult for the dead queen survived into the 4th Dynasty, and is mentioned in the Saqqara tomb of the courtier Metjen.

We know just one other fact about 2nd Dynasty queenship. The historian Manetho, commissioned to record a history of Egyptian kingship for Ptolemy II, tells us that during the reign of the otherwise unknown King Binothris (who is widely assumed to be the well-known King Nynetjer) '...it was decided that women might hold kingly office'. Whether Manetho is correct in pinpointing a specific moment when this decision was made is to a certain extent irrelevant; it is an undoubted fact that women were allowed to serve as kings of Egypt.

DYNASTY 3
2650–2575

Djoser = =
Hetephernebty

Sekhemkhet = ?

Khaba = ?

Huni = ?

DYNASTY 4
2575–2450

Snefru = = **Hetepheres I**

Khufu = = **Henutsen, Meritetes**

Djedefre = = **Khentetka,
Hetepheres II?**

Khafre = = **Meresankh III, Khamerernebty I? Persenet?
Hekenuhedjet?**

Menkaure = = **Khamerernebty II**

Shepseskaf = ? = **Bunefer**

DYNASTY 5
2450–2325

Userkaf = ? = **Khentkawes I**

Sahure = = **Neferethanebty**

Neferirkare = = **Khentkawes II**

Shepseskare = ?

Neferefre = ?

Nyuserre = = **Reptynub**

Menkauhor = = **Meresankh IV**

Djedkare = ?

Unas = = **Nebet, Khenut**

Names of queens in **bold**
= = known marriage
= ? = possible marriage
= ? queen unknown

DYNASTY 6
2325–2175

Teti = = **Iput I, Khuit**

Userkare = ?

Pepi I = = **'Weret-Yamtes',
Nebwenet, Inenek-Inti, Meritetes,
Ankhnespepi I, Ankhnespepi II,
Nedjeftet**

Merenre I = ?

Pepi II = = **Neith, Wedjebten,
Iput II, Ankhnespepi III,
Ankhnespepi IV**

Merenre II = ?

Nitocris

DYNASTIES 7 & 8
2175–2125

*A confused series of kings named
Neferkare*

EARLY DYNASTIC
PERIOD ENDS

OLD KINGDOM
BEGINS

Djoser (**Hetephernebty**)
Sekhemkhet
Khaba
Huni

Snefru (**Hetepheres I**)
Khufu (**Henutsen &
Meritetes**)
Djedefre (**Khentetka &
Hetepheres II?**)
Khafre (**Meresankh III, Khamerernebty I?,
Persenet?, Hekenuhedjet?**)
Menkaure (**Khamerernebty II**)
Shepseskaf (**Bunefer**)
Userkaf (**Khentkawes I**)
Sahure
(**Neferethanebty**)

DYNASTY 3

DYNASTY 4

DYNASTY 5

2750 | 2700 | 2650 | 2600 | 2550 | 2500 | 2450

Wife of Khafre

Khamerernebty II

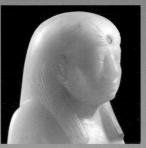
Ankhnespepi II

QUEENS OF THE PYRAMID AGE
The Old Kingdom 2650–2125 BC

DJOSER, first king of the 3rd Dynasty, abandoned the Abydos cemeteries for burial in the north. Here, his impressive stone pyramid complex confirmed Djoser's absolute control over his vast land. Pyramid building would be the defining characteristic of the next 500 years, stimulating the economy and inspiring artists and craftsmen.

In the 4th Dynasty, Snefru built Egypt's first true or straight-sided pyramid. He also developed the more streamlined pyramid complex to be used by all future kings – a linear arrangement of valley temple opening on to a canal and connected by a lengthy causeway to a mortuary temple, with the pyramid beyond. The building achievements of this time are best illustrated by Khufu's Great Pyramid complex at Giza, and his son Khafre's Great Sphinx.

Pyramid building was strongly connected with the cult of Re of Heliopolis. This interest in solar religion peaked during the 5th Dynasty when sun temples were added to the royal mortuary provision. The king, already the living Horus, was now the son of Re while his queen became Re's feminine counterpart, the goddess Hathor.

This prosperity could not last. The 6th to 8th Dynasties saw unwieldy bureaucracy, low Nile levels and the collapse of central authority as Egypt fragmented into a series of independent city states and their satellite communities.

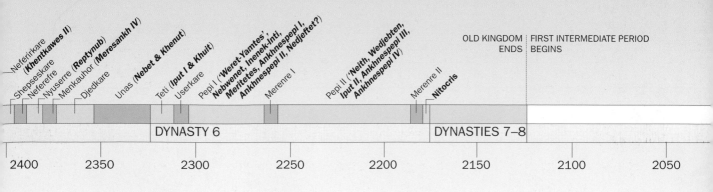

Neferirkare (**Khentkawes II**)
Shepseskare
Neferefre
Nyuserre (**Reptynub**)
Menkauhor (**Meresankh IV**)
Djedkare
Unas (**Nebet & Khenut**)
Teti (**Iput I & Khuit**)
Userkare
Pepi I (**'Weret-Yamtes', Nebwenet, Inenek-Inti, Meritetes, Ankhnespepi I, Ankhnespepi II, Nedjeftet?**)
Merenre I
Pepi II (**'Neith, Wedjebten, Iput II, Ankhnespepi III, Ankhnespepi IV**)
Merenre II
Nitocris

OLD KINGDOM ENDS | FIRST INTERMEDIATE PERIOD BEGINS

DYNASTY 6   DYNASTIES 7–8

2400   2350   2300   2250   2200   2150   2100   2050

DYNASTY 3
2650–2575

Hetephernebty

DYNASTY 4
2575–2450

Hetepheres I

Djoser sits on his throne, one hand in his lap, the other (now vanished) holding his ceremonial flail. He is supported by three royal women whose miniature size serves to emphasize the king's greatness. This is one of 36 surviving fragments from Djoser's limestone shrine dedicated to the god Re at Heliopolis. (*Below*) Fragment of one of Djoser's limestone boundary stelae from his Step Pyramid complex at Saqqara.

FAMILY AND TITLES	
HETEPHERNEBTY	**HETEPHERES I**
Husband	*Husband*
Djoser (Netjerykhet)	Snefru
Parents	*Father*
Unknown	Huni?
Son	*Mother*
Unknown	Meresankh I?
Daughters	*Son*
Intkaes,	Khufu (known to the
Hetephernebty II?	Greeks as Cheops)
Titles	*Titles*
She who Sees	God's Daughter of
Horus, King's	his Body, King's
Daughter, Great of	Mother
Sceptre	*Burial place*
Burial place	Giza?
Saqqara?	

HETEPHERNEBTY

Hetephernebty, 'King's Daughter, the One who Sees Horus', is named on approximately 100 boundary stelae erected to define the limits of Djoser's Saqqara pyramid complex. Over the river at Heliopolis, an inscribed fragment from a stone shrine dedicated by Djoser to the sun god Re (and now irredeemably smashed) shows two miniature women standing beside the leg of a gigantic seated king. The women are simply dressed and lack any form of regalia, but an inscription names them as 'King's Daughter Intkaes and She who sees Horus and Seth Hetephernebty'. A third, anonymous, female figure stands behind the king's leg, extending her left arm to embrace or support the king's ankle. Are we looking at the queen plus two daughters, or are these women perhaps the King's Wife Hetephernebty, the King's Mother Nimaathap and the King's Daughter Intkaes? Either way, it is obvious from her size that the queen is considerably closer in status to her miniature daughter(s) than to her colossal, god-like husband. Bigger was better in Egyptian art, allowing semi-divine kings to tower over mere mortals. King's Sons are often omitted from family statues, emphasizing the importance of female support to the god-king.

Queen Hetephernebty may also be the owner of one of the four pairs of feet, two large and two small, which stand on a broken statue base recovered from her husband's Step Pyramid complex. Again experts are divided over the interpretation of these anonymous feet, with some believing that they represent the king, his mother Nimaathap, wife Hetephernebty and daughter Intkaes, others that they represent the king, queen and their two daughters Intkaes and Hetephernebty junior.

We know little else about Queen Hetephernebty, and cannot even be certain where she was buried. Djoser intended to lie in his pyramid alone, but he had made some provision for his family. His Step Pyramid started life as an unusual square stone mastaba with a burial shaft beneath. Only when this mastaba (known to Egyptologists as M1) was substantially complete was it first of all extended on all sides to create a square two-stepped mastaba (M2), and then enlarged again only on the east side to make a rectangular two-stepped mastaba (M3). Further extensions (P1 and P2) would subsequently convert the mastaba into the bottom step of a six-stepped pyramid.

Along the east side of the second-phase mastaba (M2), Djoser's architect Imhotep sank eleven vertical shafts. These, each approximately 98 ft (30 m) deep, dropped to galleries that ran westwards under the mastaba/pyramid. The first five galleries were to be used by close family members and were equipped with at least six calcite sarcophagi. They were robbed in antiquity, but a burial chamber incorporated in the gallery at the end of shaft III has yielded the hip bone of an anonymous young

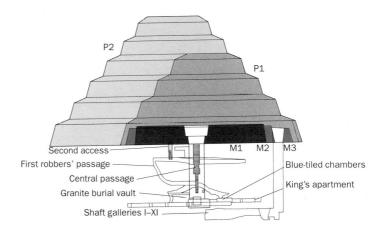

Djoser extended and re-extended his stone mastaba until it became an imposing stairway (the famous Step Pyramid) that would allow the dead king to ascend to the sky. Shafts beneath the original mastaba were provided for lesser royal burials.

woman, while shaft V yielded a gilded wooden coffin housing a body variously identified as a young boy or a young woman. Shafts VI–XI led to storage galleries where Djoser stockpiled up to 40,000 hard stone vessels, many taken from earlier Saqqara tombs. Unfortunately the shafts were rendered inaccessible by the easterly mastaba extension (M3), forcing the still-living members of Djoser's family to build tombs elsewhere.

The subsequent 3rd Dynasty kings are shadowy beings whose lives are ill-documented and whose queens are unrecorded. It is with the advent of the 4th Dynasty that we suddenly start to gain an understanding of the complexities of royal family life.

HETEPHERES I

Snefru was to be remembered as a king with an eye for beautiful women. The fictional Middle Kingdom Westcar Papyrus tells how he staved off boredom by watching the most nubile of the palace maidens row up and down the palace lake, excitingly dressed in barely-there fishnet robes of his own design. It is therefore appropriate that we know more about the women of Snefru's extensive and interconnected family than we do about their predecessors. His mother, however, remains something of a mystery. Our only references to Meresankh I, who may have been the wife of the last 3rd Dynasty king Huni, come from the Cairo Annals Stone and from a New Kingdom graffito scrawled at Snefru's Meidum pyramid complex, which associates her with the divine cult of her dead son.

To the north of the Meidum pyramid a series of mastabas was built for high-ranking members of Snefru's court, including the unfortunate

(*Opposite above*) The Meidum tomb chapel of Atet was decorated with incised reliefs filled with coloured paste, a technique apparently invented by Atet's husband Nefermaat, King Snefru's son. Here we can see the two sons of Atet, Seref-Ka and Wehem-Ka, kneeling as they trap birds in a net. Below, a child (another possible son) plays with his pet monkeys.

(*Opposite below*) Snefru's Meidum pyramid was built as a step pyramid and then converted to a true or straight-sided pyramid. The pyramid was abandoned when it became structurally unsound, and later collapsed.

(*Right*) Rahotep, another son of Snefru, and his wife Nefret, discovered in their Meidum mastaba in 1871. Their eyes, inlaid with rock crystal and quartz, give the statues a particularly life-like appearance and terrified the local workmen charged with excavating their tomb. Cairo Museum.

King's Sons who predeceased their father. Some of these King's Sons were buried with their wives – women whose hopes of becoming queen had died with their husbands. The 'Eldest Son of the King' Nefermaat and his wife Atet shared a large decorated mastaba (M16). Nearby the 'Priest of Heliopolis, Overseer of the Task Force, King's Son of his Body and Director of Bowmen' Rahotep was buried with his wife Nefret (M6a); the stunning painted statues recovered from their offering chapel are amongst the highlights of the Cairo Museum. The Meidum burials represent those members of the royal family who died before the Meidum pyramid was abandoned; those who died later were buried in the new mastaba cemetery at Dahshur. Entirely missing are the burials of Snefru – who was presumably interred in the Dahshur Red Pyramid – and his consort and sister or half-sister, Hetepheres I. For clues to Hetepheres' burial, we need to look at the Great Pyramid complex built by her son Khufu.

(*Opposite*) The three pyramids at Giza, with Khufu's Great Pyramid in the foreground. Khufu's three diminutive queens' pyramids lie to the east of his own (centre foreground). Around the major pyramids lie the tombs of the elite. Those lucky enough to be buried alongside their king could hope to share some of the privileges of the royal afterlife.

A chance discovery

To the east of his Great Pyramid, Khufu built three small queens' pyramids complete with mortuary chapels. None of the three is specifically labelled, but the northernmost pyramid (G1a) has been assigned to Hetepheres I, 'God's Daughter' (of Snefru's predecessor Huni?), wife of Snefru and King's Mother to Khufu. Like the other two small pyramids it was looted in antiquity, but some of Hetepheres' burial equipment did, against all the odds, survive.

In February 1925 an American survey team working to the north of her pyramid made the chance discovery of a deep, narrow shaft (G7000X) which had been filled with limestone blocks and hidden beneath a layer of plaster. After weeks of patient excavation the team reached the bottom of what proved to be an 88-ft (27-m) shaft. Here they found a single chamber tightly packed with funerary equipment, including a closed alabaster sarcophagus, a sealed alabaster canopic box and a vast amount of pottery. The chances seemed good that they had found an intact royal burial, but the sarcophagus could not be opened until the tomb had been emptied and this, due to the hot and dangerous working conditions, would not be for almost two years. As the clearance of the tomb progressed, it became clear that this was not the intact primary burial that George Reisner and his team had hoped for. When the sarcophagus was finally opened it was found to be empty, although the canopic chest still held four packets of preserved human organs.

How can we explain this curious chamber? George Reisner believed that he had excavated a reburial. Hetepheres must have been interred elsewhere, perhaps nearby her husband's Dahshur pyramid, and her tomb must have been robbed almost as soon as it was sealed. The transfer of her remaining grave goods to the greater security of the Giza cemetery would then make perfect sense. It might even have occurred without Khufu's knowledge. This would certainly explain the missing body. Tomb robbers tended to make a beeline for mummies as they knew that

PERSONAL HYGIENE

'To expel stinking from the body of a man or woman: ostrich-egg, shell of tortoise and gallnut from tamarisk are roasted and the body is rubbed with the mixture.... Recipe for a tongue that is ill: bran, milk and goose grease are used to rinse the mouth....' [3]

Cleanliness and good grooming were a necessity rather than a luxury for Egypt's elite. Both men and women valued cleanliness as an obvious means of setting them apart from the masses who could not afford the comfort of personal hygiene.

The more fastidious Egyptians removed all their body hair – and their body lice – using tweezers, flint knives and metal razors, with oil providing a useful shaving lotion. Bald heads could then be covered by wigs when appropriate. There was no soap, but natron and soda could be used as a detergent. Toothbrushes, too, were unknown, although the historian Pliny tells us that the Egyptians cleaned their teeth with a unique toothpaste made from plant roots. Chewed twigs were used to apply the paste.

The clean face could then be decorated with green (malachite) and grey (galena) eye paint or kohl, which was believed to have healing and protective powers against the fierce rays of the sun. The presence of stone cosmetic palettes in Predynastic graves of both sexes shows just how deeply embedded this tradition had become.

The funerary equipment of Hetepheres (see box p. 44) naturally included a full cosmetic set including miniature alabaster pots for her perfumes, ointments and kohl, a gold knife, a gold razor and handful of flint blades to shave both her limbs and her head, and a nail pick or needle.

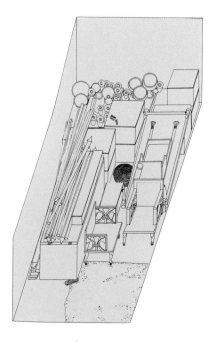

(*Below and below right*) The packed chamber containing the disorganized and very fragile burial equipment of Queen Hetepheres, with a reconstruction drawing showing how the grave goods may have looked when originally deposited.

they would have highly portable, and highly valuable, charms and amulets hidden beneath their bandages. More recently it has been suggested by Mark Lehner that the shaft may have been Hetepheres' original tomb – a pyramid whose superstructure was never built, and which was eventually abandoned. While most of Hetepheres' grave goods, including her body, were subsequently interred in her queen's pyramid, some of the bulkier items were left sealed at the bottom of the abandoned shaft.

FIT FOR A QUEEN: THE TREASURES OF HETEPHERES I

In 1925 a team led by the American archaeologist George Reisner found an incredible cache of grave goods belonging to Queen Hetepheres. Included was a collection of elegant wooden furniture incorporating gold foil and metal fittings and inscribed with Snefru's name – our only definite link between Hetepheres and her husband. When discovered, the wooden elements of the furniture were shrunken and badly decayed and many of the inlays had fallen out, but they have since been restored (and, in the case of the wood, replaced) by a team of experts and craftsmen so that we may once again admire the bed and head-rest, canopy, curtain box (the curtains were presumably stolen in antiquity) and pair of armchairs which once graced the queen's bedroom. A carrying chair, highly reminiscent of the chair featured on the Narmer Macehead, was specifically labelled in miniature gold hieroglyphs set in a strip of ebony as the property of the 'Mother of the King of Upper and Lower Egypt, the Follower of Horus, She who is in Charge of the Affairs of the [Harem?], the Gracious One whose every Utterance is done for her, Daughter of the God's Body, Hetepheres'.

Her gold-covered jewelry box, helpfully labelled 'box containing rings…Mother of the King of Upper and Lower Egypt, Hetepheres', held not rings but 20 silver bracelets of varying diameter decorated with inlaid butterflies formed from turquoise, lapis lazuli and carnelian. Contemporary scenes show that this style of bracelet, popular with both men and women, royalty and commoners, was worn several to each arm.

(Above) Hetepheres' restored bedroom furniture. Her curtains and bedding vanished in antiquity.

(Left) These inlaid silver bracelets were found in the collapsed remains of a wooden jewelry box covered inside and out with gold leaf. Silver was a more precious metal than gold. The queen is depicted on her carrying-chair wearing 14 similar bracelets on one arm.

(Below) Detail of Hetepheres' empty curtain box, decorated with the cartouche of her husband, Snefru.

DYNASTY 4
2575–2450

Henutsen
Meritetes
Khentetka
Hetepheres II
Meresankh III
Khamerernebty I
Persenet
Hekenuhedjet
Khamerernebty II
Bunefer

Hetepheres II, daughter of Khufu, married as many as three royal brothers, yet never produced an heir to the throne.

FAMILY AND TITLES	
HENUTSEN	King's Wife
Husband	*Burial place*
Khufu (also known as Cheops)	Unknown
Parents	
Unknown	**HETEPHERES II**
Son	*Husbands*
Khafre?	Kawab, Djedefre?
Titles	Khafre?
King's Daughter	*Father*
Burial place	Khufu
Giza (G1c)	*Mother*
	Unknown
MERITETES	*Daughter*
Husband	Meresankh III
Khufu	*Titles*
Father	King's Daughter,
Snefru	King's Wife, Great of
Mother	Sceptre
Unknown	*Burial place*
Sons	Giza (G7530+7540)
Djedefre?, Kawab	
Titles	**MERESANKH III**
Great of Sceptre,	*Husband*
King's Wife	Khafre (also known
Burial place	as Chephren)
Giza (G1b)	*Father*
	Kawab
KHENTETKA	*Mother*
Husband	Hetepheres II
Djedefre	*Son*
Parents	Nebemakhet?
Unknown	*Titles*
Children	King's Daughter,
Unknown	King's Wife, Great of
Titles	Sceptre
She who Sees	*Burial place*
Horus and Seth,	Giza (G7530+7540)

HENUTSEN AND MERITETES

The southernmost and best-preserved of Khufu's queens' pyramids (known today as G1c) has been cautiously assigned, on the basis of a 26th Dynasty stela, to the otherwise obscure King's Daughter (of Snefru?) Henutsen. Henutsen is assumed to have been Khufu's wife and the mother of the builder of the second Giza pyramid, Khafre. Her pyramid was built some time after the other two, perhaps by her son, and may not have formed part of Khufu's original complex.

The middle pyramid (G1b) probably belonged to the King's Wife 'Great of Sceptre' Meritetes, another daughter for Snefru and wife for Khufu, and a possible mother for Djedefre, the king whose reign came between Khufu and Khafre. Meritetes is also known to have been the mother of Crown Prince Kawab who predeceased Khufu.

KHENTETKA

The next king, Djedefre, has been treated with an unjustified degree of suspicion. For several years it was believed that he was Khufu's son by a beautiful blonde Libyan queen, and that he had seized the throne by murdering the true heir, his brother Kawab. There is, however, no evidence to support the existence of any Libyan queen, blonde or otherwise. The yellow hair, deduced from the 'blonde' or 'red' hair shown in tomb images of Queen Hetepheres II (sister of Djedefre, and therefore daughter to the fictitious Libyan queen) was in fact a misinterpretation of Hetepheres' exotically coloured and elaborately striated wig.

Djedefre abandoned Giza to build his pyramid in the already ancient

QUEENS OF THE 4th DYNASTY

Queen
KING
Other royal male
?
= possible marriage
= marriage
? possible offspring

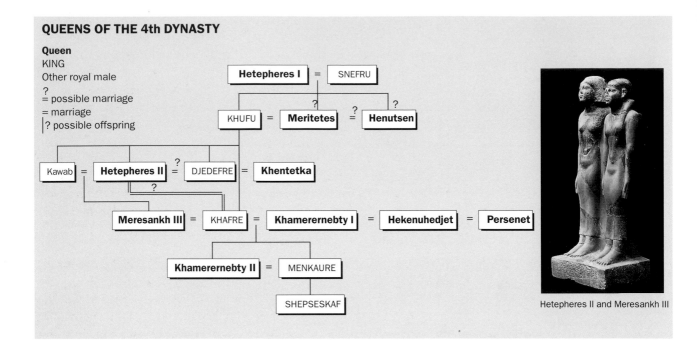

Hetepheres II and Meresankh III

In this statue fragment, recovered from 'Djedefre's Starry Sky', Djedefre's Abu Roash pyramid complex, the small-scale Khentetka kneels supportively beside her husband's foot. The pyramid complex originally included over 20 statues of the king.

desert cemetery of Abu Roash. The Late Period masons who later stripped the site dumped Djedefre's smashed statues in his empty boat pit. Amongst the 120 statues and statue fragments were various representations of his consort, Khentetka. Her best-preserved image shows the miniature queen kneeling submissively beside her colossal husband's leg.

HETEPHERES II

It has been suggested that Djedefre may also have married his sister Hetepheres, widow of his brother Kawab. Widowed for a second time by Djedefre's untimely death, she is then suspected of marrying a third brother, Khafre. If this is the case it is very unusual; few royal widows remarried once, let alone twice, and it may be that her second two marriages were honorary ceremonies designed to maintain her position at court. Certainly Hetepheres II never produced the heir who would have allowed her to become a King's Mother, and this may explain why, although she had built a joint tomb with her first husband Kawab, she was eventually buried with her daughter Meresankh III in an elaborately decorated double tomb at Giza.

(*Opposite*) Ten anonymous female figures depicted in the harem-like underground north annex in the Giza tomb of Meresankh III. Elsewhere in the tomb stand six male scribes, and there are two separate pairings of Meresankh and her mother Hetepheres II.

Rustling the papyrus: Hetepheres II and her daughter Meresankh III take to the waters in a flimsy papyrus boat. With no king present, Hetepheres becomes the dominant figure, and the younger queen supports her mother by embracing her with her left arm.

MERESANKH III

Although her tomb credits her with the titles 'King's Daughter, King's Wife', the former is used with its occasional extended meaning of grand-daughter as Meresankh was the daughter of Khufu's son Kawab, and wife and niece of Khafre. Like her mother, she too failed to become a King's Mother. On the wall of their tomb we can see mother and daughter sailing in a papyrus boat as they participate in the religious ritual of 'rustling the papyrus' for the goddess Hathor. The younger queen, dressed in an elaborate beaded dress and wearing a necklace, anklets and a diadem on her short hair, stands supportively behind her mother with her left arm encircling her waist. Hetepheres II, as youthful in appearance as her daughter, prefers a plain dress and a long wig. A pair statue, recovered from the same tomb, shows Hetepheres embracing and supporting 'her daughter, the King's Wife whom she loves'. Again Meresankh favours a short hairstyle that, possibly her own hair rather than a wig, may be an indication of her more junior status when appearing with her mother. A small annex to the tomb houses a unique arrangement of ten rock-cut, anonymous female figures – royal women? – standing in a row.

Meresankh's tomb is remarkable in giving both the date of her death and the date for her funeral. Although Herodotus tells us that the normal period for embalming was 70 days, it seems that Meresankh spent an incredible 272 days with the undertakers waiting, perhaps, for the masons to finish their work on her tomb. Her burial has yielded a set of canopic jars, the earliest known, and the badly battered skeleton of a woman in her mid-50s with very worn teeth.

KHAMERERNEBTY I, PERSENET AND HEKENUHEDJET

Three other wives – Khamerernebty I, Persenet and Hekenuhedjet – have been suggested for Khafre, their relationships deduced from a series of cryptic references in their own and their children's tombs. A broken statue head, discovered close by the pyramid of Khafre and so rather tentatively dated to his reign, may represent one of the three. The head shows, for the first time, a queen wearing a royal headdress: the vulture headdress. Additional fragments of vulture headdress-wearing statuary have been recovered from the pyramid complexes of Khafre and Menkaure, but are too badly broken to identify.

KHAMERERNEBTY II

The succession after Khafre is somewhat muddled, but eventually the throne passed to his son Menkaure, born to Khamerernebty I. Menkaure and his Giza pyramid have, for no apparent reason, attracted a whole host of legends. Reading the classical authors, we find that the king had his beloved daughter (whom he may or may not have raped) entombed inside a gigantic gold-covered, wooden cow. Or that his pyramid was actually built by the beautiful courtesan Rhodophis. The classical historian Strabo developed this last theme into a Cinderella-like story where Rhodophis' fragrant sandal was stolen by an eagle that dropped it in the king's lap. The king, overwhelmed by the sandal's perfume, ordered a search for its owner and Rhodophis eventually became his wife.

Menkaure built at least two queens' pyramids (GIII-a and GIII-b; a third small-scale pyramid, GIII-c, was almost certainly his own satellite pyramid) to the south of his main pyramid. GIII-b has yielded the remains of an anonymous young woman. One woman who was not interred in a queens' pyramid is Rekhetre, who in her tomb claims the titles King's Daughter and King's Wife; but without names of father or husband, any link with Menkaure has to be speculative.

The easternmost and most complete of the queens' pyramids, GIII-a, may have been used for the burial of Menkaure's sister-consort Khamerernebty II, daughter of Khamerernebty I. However, as a twice-life-sized statue of Khamerernebty II – the only surviving colossal statue of an Old Kingdom queen – was found in the tomb of Khamerernebty I, it is possible that mother and daughter shared a tomb. This ill-preserved statue lacks any form of distinguishing regalia. It is the queen's impressive size,

This broken 4-inch (10-cm) high alabaster sculpted head provides the first evidence for the use of the queen's vulture headdress. It is one of a very limited number of Old Kingdom royal female statues, and is dated, on stylistic grounds, to the 4th Dynasty.

KHAMERERNEBTY II

Husband	*Son*
Menkaure (known to the Greeks as Mycerinus)	Khuenre
	Titles
Father	King's Daughter, King's Wife, Great of Sceptre
Khafre	
Mother	*Burial place*
Khamerernebty I	Giza (GIII-a?)

THE VULTURE HEADDRESS AND URAEUS

The vulture crown or headdress, as its name suggests, has the appearance of a rather limp bird draped over the wearer's head, with the body forming a close-fitting cap, the feathered wings drooping either side of the face, the legs hanging down the back of the wearer's head and the vulture's head and neck rising from the wearer's forehead.

The vulture headdress was originally the divine headdress worn by Nekhbet, the vulture goddess of southern Egypt and, in some mythologies, mother of the king. It was subsequently adopted by other goddesses.

This headdress was to become a standard part of the queen's regalia, but during the 4th Dynasty (and bearing in mind that we have too few Old Kingdom examples to form any kind of scientific study) it may have been reserved for King's Mothers. It seems obvious that the headdress was being used to stress the connection between the queen and/or queen mother and the divine, while highlighting the widening gulf between the queen consort and other women, including the women in the royal harem. What we cannot tell is whether this queenly divinity was an entirely new phenomenon, or whether it had been understood, but unrecorded, since the time of Queen Neithhotep.

The Egyptians recognized a wide variety of snake gods, good and bad, male and female. Apophis was the most malevolent of all. A gigantic, aggressive serpent, he nightly attacked the solar boat of the sun god Re. Fortunately Re had Mehen, a tightly coiled snake, to protect him.

Female snakes were seen as protective and nurturing. Meretseger, 'She who Loves Silence', guarded the dead of the Theban necropolis and was a popular object of worship for the New Kingdom workmen who laboured in the Valley of the Kings. Renenutet, a deadly hooded cobra, was celebrated as goddess of the harvest. She protected granaries, houses and families and, as

Sithathoriunet's diadem, recovered as part of the 12th Dynasty Lahun treasure in 1914. The single uraeus is worn by royal women from the 6th Dynasty onwards, becoming standard in the Middle Kingdom.

the divine nurse, cared for both babies and the king.

Wadjyt, 'The Green One', the snake deity of Lower Egypt and the Nile Delta, introduced a variant to the vulture headdress by replacing the bird's head with a snake's head or 'uraeus' – a cobra that decorates and protects the royal crown. This modified vulture headdress would be worn by queen consorts from the 6th Dynasty onwards, emphasizing the link both between the queen and motherhood (vultures and snakes being regarded as archetypal good mothers) and between the queen and the uraeus-wearing king.

The development of the uraeus is explained in the creation myth of Heliopolis. The creator god Atum sent his Eye (a form of the goddess Hathor) to search for his missing children. When the Eye returned with the children she found that she had been replaced by the sun. Enraged by this betrayal she transformed herself into a cobra, and Atum, first king of Egypt, placed the snake goddess on his brow.

The vulture headdress, here worn in combination with the modius or platform crown by the deceased 18th Dynasty queen Ahmose-Nefertari. This image, painted 150 years after her death, comes from the Theban tomb of Nebamun and Ipuky (TT 181).

Three queens' pyramids lie to the south of Menkaure's own, much larger, pyramid at Giza.

and the fact that she sits on a throne, that confirms her royal status.

Menkaure's two pyramid temples have provided an unprecedented series of hard stone statues and statue groups plus several part-finished works. We have images of the king alone, dyads (pair statues) showing the king with an unnamed consort, and triads (triple statues) that show the king standing between Hathor and one of a variety of deities who represent the regions where Hathor was worshipped. Hathor, in this funerary context, may be interpreted as a symbol of motherhood and royal rebirth. The most famous Menkaure piece is a greywacke dyad recovered from the valley temple by George Reisner in 1910, and now housed in Boston. Menkaure, dressed in the kilt, headcloth and false beard but lacking a uraeus, stands beside a lady whose lack of headdress proclaims her to be mortal, and whose affectionate pose suggests that she is a wife. By convention, but without any evidence, she is identified as Khamerernebty II. The queen wears a skin-tight sheath dress and long, smooth tripartite wig pushed far enough back from her forehead to reveal the natural hair beneath. She has no distinguishing regalia and no jewelry. Her left arm extends across her body so that her hand touches her husband's left arm, while her right arm encircles her husband. Her face is rounded, youthful and distinctly similar to the face given to Hathor in her husband's other statuary. The king is the embodiment of a semi-divine being – handsome, muscular, severe yet faintly smiling. His serene queen is almost equal size with her husband.

(*Opposite*) Menkaure and the wife conventionally identified as Khamerernebty II. The polished greywacke stone is beautiful to modern eyes, but the ancient Egyptians would have painted this as they painted all their statues. There are traces of the original red paint on the king's face, neck and ears, and some black paint on the queen's wig. Museum of Fine Arts, Boston.

BUNEFER

Menkaure was succeeded by his son Shepseskaf, a king happy to abandon the expensive pyramid tomb in favour of a stone mastaba known today as the Mastabat Faraoun ('pharaoh's bench'), which he built in the new Saqqara south necropolis. Shepseskaf made no funerary provision for either his queens or the bureaucratic elite, and the lady Bunefer – associated with him as either his daughter or his queen – was buried at Giza.

DYNASTY 5
2450–2325

Khentkawes I
Neferethanebty
Khentkawes II
Reptynub
Meresankh IV
Nebet
Khenut

Khentkawes I depicted on the granite doorjamb of her Giza tomb. The queen is wearing a dress, yet bears kingly regalia.

(*Below*) The queen's title may be read with equal validity as either 'Mother of the Two Kings of Upper and Lower Egypt' (*mwt-nswy-bity*; translation proposed by Vladimir Vikentiev) or as 'King of Upper and Lower Egypt and Mother of the King of Upper and Lower Egypt' (*nsw-bity-mwt-nsw-bity*; translation proposed by Hermann Junker).

KHENTKAWES I

Shepseskaf's tomb may have inspired the unusual Giza mastaba of the 5th Dynasty Queen Khentkawes I. Her tomb (LG100), built on natural outcrop of rock so that it appeared as a two-stepped hybrid between a royal pyramid and a non-royal mastaba, was an impressive 149 x 150 x 57 ft (45.5 x 45.8 x 17.5 m) in size and included a mortuary temple, antechamber, burial chamber and storerooms. It even had its own small 'pyramid village' to house the priests who would maintain her cult. Excavated by Selim Hassan in 1931–32, the mastaba yielded fragments of an alabaster sarcophagus but no other signs of burial.

Khentkawes was obviously a woman of considerable importance, but who exactly was she? Her titles, carved on the granite doorway leading to the mortuary chapel, included one important, ambiguous phrase which can be translated either as 'Mother of Two Kings of Upper and Lower Egypt', or as 'King of Upper and Lower Egypt and Mother of the King of Upper and Lower Egypt'. Egyptologists originally accepted the first translation, understanding it to mean that Khentkawes was a King's Mother who had given birth to two kings, Sahure and Neferirkare, the second and third kings of the 5th Dynasty. However, Khentkawes' doorjamb shows her sitting on a throne, wearing a false beard and uraeus and carrying a sceptre. The single uraeus, which links the wearer both with kingship and more specifically with the snake goddess Wadjyt, will not become standard queens' wear until the Middle Kingdom. Khentkawes' damaged name is not presented in a cartouche – the oval loop which, from the 3rd Dynasty onwards, had replaced the *serekh* as the signifier of a king's name – but the blatant assumption of kingly regalia suggests that

FAMILY AND TITLES

KHENTKAWES I	KHENTKAWES II
Husband	*Husband*
Userkaf?	Neferirkare (Kakai)
Parents	*Parents*
Unknown	Unknown
Sons	*Sons*
Sahure?	Neferefre, Nyuserre
Neferirkare?	*Titles*
Titles	King's Wife, King's
King?, King's	Mother
Mother	*Burial place*
Burial place	Abusir
Giza (LG100)	

Khentkawes' enormous two-stepped mastaba tomb, partially carved from a natural outcrop of rock, was originally believed to be a fourth, unfinished, Giza pyramid. The tomb was extended during the 5th Dynasty. In the background can be seen the pyramid of Khafre.

Khentkawes served as a temporary ruler of Egypt, presumably acting as regent for one or more of her sons who are, most unfortunately, nowhere named. Her reward – like Meritneith's before her – was a splendid tomb alongside her fellow rulers.

The Westcar Papyrus

The Westcar Papyrus shows us another version of events leading up to Khentkawes' regency, by telling the story of a divine birth. This story starts in the 4th Dynasty. King Khufu has summoned an elderly wise man, Djedi, to entertain him with magic. Having delighted his king by bringing a series of decapitated animals back to life, Djedi starts to prophesy, speaking of the triplet sons who are soon to be born to the lady Redjedet, wife of a priest of Re. The story then shifts into the future. Redjedet goes into labour and nothing can ease her pains. Re, the father of her unborn children, sees her suffering and sends the goddesses Isis, Nephthys, Meskhenet and Heket to help her. Escorted by Khnum the creator god, they arrive at her house disguised as dancing girls.

As Redjedet squats to give birth Isis stands in front of her, Nephthys behind her, and Heket performs magic to speed the delivery. Isis greets the first baby, making a pun on the name Userkaf: 'Do not be so strong in your mother's womb, you whose name means Strong.' The baby is washed, his umbilical cord severed, and he is placed on a cushion. Meskhenet then confirms his fate: 'A king who will rule over the entire land.' And Khnum gives him the gift of health.

As two more future kings are born, the same sequence of events is followed and Isis again names the babies: 'Do not kick in your mother's womb, you whose name means Kicker' (Sahure) and 'Do not be dark in your mother's womb, you whose name means Dark (Neferirkare Kakai).'

This story is obviously not an accurate historical account of events at the beginning of the 5th Dynasty. It is a piece of royal propaganda designed to stress the divine birth of Userkaf, Sahure and Nyuserre as sons of the sun god Re, and its format will reappear in the New Kingdom, when Hatshepsut, Amenhotep III and Ramesses II will claim to be the children of Amun. This close association with the god leaves their mother Redjedet – presumably a corruption of the name Khentkawes – in the curious position enjoyed by all King's Mothers. She is a mortal woman who has enjoyed the most intimate of relationships with a god.

If we refer to more conventional historical sources we see that Shepseskaf was followed on the throne by Userkaf, a man of unknown origins who tells us nothing of his parentage although we can speculate that he was a member of the wider royal family, possibly a grandson of Djedefre or a son of Menkaure. It seems likely, but is nowhere explicitly stated, that Userkaf was married to Khentkawes I. Userkaf reigned for only eight years; it is therefore entirely possible that his son and successor Sahure would needed his mother's guidance. Userkaf had raised one of the largest queens' pyramid complexes ever built next to his own Saqqara pyramid. Today this lies in ruins, its owner's name unknown. If we are right in our assumption that it was built for Khentkawes, it was never occupied.

NEFERETHANEBTY

Sahure's wife Neferethanebty is named in his mortuary temple, along with their children, but we know little more about her.

KHENTKAWES II

Sahure's successor, Neferirkare, was not his son. Although their relationship is never explained, the Westcar Papyrus suggests that the two might have been brothers. The new king started to build a pyramid for his consort, Khentkawes II, on the south side of his own Abusir pyramid complex. Ten years later Neferirkare's untimely death forced the abandonment of the queen's pyramid; when work restarted the masons, now working for Khentkawes' son, thriftily incorporated blocks 'borrowed' from Neferirkare's own unfinished complex. Once

Khentkawes' pyramid stood 55 ft (17 m) high. Today it is a low, shapeless mound. However, the burial chamber has yielded pieces of a pink granite sarcophagus and fragments of mummy bandages, and it seems reasonable to assume that it was used for the queen's burial.

Contemporary papyri tell us that Khentkawes' mortuary temple included at least 16 statues of the queen. These are now lost. However, we can still see Khentkawes carved in low relief on the temple walls and pillars. Here, included amongst uncontroversial images of religious and family life, Khentkawes is wearing a uraeus, and once again we meet the ambiguous title 'Mother of Two Kings of Upper and Lower Egypt' or 'King of Upper and Lower Egypt and Mother of the King of Upper and Lower Egypt'. Originally this led to a huge amount of confusion as Egyptologists assumed, not unnaturally, that Khentkawes I and Khentkawes II were one and the same lady. Today we recognise that they are different, identically named women each faced with a dynastic crisis. Khentkawes I ruled Egypt on behalf of at least one infant son. Whether Khentkawes II ruled on behalf of one son, or was 'merely' the mother of two kings (Neferefre and Nyuserre) is less clear.

REPTYNUB, MERESANKH IV, NEBET AND KHENUT: THE LAST QUEENS OF THE 5TH DYNASTY

The list of the final queens of the 5th Dynasty is incomplete. We have a handful of names (Reptynub wife of Nyuserre, Meresankh IV wife of Menkauhor, Nebet and Khenut wives of Unas), a host

Unas provided his queens Nebet and Khenut with an unusual double mastaba situated to the northeast of his own pyramid at Saqqara .

of royal children, and a few kings who lack named wives (Neferefre, Shepseskare, Djedkare) although if size of monument is any indicator of status, Djedkare's anonymous wife must have been a woman of considerable authority. Unas, last king of the 5th Dynasty, built his pyramid at Saqqara, where it became the first to include spells from the Pyramid Texts. He was succeeded by his son and/or son-in-law Teti, son of Queen Sesheshet and husband of his daughter Iput.

Unas was the first king to decorate his tomb with spells from the Pyramid Texts, written to help the dead king in his quest for eternal life.

DYNASTY 6
2325–2175

Iput I
Khuit
'Weret-Yamtes'
Nebwenet
Inenek-Inti
Meritetes
Nedjeftet
Ankhnespepi I

Ankhnespepi II
Neith
Wedjebten
Iput II
Ankhnespepi III
Ankhnespepi IV
Nitocris

IPUT I

Teti built two queens' pyramids in the north Saqqara cemetery. Iput I's tomb started life as a conventional mastaba but after her death was converted by her son, Pepi I, into a small, steep, entranceless pyramid. Pepi may have felt a special obligation to his mother, as it is possible that she served as regent during the first years of his reign. Iput's burial was looted in antiquity, but her middle-aged bones and a small quantity of gold jewelry were found lying in a cedarwood coffin inside her limestone sarcophagus. A more youthful Iput appears on a broken block from Coptos, where she stands behind her son as he offers to the god Min. Iput wears the vulture headdress and carries both a staff and an *ankh* – the symbol of life reserved for gods and royalty, which may indicate that she is dead.

KHUIT

Khuit's tomb was designed from the beginning to be a pyramid. As pyramids were always more prestigious than mastabas, it seems that she was, during her husband Teti's lifetime at least, considered the more important queen. This suggests that Khuit may have been the mother of Teti's short-lived and little-known successor Userkare, a monarch with no recorded parentage and no known tomb. To add further to the dynastic confusion, Manetho tells us that Teti was assassinated by either his bodyguards or his eunuchs (translations vary, but there is no evidence to indicate that Egyptian kings were ever attended by eunuchs), a startling and unconfirmed statement.

On this scene from Coptos, Pepi I offers to the ithyphallic god Min. Behind him stands his mother, Iput I. Behind Min are a series of tall lettuce plants, lettuce being considered both an aphrodisiac and a symbol of fertility.

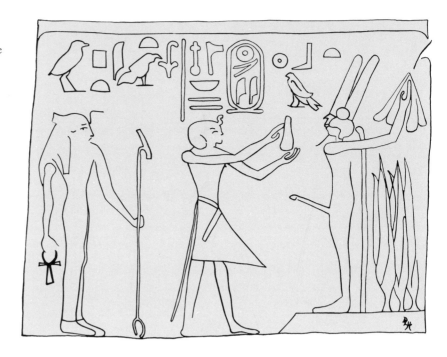

Weni's autobiography, carved on a limestone slab in his mud-brick Abydos tomb chapel and now housed in Cairo Museum. The anonymous queen 'Weret-Yamtes' is named in the fourth column from the left (highlighted).

FROM 'WERET-YAMTES' TO NEDJEFTET: THE MANY WIVES OF PEPI I

Our only reference to 'Weret-Yamtes', wife of Pepi I, comes from the Abydos tomb-chapel of the courtier Weni, where it forms a brief episode in his much longer autobiography. In his own words, he tells us how:

When there was a secret charge in the royal harem against Queen Weret-Yamtes, His Majesty made me hear it alone. No chief judge or vizier, no official was there, only I alone.... Never before had one like me heard a secret of the king's harem; but His Majesty made me hear it, because I was worthy in his majesty's heart beyond any official of his....

Unfortunately this is where the story stops and, although Weni's autobiography continues, we never discover the nature of the queen's offence nor, indeed, her punishment. We don't even know her true name; the name given by Weni, Weret-Yamtes or Great of Sceptre, is an alias (a title without a name) used to preserve the royal dignity. The king, no doubt, would have liked to keep the whole sorry affair secret.

The fact that there was serious trouble in the harem, taken together with the suggestion that Teti was assassinated (a crime which Weni, who also served under Teti, neglects to mention), confirms our growing awareness that the 6th Dynasty kings were suffering from an acute loss of status brought about by an unfortunate combination of circumstances: economic and agricultural problems caused by the increasing dryness, the inefficiencies of an ever-expanding bureaucracy, and political unrest stirred by an increasingly powerful provincial elite. *Maat* may not have deserted Egypt, but away from Memphis, confidence in the kings was starting to waver.

The threat of civil unrest may explain why Pepi I made an unprecedented series of diplomatic marriages linking the royal family to the local governors, whose fortunes were waxing as the crown's were waning. It is difficult to determine exactly how many times he married, but he built at least six queens' pyramids close by his own south Saqqara pyramid and, as pyramids were reserved for the most important consorts and King's Mothers, we can assume that he married many more times, perhaps even selecting a wife from each nome (province). The pyramids were dedicated to queens **Nebwenet**, **Inenek-Inti**, **Meritetes**, Ankhnespepi II (see section below) and Ankhnespepi III (spouse of Pepi II, may have been intended for the disgraced 'Weret Yamtes'), and an anonymous 'Elder Daughter of the King'. Another possible wife, **Nedjeftet**, is mentioned on a broken relief.

ANKHNESPEPI I

In the last few years of his reign Pepi I married two sisters, the daughters of the influential Khui of Abydos whose son, Djau, was destined to serve as vizier. Both sisters were most appropriately, and most confusingly, named Ankhnespepi ('She Lives for King Pepi I') and both are also called by its variant, Ankhnesmerire, 'She Lives for King Merire [Pepi I]', names which they most probably assumed at the time of their marriage.

Each sister bore the elderly king a son. The elder son, Merenre I, born to the elder daughter Ankhnespepi I, ruled for no more than nine years before the throne passed to his young half-brother Pepi II, son of Ankhnespepi II, and the role of King's Mother passed from sister to sister. Manetho tells us that Pepi II, having inherited the throne as a six-year-old, reigned for an extraordinary 94 years, an almost unbelievable achievement in a society where those who escaped the perils of birth and childhood were unlikely to live for longer than 40 or 50 years. It may be that Manetho has confused the numbers 64 and 94, but even so, Pepi enjoyed an exceedingly long reign.

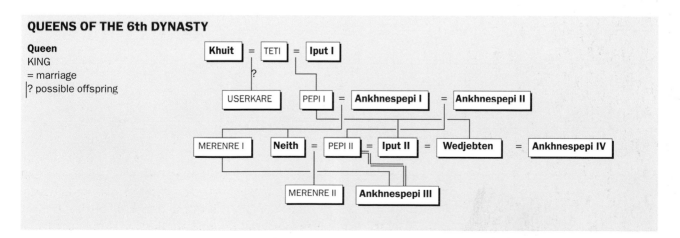

QUEENS OF THE 6th DYNASTY

Queen
KING
= marriage
? possible offspring

(Opposite) The Brooklyn Museum
statue of Ankhnespepi II and her son,
Pepi II. The statue is of unknown
provenance, but its reference to creator
god Khnum suggests that it may have
originated in Elephantine. Unusually,
this statue presents the observer with
two front views.

(Below) The name and titles of Iput II,
sister and wife of Pepi II, on the remains
of her ill-preserved South Saqqara
pyramid complex. Iput does not bear the
title King's Mother and it is clear that
pyramids, hitherto reserved for Kings'
Mothers and the most important of royal
women, were now being built for a wider
range of queens.

ANKHNESPEPI II

Nowhere is it explicitly stated that Ankhnespepi II ruled as regent for her young son Pepi II. However, an alabaster statue, now housed in the Brooklyn Museum, goes a long way towards explaining their close relationship. The queen, 'Mother of the King of Upper and Lower Egypt, the God's Daughter, the revered one beloved of [the god] Khnum', wears a sheath dress, tripartite wig and vulture headdress whose vulture head has been broken off. She sits on a box throne with Pepi (obviously a child yet shown with an adult body and dressed in a king's kilt and headcloth) sitting at right angles across her lap so that as she gazes straight ahead he looks to her right. The queen supports Pepi with her left arm, and places her right arm comfortingly across his knees. He holds her right hand in his left. This is one of the few royal sculptures to show a tender scene,

and one of the few to show a king of Egypt as smaller and therefore less significant than another mortal. Clearly the queen is a person of immense importance. It may be that this is in fact her statue, and that the miniature king is only incorporated as a means of emphasizing her role in the royal family, but it seems more reasonable to deduct that the queen and king are here assuming the roles of the divine mother Isis and her infant son Horus.

NEITH TO ANKHNESPEPI IV

The three principal queens of Pepi II were buried in small-scale pyramid complexes beside his own far larger Saqqara complex. The largest of the three belonged to Queen **Neith**, the daughter of Pepi I and Ankhnespepi I, and therefore both half-sister and cousin of Pepi II. Here, on her temple walls, we can see Neith wearing the vulture crown with the cobra head, and carrying a papyrus sceptre.

Wedjebten, also a daughter of Pepi I, had a smaller pyramid complex but two perimeter walls. The pyramid complex built for **Iput II** has today almost entirely disappeared, but enough remains to allow us to read her titles and see that she was never a King's Mother; maybe her son died before he could succeed his long-lived father. Iput's complex housed an intrusive First Intermediate Period burial. **Ankhnespepi III** was the daughter of

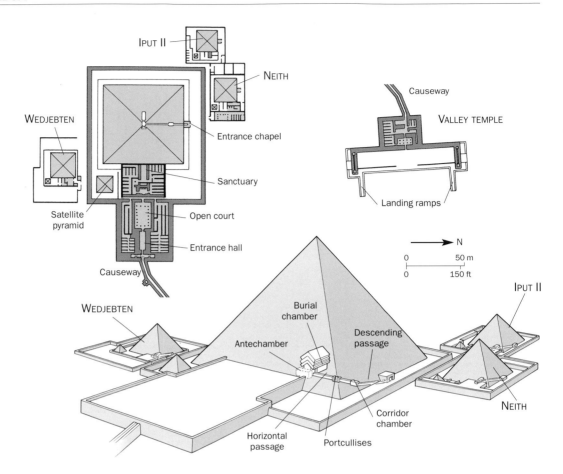

The South Saqqara pyramid complex of Pepi II, 'Pepi's life is Enduring', showing the location of the three queens' pyramids. The small satellite pyramid to the southwest of the main pyramid was provided as part of the king's own funerary ritual, and should not be confused with a queen's pyramid.

Neith, sister-wife of Pepi II, here depicted in her Saqqara pyramid chapel. Neith's plundered pyramid has yielded an unprecedented 16 model ships.

Merenre, son of Pepi I. She was buried in a pyramid near the pyramid of Pepi I, where her sarcophagus was carved out of a massive flooring block.

Queen **Ankhnespepi IV** was yet another wife of Pepi II whose son, the insignificant king Neferkare Nebi, is thought to have ruled during the

8th Dynasty. The lid of her coffin, recovered from the western storeroom in the pyramid complex of Iput II, was carved with a royal history which, as yet unpublished, is reported to record events during the turbulent 6th Dynasty, including the abrupt end of Teti's reign.[4]

NITOCRIS

Pepi II had outlived many of his children and grandchildren, and his death left the dynastic succession in confusion. The ephemeral Merenre II, possibly the son of Queen Neith, succeeded him, and he in turn was apparently followed by his sister, Nitocris, who is described by Manetho as 'the most noble and lovely woman of her time, fair skinned, with red cheeks'.

The accession of a woman to the throne of Egypt is a sure and certain sign that things have gone badly wrong. Under normal circumstances a female reign is a temporary reign – a mother rules for her son and steps down when he becomes old enough to reign alone. However, in this case, there is no evidence that Nitocris had a son and it seems that she was accepted by her people as a female king acting to preserve her dynastic line. Herodotus tells the rather dramatic tale of her accession:

...[Nitocris] succeeded her brother. He had been king of Egypt, and had been put to death by his subjects, who then placed her upon the throne. Determined to avenge his death, she devised a cunning scheme by which she destroyed a vast number of Egyptians. She constructed a spacious underground chamber and, on pretence of inaugurating it, threw a banquet, inviting all those whom she knew to have been responsible for the murder of her brother. Suddenly, as they were feasting, she let the river in upon them by means of a large, secret duct.[5]

To Herodotus' evident approval the brave queen then committed suicide rather than face the wrath of her people. Entertaining though this story is, it is most unlikely to be true. We are left with a lingering feeling that Herodotus is confusing two events – the murder of Teti (if it really happened) and the reign of a powerful queen. It is therefore unfortunate that this remarkable lady has left neither monument nor tomb and, although the 19th Dynasty Turin Canon does allocate 'Neitaqerti' a brief reign of two years, one month and one day, many Egyptologists have expressed doubts that she actually existed, suggesting that 'Neitaqerti' may actually be a misrecorded fragment of a male king's name.

THE FIRST INTERMEDIATE PERIOD
2125–2010 BC

DYNASTIES 9 & 10
2125–1975

A series of local rulers based at Herakleopolis

DYNASTY 11 (Theban rule)
2080–2010

A series of local kings including Mentuhotep I, Intef I, Intef II and Intef III, based at Thebes

THE MIDDLE KINGDOM
2010–1630 BC

DYNASTY 11 (National rule)
2010–1938

Mentuhotep II = = **Nefru II, Tem, Henhenet, Sadeh, Ashayt, Kawit? Kemsit?**

Mentuhotep III = ? = **Imi**

Mentuhotep IV = ?

DYNASTY 12
1938–1755

Amenemhat I = = **Neferitatjenen**

Senusret I = = **Nefru III**

Amenemhat II = ?

Senusret II = = **Khnemetneferhedjet I, Nefret, Itaweret, Khnemet**

Senusret III = = **Sithathoriunet, Mertseger, Khnemetneferhedjet II**

Amenemhat III = = **Aat, Hetepti?**

Amenemhat IV = ? = **Sobeknefru**

Sobeknefru

DYNASTIES 13 & 14
1755–1630

A confused series of local rulers

THE SECOND INTERMEDIATE PERIOD
1630–1539 BC

DYNASTY 15
1630–1520

Foreign Hyksos rulers based in the Delta, amongst whom:
Apepi = ? = **Tany** *(the only recorded queen)*

DYNASTY 16

Numerous ephemeral kings

DYNASTY 17
1630–1539

A series of Theban rulers culminating with:
Senakhtenre Taa I = = **Tetisheri**

Seqenenre Taa II = = **Ahhotep I, Inhapy, Sitdjehuty**

Kamose = ? = **Ahhotep II**

Names of queens in **bold**
= = known marriage
= ? = possible marriage
= ? queen unknown

OLD KINGDOM ENDS | FIRST INTERMEDIATE PERIOD BEGINS | FIRST INTERMEDIATE PERIOD ENDS | MIDDLE KINGDOM BEGINS

Local rulers (Herakleopolis)

Local rulers (Thebes)

Mentuhotep II (**Nefru II, Tem, Henhenet, Sadeh, Ashayt, Kawit?, Kemsit?**)

Mentuhotep III (*Imi*)

Mentuhotep IV

Amenemhat I (***Neferitatjenen***)

Senusret I (***Nefru III***)

Amenemhat II

DYN. 9–10 | DYNASTY 11 (Thebes) | DYNASTY 11 | DYNASTY 12

2200   2150   2100   2050   2000   1950   1900

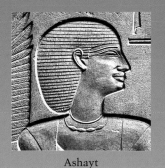
Ashayt

Khnemetneferhedjet I

Nefret

Ahhotep I

CHAOS AND REBIRTH

The First Intermediate Period 2125–2010 BC
The Middle Kingdom 2010–1630 BC
The Second Intermediate Period 1630–1539 BC

THE SCRIBE IPUWER recounts that crime was rife in the First Intermediate Period but, although there were occasional food shortages, this period was by no means a Dark Age.

The independent local governors of the Valley and the Delta formed alliances until two powerful dynasties emerged: a northern dynasty at Herakleopolis and a southern dynasty at Thebes. Finally the Thebans, led by Mentuhotep II, reunited Egypt and established a new northern capital city, Itj-Tawy. The Middle Kingdom rulers relaxed their semi-divine pretensions – their statuary revealing a more human, careworn face of kingship – and their queens, denied any real political role, all but vanished from the royal monuments. It seems that the women of the Middle Kingdom restricted themselves to family concerns.

Discontent amongst local governors and a succession of weak kings including a female pharaoh heralded the collapse of the Middle Kingdom. The Second Intermediate Period saw southern Egypt, ruled from Thebes, uncomfortably sandwiched between the Nubian Kingdom of Kush and the Palestinian 'Hyksos' who ruled the north from Avaris. In 1539 the Theban king Ahmose expelled the Hyksos and reunited his land.

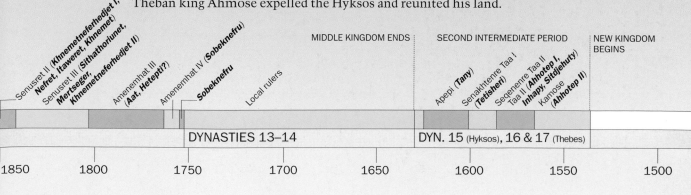

Senusret II (*Khnemetneferhedjet I, Nefret, Itaweret, Khnemet*)
Senusret III (*Sithathoriunet, Mertseger, Khnemetneferhedjet II*)
Amenemhat III (*Aat, Hetepti?*)
Amenemhat IV (*Sobeknefru*)
Sobeknefru
Local rulers

MIDDLE KINGDOM ENDS

Apepi (*Tany*)
Senakhtenre Taa I (*Tetisheri*)
Seqenenre Taa II (*Ahhotep I, Inhapy, Sitdjehuty*)
Taa II
Kamose (*Ahhotep II*)

SECOND INTERMEDIATE PERIOD

NEW KINGDOM BEGINS

DYNASTIES 13–14

DYN. 15 (Hyksos), 16 & 17 (Thebes)

1850 1800 1750 1700 1650 1600 1550 1500

DYNASTIES 9 & 10
2125–1975

DYNASTY 11
(National rule)
2010–1938

Obscure queens

Nefru II
Tem
Henhenet
Sadeh
Ashayt
Kawit
Kemsit
Imi

(*Above right*) The 11th Dynasty queen Nefru II has her hair dressed. Part of a relief from her tomb chapel in the precincts of the Mentuhotep tomb complex at Deir el-Bahari (TT 319).

(*Below*) Scene from the Wadi Shatt el-Rigal showing, from left, Iah, Mentuhotep II, Intef III and the treasurer Khety.

The queens of the 9th and 10th Dynasties are, like their husbands and sons, ephemeral beings whose history goes largely unrecorded.

QUEENS OF THE 11TH DYNASTY

The first kings of the 11th Dynasty made grandiose claims to govern the whole of Egypt, but actually controlled only the south. Nebhepetre Mentuhotep II (his name is correct, but his number is uncertain) was the first to rule over a united land. The new king established his divine credentials by claiming the title 'Son of Hathor'. In fact he was the son of the local king Intef III and his wife, the King's Mother and priestess of Hathor, Iah. We can see Intef and Iah as they stand with their son, Mentuhotep, on a rock carving in the Wadi Shatt el-Rigal in Upper Egypt. Mentuhotep, as the dominant figure, stands twice-life-sized wearing the red and white crowns of Upper and Lower Egypt. He faces his father who wears a simple headcloth and uraeus. Behind Intef stands the treasurer Khety. Behind Mentuhotep stands his mother. She wears a tight sheath dress and a tripartite wig but no queenly regalia, and she carries a lotus and a staff.

FROM NEFRU II TO KEMSIT: THE WOMEN OF DEIR EL-BAHARI

Mentuhotep II ruled from Thebes, where his 52-year reign allowed him ample time to build an impressive tomb – a curious tiered temple, possibly topped with a small pyramid – in the shelter of a natural bay at Deir el-Bahari, on the west bank of the Nile. Within his complex he built tombs for two significant wives. The King's Mother **Tem** (mother of Mentuhotep III) was provided with a tomb at the rear of his mortuary temple while his sister-wife **Nefru** had a separate rock-cut tomb in the forecourt.

Separate shaft graves and limestone chapels were provided for a further six women of slightly lower status who, as the entrances to their burials were covered by the king's own building works, must have died at roughly the same time, relatively early in his reign. The graves were allocated to the King's Wives **Henhenet**, **Sadeh** and **Ashayt**, the unexplained ladies **Kawit** and **Kemsit** (who are assumed to be royal wives), and Muyet who was approximately five years old when she died and was probably a King's Daughter. The five adult women, none of whom was more than 22

WIGS AND HAIRDRESSING

The barber labours until dusk. He travels to a town, sets himself up in his corner, and moves from street to street looking for a customer. He strains his arms to fill his stomach, like the bee that eats as it works.[6]

Kawit's beautifully carved sarcophagus features one of several Middle Kingdom hairdressing scenes. The deceased sits on a chair holding a polished metal mirror in her left hand and a bowl in her right. In front of her stands a male servant pouring water, while behind her a female servant dresses her short wig.

Coming from a culture where pictures are words and words are represented by pictures, this scene can be interpreted both as a literal representation of the queen's daily toilette, and as a coded image of rebirth with the pouring representing the sexual act (a similar sounding word, 'seti', means to pour and to ejaculate), the mirror representing femininity and fertility, and the hairdressing hinting at eroticism. The loosening of the hair was well understood to be the first step of the confident seductress.

To cause the hair to fall out: burnt leaf of lotus is put in oil and applied to the head of a hated woman.[7]

Many of Egypt's elite shaved their heads, wearing elaborate wigs of human hair on formal occasions. Those unable to afford such splendid creations were forced to don unconvincing and very itchy date-palm fibre wigs. Female wig styles changed more rapidly than fashions in either clothing or jewelry, moving from the rather plain styles worn during the Old Kingdom to the longer, heavier, elaborately braided styles favoured during the New Kingdom.

In a scene full of symbolism, Queen Kawit has her wig dressed. From her limestone sarcophagus, Deir el-Bahari.

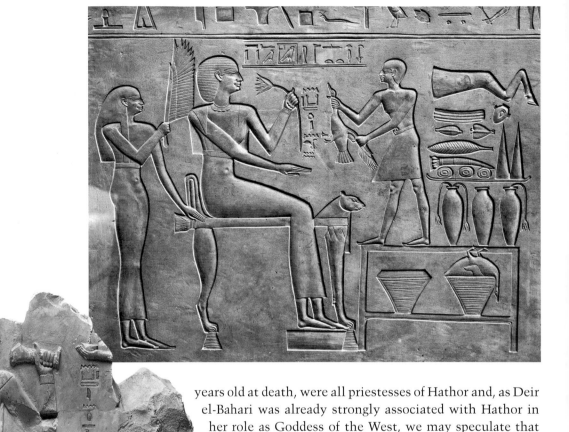

years old at death, were all priestesses of Hathor and, as Deir el-Bahari was already strongly associated with Hathor in her role as Goddess of the West, we may speculate that their graves mark the site of a Hathoric cult centre. Speculation that all six wives died together, killed by an unspecified epidemic, an accident or something more sinister, is perhaps a speculation too far. We know that Henhenet, at least, died of natural causes. Her mummy shows that she suffered an agonizing death in childbirth: her abnormally narrow pelvis had made it impossible for her to deliver a full-sized baby, and she had suffered a vestico-vaginal fistula, a tear running from her bladder to her vagina. Tragedies like this were all too common as, although Egypt's doctors were famed throughout the Mediterranean world, the lack of medical skill made childbirth a dangerous time for all concerned.

(*Top*) In a scene carved on the exterior of her sarcophagus, Queen Ashayt smells the blue lotus, a flower believed to have powers of rejuvenation. A similar scene is painted inside the sarcophagus.

(*Above*) A fragment of a painted limestone relief showing Queen Kemsit, recovered from her tomb chapel within the Mentuhotep II complex at Deir el-Bahari.

IMI

Mentuhotep II was succeeded by Mentuhotep III, son of Queen Tem. Twelve years later Mentuhotep IV, son of a woman named Imi whom we must assume was a wife of Mentuhotep III, took the throne. His reign was to be the last of the 11th Dynasty.

WOMEN'S HEALTH AND CHILDBIRTH

Egypt's unique mortuary practices allowed her undertakers to look deep beneath their subjects' skin. In spite of this, doctors had little understanding of the human body, and the function of the brain was never appreciated. During mummification, when the heart, lungs, liver, intestines and stomach were carefully preserved, the brain was simply thrown away. Nevertheless, the 18th Dynasty Ebers Medical Papyrus included a useful section dealing with women's health, concentrating on such all-important matters as conception, pregnancy and breastfeeding:

Prescription to cause a woman's womb to go back to its proper place: tar that is on the wood of a ship is mixed with the dregs of excellent beer, and the patient drinks this.

One crucial mistake was the belief that the womb might float freely about the abdomen. A healthy woman was understood to have a clear passageway linking her (fixed) womb to the rest of her body. Any blockage in this passageway would, of course, make the woman infertile. And so, hopeful mothers-to-be were tested by inserting a garlic or onion pessary into the vagina. If, a few hours later, the patient's breath smelt of onion, it was clear that she was able to conceive! Alternatively, a trained physician could learn much by examining a lady's face:

If you find one of her eyes similar to that of an Asiatic and the other like that of a southerner, she will not conceive.

To discover the sex of an unborn child, the pregnant woman's urine could be sprinkled on both wheat and barley. A flourishing crop of barley would indicate a boy, wheat a girl.

Most mothers breastfed their babies for up to three years, which may have acted as a natural contraceptive. Royal women, however, employed wet-nurses, recruiting not lowly servants but the wives of top government officials.

(Above) The midwife's tools included birthing blocks, a sharp obsidian knife and perhaps, during the Middle Kingdom, these curious curved batons carved out of hippopotamus teeth. They may have been used to draw a protective magical border around the mother, in the same way that amulets and charms were used.

(Below) The image of a mother suckling her child at her left breast symbolized successful motherhood, and often featured in both secular and religious art. Mothers were advised that good milk smelt pleasant, while bad milk stank 'like the stench of fish'.

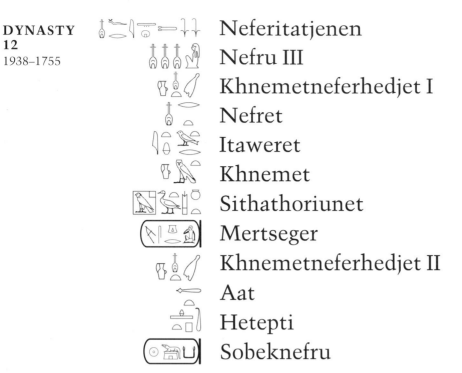

DYNASTY 12
1938–1755

Neferitatjenen
Nefru III
Khnemetneferhedjet I
Nefret
Itaweret
Khnemet
Sithathoriunet
Mertseger
Khnemetneferhedjet II
Aat
Hetepti
Sobeknefru

DYNASTIES 13 & 14
1755–1630

Obscure queens

FAMILY AND TITLES

NEFERITATJENEN
Husband
  Amenemhat I
Parents
  Unknown
Son
  Senusret I
Daughters
  Nefru III,
  Nefrutasherit?,
  Kayet?
Titles
  King's Mother
Burial place
  Lisht?

NEFRU III
Husband
  Senusret I
Father
  Amenemhat I
Mother
  Neferitatjenen
Son
  Amenemhat II
Titles
  King's Daughter,
  King's Wife, King's
  Mother
Burial place
  Lisht

NEFRET
Husband
  Senusret II
Father
  Amenemhat II?
Mother
  Keminub?
Titles
  King's Daughter,
  Great of Sceptre,
  Mistress of the Two
  Lands
Burial place
  Lahun

SITHATHORIUNET
Husband
  Senusret III
Father
  Senusret II
Mother
  Unknown
Son
  Amenemhat III?
Titles
  King's Daughter,
  King's Wife
Burial place
  Lahun

NEFERITATJENEN

The vizier Amenemhat, now King Amenemhat I, moved his court north-wards and founded a new capital city, Itj-Tawy. Itj-Tawy is today lost, but is assumed to have been in the Faiyum region. Here, taking his cue from the Old Kingdom monarchs, Amenemhat abandoned the more restrained Theban-style rock-cut tomb and built a pyramid in the new royal ceme-tery of Lisht. Around his pyramid enclosure he built 22 burial shafts for the more important royal women. Included amongst these was, we must assume, Amenemhat's consort Neferitatjenen, the mother of his son and co-regent Senusret and his daughter Nefru.

After 30 years on the throne, Amenemhat was murdered. Unlike most murder victims, he was able to write a letter to his son detailing the horrific chain of events leading up to, and including, his death. 'His' letter was actually composed by the scribe Khety, who wrote from the viewpoint of the dead king to increase the dramatic effect:

As I began to drift into sleep, the very weapons that should have been used to protect me were turned against me while I was like a snake of the desert. I awoke with a jump, alert for the fight, and found that it was a combat with the guard. Had I been able to seize my weapon I would

A New Kingdom scribe's copy of the Middle Kingdom text 'The Instructions of King Amenemhat'. Initially scholars believed that Amenemhat had survived the assassination attempt. Today it is accepted that the king died and so cannot have written about his experience. The account of his death conveys the king's bitterness, and his shock at being attacked in the place where he should have been most secure.

have beaten back the cowards single-handed, but no one is strong at night.... I had not expected it and had not predicted the treachery of my servants. Had any woman ever marshalled troops? Are rebels nurtured in the palace? [8]

Egypt's scribes shied away from recording anything that might suggest an absence of *maat*, and so accounts of crimes against the royal family are few and far between. It therefore comes as little surprise that we have no more official record of Amenemhat's death by unnatural causes. However, Khety's account is backed up, somewhat obliquely, by the fictional Middle Kingdom story of Sinuhe, which tells how the eponymous hero runs away from Egypt upon learning of the king's death. Why would Sinuhe run away if the elderly Amenemhat had died of natural causes? And, indeed, why would he run away if he weren't frightened that he would somehow be implicated in the death? We know, because he tells us, that Sinuhe was in the service of the royal harem: 'I was an attendant who waited on his lord, a servant of the royal harem assigned to the Princess Nefru, wife of King Senusret and daughter of King Amenemhat.' The inference that the king has fallen victim to a harem plot to disrupt the intended succession hovers unspoken. If this was the case, it was a plot that was only partially successful. The king might have died, but he was succeeded as he had planned by Senusret I.

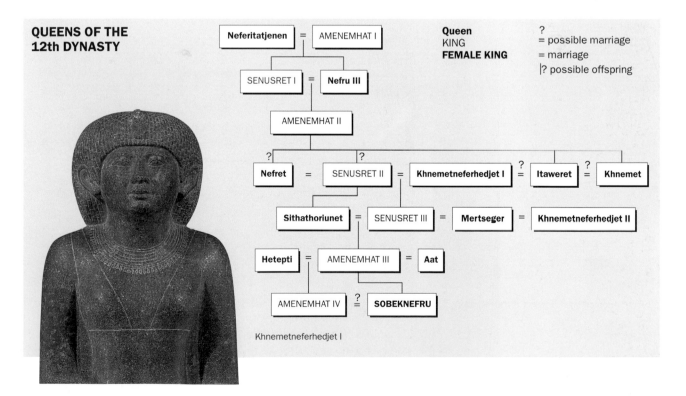

QUEENS OF THE 12th DYNASTY

Neferitatjenen = AMENEMHAT I

SENUSRET I = Nefru III

AMENEMHAT II

Nefret = SENUSRET II = Khnemetneferhedjet I = Itaweret = Khnemet

Sithathoriunet = SENUSRET III = Mertseger = Khnemetneferhedjet II

Hetepti = AMENEMHAT III = Aat

AMENEMHAT IV = SOBEKNEFRU

Queen
KING
FEMALE KING

? = possible marriage
= marriage
|? possible offspring

Khnemetneferhedjet I

NEFRU III

Senusret I built his pyramid to the south of his father's complex, surrounding it with an unprecedented nine subsidiary pyramids for wives and daughters. These were not all planned from the outset, but added gradually over the years, with the last pyramid perhaps built several years after Senusret's death. Queen Nefru's pyramid, which presumably was part of the original plan, was the largest of the nine. This queen puts in a re-appearance at the end of Sinuhe's story when, together with the royal princesses, she greets the traveller on his return to Egypt, singing and shaking her rattle as she offers praise to Hathor for his safe return.

The 12th Dynasty queens adopted an increasing range of titles including 'Mistress of the Two Lands', 'Lady of the Two Lands' and 'Mistress of Upper and Lower Egypt'. But their expanding titulary was not matched by a high public profile. From this point on, our history of the 12th Dynasty queens effectively becomes a survey of the Middle Kingdom pyramid fields, as all the available evidence comes from funerary contexts. We know, for example, that Amenemhat II – Senusret's son by Queen Nefru III – built his pyramid to the east of the Red Pyramid at Dahshur. But a lady called Keminub, once assumed to be the wife of Amenemhat II, is now dated on the basis of inscribed objects from her badly preserved Dahshur burial, to the 13th Dynasty. The name of her husband goes unrecorded.

FROM KHNEMETNEFERHEDJET I TO KHNEMET

Amenemhat's successor, and probable son, Senusret II, was married to **Khnemetneferhedjet I** (the mother of his son Senusret III) and to his sister **Nefret**. A further two wives, **Itaweret** and **Khnemet**, both daughters of Amenemhat II, have been proposed although, as both were buried in their father's funerary complex, their status as wives cannot be confirmed.

Nefret is today the most visible of Senusret's queens, as two above life-sized, polished black granite statues of Nefret have been recovered from the late Ramesside/Third Intermediate Period Delta city of Tanis. Clearly this was not their original location. All of Egypt's kings were happy to plunder earlier sites in order to provide their modern cities with a range of impressive antiquities, and we may speculate that these fine pieces originally formed a part of Nefret's funerary provision at Lahun, then spent some time ornamenting the new Ramesside city of Per-Ramesse before being moved during late Ramesside times to Tanis. Both statues, now housed in the Cairo Museum, show the seated queen wearing a shift dress and a 'Hathor-style' tripartite wig with the two front sections of hair bound with ribbons and wrapped around flat disk-shaped weights. Nefret wears a pectoral inscribed with her husband's cartouche, and a single uraeus.

(*Opposite*) Black granite statue of Queen Nefret, recovered from Tanis. Nefret's pectoral is very hard to distinguish here, but is similar in style and workmanship to the pectoral of Sithathoriunet recovered from Lahun (see p. 76). Cairo Museum.

SITHATHORIUNET, MERTSEGER AND KHNEMETNEFERHEDJET II

Senusret III built his pyramid at Dahshur. Here an underground gallery gave access to the substructures of four queens' pyramids. Directly beneath was a gallery built to house the burials of the royal daughters, which has yielded both funerary equipment and jewelry (see pp. 76–77). Senusret's three wives were his half-sister Sithathoriunet, Mertseger and Khnemetneferhedjet II.

AAT AND HETEPTI

Senusret's son, Amenemhat III, built two pyramids, one at Dahshur and one at Hawara. His Dahshur pyramid was abandoned when it became structurally unsound, but it was not left empty. On the south face of the pyramid two separate entrances led to two tombs built within the pyramid mass and linked via a corridor both to each other and to the king's unused chambers. One tomb, belonging to Queen Aat, has yielded a pink granite sarcophagus similar to that provided for the king's abandoned burial, a canopic chest, sundry burial equipment and enough skeletal material to show that Aat died in her mid-30s. The other tomb,

'Amenemhat is Mighty': the Dahshur pyramid of Amenemhat III, now – thanks to its exposed mud-brick core – better known as the Black Pyramid. In the background is the Old Kingdom Bent Pyramid of King Snefru.

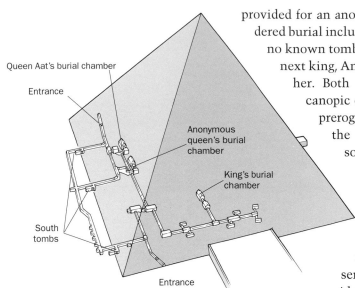

Queen Aat's burial chamber

Entrance

Anonymous queen's burial chamber

King's burial chamber

South tombs

Entrance

Section through the abandoned Dahshur pyramid of Amenemhat III, showing provision for the burial of two queens.

provided for an anonymous lady, has yielded the remains of a plundered burial including another pink granite sarcophagus. As there is no known tomb for the King's Mother Hetepti, mother of Egypt's next king, Amenemhat IV, it may be that this tomb belonged to her. Both tombs included a 'Ka chamber' to house the canopic chest, a chamber that had up until now been the prerogative of kings. The increasing democratization of the afterlife was allowing dead queens to assume some kingly privileges.

Princess Ptahnefru

Amenemhat III was to be the last powerful king of the Middle Kingdom. His reign had seen accomplished building works, ambitious irrigation and land reclamation schemes and a series of successful mining expeditions, and this evident prosperity makes it difficult to understand how such a robust dynasty could suddenly fail. It has been suggested that the over-large royal family was plagued with infighting at this time, but there is little evidence to support this theory, and it may be that the 12th Dynasty suffered from something as simple as a lack of a suitable male heir.

Support for this hypothesis comes from the burial chamber of Amenemhat's Hawara pyramid. Here an additional sarcophagus was included for the burial of the King's Daughter Ptahnefru, either Amenemhat's own daughter or, less likely, his sister. It is difficult to reconstruct the precise sequence of events in the burial chamber, but it seems that Ptahnefru, having died unexpectedly, was interred in her father's tomb while the builders completed her own monument. She was then moved just over a mile away to her own pyramid, a structure that is today almost totally destroyed and disastrously waterlogged. This pyramid was investigated by Labib Habachi (1936) and Naguib Farag (1956), and has yielded a series of grave goods including a beaded falcon collar, flail, apron, bracelet, strips of rotted mummy bandage and a granite sarcophagus inscribed with Ptahnefru's name. Unfortunately Ptahnefru's body had been destroyed by the infiltrating floodwater. The evidently close relationship between Amenemhat III and his daughter, combined with Ptahnefru's assumption of a cartouche in her later inscriptions, suggests that she, rather than a royal son, was being groomed to follow her father on the throne.

SOBEKNEFRU

With Ptahnefru already dead, Amenemhat IV succeeded Amenemhat III and enjoyed a brief reign. He in turn was followed by his probable half-sister and probable wife King Sobeknefru (known as Nefersobek to early Egyptologists and Scemiophris to the classical historians). Sobeknefru,

SOBEKNEFRU	
Throne name Sobekkare	*Children* Unknown
Husband Amenemhat IV?	*Title* King's Daughter, King
Father Amenemhat III	*Burial place* Unknown
Mother Unknown	

British Museum cylinder seal displaying the Horus name of Sobeknefru in a falcon-topped *serekh*. The queen used a mixture of feminine and masculine titles, an ambiguity also reflected in the clothes she is depicted wearing.

determined to prove the legitimacy of her claim to the throne, consistently associated herself in her inscriptions with her powerful father rather than her less than impressive brother/husband. There is some evidence that she may even have been the first to deify Amenemhat III as a god of the Faiyum; this would certainly have made good political sense, as the daughter of a god would be regarded as an eminently suitable king. There is absolutely nothing to suggest that Sobeknefru was a temporary regent ruling on behalf of an infant son. Instead a glazed cylinder seal, now in the British Museum, confirms her true status by recording her name in a cartouche followed by her female Horus name 'Beloved of Re' presented in a *serekh* topped by a falcon, underneath which are the 'Two Ladies', represented by the goddesses of Upper and Lower Egypt.

The Turin Canon gives Sobeknefru a reign of just 3 years, 10 months and 24 days. This allowed her little time to leave her mark on the archaeological record. We would expect her to have been buried in style beneath a king's pyramid. However, although we do have some ownerless pyramids of the late 12th and early 13th Dynasties (at least one at Dahshur and two at Mazghuna), Sobeknefru as yet has no identified tomb. Recovered architectural fragments suggest that her building activities were centred on the Faiyum region, and this is presumably where she was buried, although an inscription dating to the third year of her reign, discovered at the Nubian fortress of Kumma, confirms that she did rule the entire length of Egypt. The end of her reign is obscure, but there is nothing to suggest that she died anything other than a natural death.

Sobeknefru's statuary

We have at least three headless statues of Sobeknefru, found at Avaris but presumably originating in the Faiyum region. The most remarkable of these, now displayed in the Louvre Museum, Paris, is a red quartzite piece which shows the queen's obviously female torso dressed in a conventional (female) shift dress, but with a (male) king's kilt worn over the top, and a (male) king's *nemes* headcloth on her now vanished head. In other images Sobeknefru is entirely feminine in appearance, but assumes a male pose as she tramples the enemies of Egypt in archaic ritual.

Sobeknefru and her artists are here struggling to conform to many centuries of tradition extending right back to the time of the Narmer Palette. A king of Egypt should always look, dress and act like every other king: tall, muscular, kilted, fit, capable of killing enemies and undeniably male. No matter what the king looked like in real life – and modern mummy studies have confirmed that some kings were far removed from this ideal – this was how the king should appear before his gods and people. Indeed, the very act of portraying the king as an idealized being would help him (or her) become

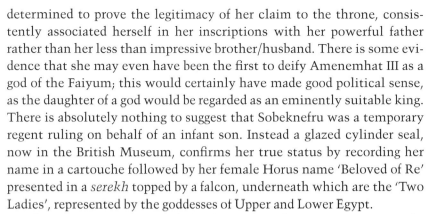

The Louvre torso of Sobeknefru showing her unique combination of male and female clothing.

THE LAHUN AND DAHSHUR TREASURES

Senusret II raised his pyramid at Lahun (also known as Illahun) close by the opening to the Faiyum. Here he provided four shaft tombs for female family members. All of these were robbed in antiquity but in one, the tomb of Senusret's daughter Sithathoriunet, Flinders Petrie and Guy Brunton discovered the 'Lahun treasure': five boxes of jewelry and toiletries hidden in a mud-filled niche by an ancient robber. Petrie himself takes up the tale:

On February 10 [1914] a tomb was being cleared which had been plundered anciently; the sarcophagus was empty, and nothing was anticipated. In clearing a recess (of about a cubic yard) at the side, which was filled with hard mud washed down into the tomb, a few rings of thin gold tubing were found, and at once reported…. As, owing to a strain, I could not go down, Brunton went to see what the meaning of the place might be…. For a week Brunton lived all day and every night in the tomb, gently extracting all the objects from the hard mud, without bending or scratching a single piece. Everything as it came up I washed in plain water with a camel-hair brush, so as not to alter the natural surface, then photographed it….[9]

The cache included a tarnished silver mirror with a beautiful obsidian and gold Hathor handle, a gold diadem decorated with colourful rosettes, and two pectorals (necklaces), one displaying the cartouche of the princess's father, Senusret II, and one displaying the cartouche of her son or stepson, Amenemhat III.

A similar Middle Kingdom treasure had been recovered 20 years earlier at the pyramid site of Dahshur. Here archaeologist Jacques de Morgan discovered jewelry and personal possessions belonging to a variety of royal women. The two caches of jewelry are so similar in style, it seems that they must have been created by the same royal craftsmen. Today, most of the Lahun Treasure is displayed in the Metropolitan Museum of Art, New York, while the rest – and the Dahshur Treasure – can be seen in the Cairo Museum.

(Above right) The reconstructed gold diadem of Sithathoriunet decorated with rosettes, streamers, double plumes and a uraeus. The diadem is wide enough to fit over a full wig. The feathers, which are 8.5 inches (215 mm) tall, would have waved slightly as she moved her head. Recovered from Lahun in 1914.

(Right) Inlaid pectoral belonging to Sithathoriunet, bearing the cartouche of her father, Senusret II, flanked by two Horus hawks. Recovered from Lahun.

(Opposite, above left) An early attempted reconstruction of some of the jewelry recovered in the Lahun treasure. The gold spacers are back-to-back lion heads, originally from a girdle.

(Opposite, above right) Pectoral belonging to Princess Mereret, daughter of Senusret III. The pectoral bears the name of her brother, Amenemhat III. Part of the Dahshur treasure recovered by Jacques de Morgan in 1894.

(Opposite, below) Cowrie shell girdle and pectoral displaying the cartouche of Senusret II and belonging to his wife, Queen Khnemet. Part of the Dahshur treasure.

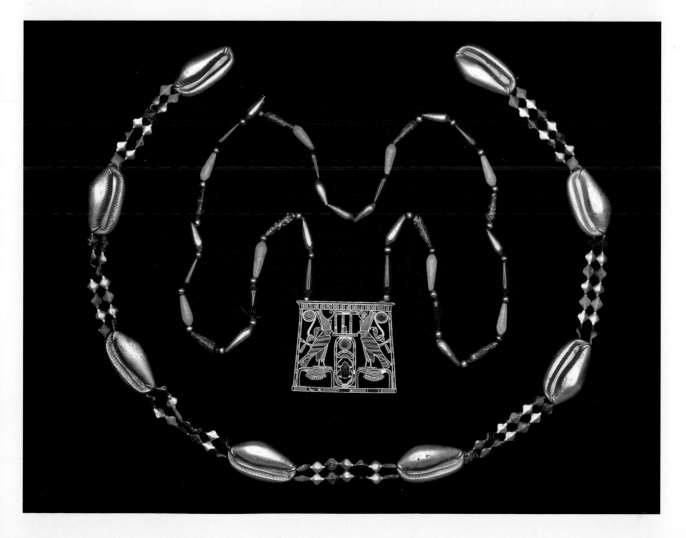

one. Without in any way denying her femininity – indeed, she almost invariably uses feminine titles – Sobeknefru is here donning the regalia which will magically transform her from queen to king. Whether or not she routinely wore these garments in 'real life' we do not know, although she would almost certainly have been required to don traditional priestly garb when performing the all-important temple rituals. We cannot be certain about the origins of Sobeknefru's statues but it seems likely that, like most Old Kingdom and Middle Kingdom royal statuary, they were designed to stand in her mortuary temple. They therefore represent the idealized dead ruler, or maybe the spirit of the idealized dead ruler, rather than the living Sobeknefru.

QUEENS OF THE 13TH AND 14TH DYNASTIES

The 70 kings of the 13th Dynasty ruled for a total of 125 years, with no one king enjoying either sufficient wealth or sufficient time to leave a permanent memorial. Nevertheless, it would be wrong to interpret the first half of the 13th Dynasty as a time of chaos and, indeed, archaeology has shown that the bureaucracy was still functioning, and both art and literature were still flourishing, during this ill-documented period. We know little about the 13th Dynasty kings, and even less about their queens. The last, weak years of the 13th Dynasty and the earliest years of the Hyksos 15th Dynasty saw a parallel, provincial 14th Dynasty claiming power in the eastern Delta.

WOMEN IN LITERATURE

Egypt's dry climate has provided us with an invaluable collection of written records: we have monumental carvings, papyrus and leather scrolls, and unofficial jottings recorded on limestone flakes and broken pottery. With less than 10 per cent of the population literate – and the overwhelming majority of those middle- and upper-class men – the written record can never give us an unbiased view of life in ancient Egypt. Nevertheless, the representation of women in contemporary literature can allow us some understanding of society's view of its womenfolk.

The earliest recovered fiction dates to the Middle Kingdom. The stories range from simple tales of adventure to sophisticated allegories capable of interpretation on many different levels. But across the range, women are noticeable by their virtual absence. As men set off to face unimaginable perils,

their wives, mothers and daughters are apparently content to stay at home waiting for their heroes to return.

Towards the end of the New Kingdom, women start to play a more prominent role in fiction. These women are not necessarily the good wives of the earlier stories. The 19th Dynasty Tale of the Two Brothers, for example, tells of the attempted seduction of an innocent young man, Bata, by his manipulative sister-in-law:

Bata found his brother's beautiful wife lounging in the cool courtyard, languidly playing with her long, dark hair. She smiled up at him…

'Mmm…', the wife murmured, running an appraising glance over his sweating torso, 'what well-developed muscles you have, and how strong you must be. I have been watching you work in the field for many days, your bare chest exposed to the sun…' To Bata's intense alarm, she jumped to her feet and took hold of

his arm, pinching his firm flesh as she did so.

'Come, let me loosen my hair. And let us spend an hour or so lying together. You will enjoy it. And afterwards I will make you some fine new clothes.' [10]

No wonder the scribes advised their young readers to steer clear of other men's wives:

If you want friendships to last in the house that you enter as a master, brother or friend, wherever you enter, beware of approaching the women! [11]

Not all fictional women were bad, however. The foreign-born wife of the Doomed Prince, a contemporary fairy story, was able to use her wits to save her husband from his preordained fate – death by snakebite.

DYNASTY 15
1630–1520

 Tany

DYNASTY 16
1630–1520

Obscure queens

DYNASTY 17
1630–1539

Tetisheri
Ahhotep I
Inhapy
Sitdjehuty
Ahhotep II

THE HYKSOS QUEENS

The six Hyksos kings of the 15th Dynasty ruled northern Egypt for just over a century. Highly Egyptianized yet retaining many Syrio-Palestinian cultural traits, they adopted full royal regalia, used hieroglyphic writing and presented their names in cartouches. Their queens, however, go unrecorded, with the exception of **Tany**, sister and possible consort of Apepi (Apophis) who is recorded on a stela fragment found at Avaris.

THE THEBAN QUEENS

The 16th Dynasty was an insignificant series of 15 minor Theban rulers contemporary with, and dominated by, the northern Hyksos kings. Then a change of ruling family heralded the start of the 17th Dynasty. The new kings were made of sterner stuff. Initially forced to coexist with the Hyksos, they had determined to reunite their country. Unfortunately the chronology, and the sequence of kings, is extremely confused at this time. Intef VII is generally acknowledged as the first of the strong Theban kings. He would eventually be buried in a large and impressive tomb with two bows and six arrows included in his coffin. A second powerful king Sobekemsaf (either Sobekemsaf I or II; experts are divided) was buried with his consort (either Nubkhaes wife of Sobekemsaf I, or Nube-mhat wife of Sobekemsaf II) beneath a small-scale pyramid, which was to be thoroughly looted during the turbulent 20th Dynasty reign of Ramesses IX. Details of this most heinous crime are preserved in the Leopold II-Amherst Papyrus, one of a group of documents known collectively as the 'Tomb Robbery Papyri'. Here the stonemason Amun-Panufer, made loquacious by torture, confesses all:

This 17th Dynasty stela from Abydos details members of Queen Nubkhaes' birth family including her three daughters and her uncle, father, mother, five brothers and five sisters. It is made clear that the queen was not of royal blood, but that she came from a long line of civil servants. Nubkhaes herself is shown making offerings to Hathor of Abydos, and to Osiris. Louvre Museum, Paris.

We went to rob the tombs as is our usual habit, and we found the pyramid tomb of King Sobekemsaf, this tomb being unlike the pyramids and tombs of the nobles that we usually rob. We took our copper tools and forced a way into the pyramid of this king through its innermost part. We located the underground chambers and, taking lighted candles in our hands, went down.... [We] found the god lying at the back of his burial place. And we found the burial place of Queen Nubkhaes, his consort, beside him, it being protected and guarded by plaster and covered with rubble.... We opened their sarcophagi and their coffins, and found the noble mummy of the king equipped with a sword. There was a large number of amulets and jewels of gold on his neck, and he wore a headpiece of gold. The noble mummy of the king was completely covered in gold and his coffins were decorated with gold and with silver inside and out, and inlaid with various precious stones. We collected the gold that we found on the mummy of the god including the amulets and jewels that were on his neck.... We set fire to their coffins....[12]

The 17th Dynasty warrior kings were happy to allow their consorts a more prominent role in state affairs. Even though the queen's status was still, and always would be, directly derived from her relationship with her husband, increasing emphasis was now placed on both the individuality of each queen and on the divinity of her role. In consequence, we suddenly find ourselves facing a line of strong, politically active women reminiscent of the powerful queens of the Early Dynastic Period. It is perhaps no coincidence that 17th Dynasty Egypt was once again a chaotic land, suffering from the almost unbearable indignity of foreign rule. The new kings, their lives dedicated to the struggle against the Hyksos, needed a reliable partner to rule while they campaigned. And who would make a more reliable partner than a loyal sister-wife?

TETISHERI

TETISHERI	
TETISHERI	*Daughters*
Husband	Ahhotep I, Inhapy,
Senakhtenre Taa I	Sitdjehuty
Father	*Titles*
Tjenna	King's Great Wife,
Mother	King's Mother
Nefru	*Burial place*
Son	Dra Abu el-Naga,
Seqenenre Taa II	Thebes

Senakhtenre Taa I was the son of Sobekemsaf II. His consort, Tetisheri, was a commoner-born queen, the daughter of Tjenna and his wife Nefru. Nevertheless, Tetisheri was considered so important a member of the royal family that after her death her grandson Ahmose established a cenotaph for her at Abydos, cult centre of the god of the dead, Osiris, and the royal ancestors.

In this mirror-image scene, two versions of Tetisheri sit, back-to-back, facing her grandson King Ahmose. The text details the king's plans to honour his dead grandmother with a cenotaph at Abydos.

The King himself said, 'I remember my mother's mother, my father's mother, the Great King's Wife and King's Mother, Tetisheri the Justified. She already has a tomb and funerary monument on the soil of the Theban province and the Abydene province, but I have said this to you because My Majesty wants to make a pyramid estate for her in the necropolis near the monument of My Majesty, its pool dug, its trees planted, its offering loaves established....' As His Majesty spoke of the matter, it was put into action. His Majesty did this because he loved her more than anything. Kings of the past never did the like for their mothers.

The stela commemorating this important decision shows the dead and deified Tetisheri wearing the vulture headdress topped with two tall feathers as she sits on a throne to receive an offering from her grandson.

Unfortunately the British Museum statuette of 'Queen Tetisheri', which for over a century has been considered a most important piece, representing the only known royal sculpture from the late Second Intermediate Period/early New Kingdom transition, has now been convincingly demonstrated to be a forgery.[13] A second, presumably genuine, inscribed but badly broken statuette of Tetisheri is owned by the French Institute in Cairo, but its whereabouts are currently unknown.

The Deir el-Bahari cache

During the Third Intermediate Period, a time of civil unrest when the security of the royal cemeteries was threatened, the priests who guarded the royal dead of the Theban necropolis opened all the known tombs, collected the mummies, stripped them of their valuables and then stored them in a series of caches dotted about the necropolis. A major cache of royal mummies was discovered in the Deir el-Bahari cliffs in the late 19th century. This collection included a female mummy once inexplicably identified as Ramesses I, but now widely known as 'Unknown Woman B'. This mummy has been tentatively identified as Tetisheri. The body is that of an elderly lady with pierced ears and prominent upper front teeth, whose skin has been stained black by resin and whose thin, white hair has been augmented by artificial extensions.

'Unknown Woman B' was unwrapped by Gaston Maspero in 1886 and re-examined by Grafton Elliot Smith in 1909. The mummy had suffered at the hands of tomb robbers: the head had been snapped off the body, and the right hand was missing. Cairo Museum.

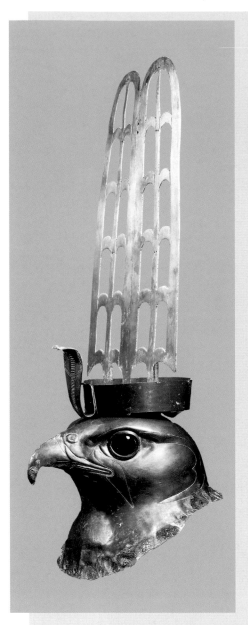

THE DOUBLE-PLUMED HEADDRESS

The double-plumed headdress, a style first seen in the 13th Dynasty, consisted of two falcon feathers set on a modius (a circular platform crown), often worn above the vulture crown and uraeus.

Illustrations suggest that these feathers were both implausibly tall and improbably balanced; but that, of course, is one of the functions of a crown, to set its wearer apart from those around her. We need not take Egyptian art at face value. Often the length of the queen's feathers is adjusted to fit the space available in the illustration.

The precise meaning of this complicated headdress is unclear, but it suggests a link both with the falcon sun god Horus, with Hathor the daughter and Eye of Horus, and with the male gods Amun of Thebes, Montu (warrior god) and Min (ithyphallic fertility god), each of whom wears tall feathers.

Goddesses will not start to wear the double plumes until the late 18th Dynasty, and it seems that the rising prominence of the queen is here being linked to the rising importance of the cult of Amun, who hitherto has been a local god of little importance beyond Thebes.

The double plumes linked Egypt's queens with a variety of solar deities, both gods and goddesses. This 6th Dynasty golden head of the Horus falcon, with polished obsidian eyes, was recovered from Hierakonpolis. Cairo Museum.

(Opposite) Ahhotep I's inner coffin lid, and a selection of grave goods recovered from the Dra Abu el-Naga tomb. The gold flies, dagger and battle axe seem to confirm Ahhotep's active role as defender of her land.

AHHOTEP I	
Husband Seqenenre Taa II	Ahmose the Younger
Father Senakhtenre Taa I	*Titles* King's Daughter, King's Sister, King's Great Wife, King's Mother, God's Wife
Mother Tetisheri	
Children Ahmose-Nefertari, Ahmose-Nebta, Ahmose the Elder,	*Burial place* Dra Abu el-Naga, Thebes

AHHOTEP I AND THE MYSTERIOUS AHHOTEP II

Seqenenre Taa II, son of Tetisheri, had married his sisters Inhapy, Sitdjehuty and Ahhotep. Now Ahhotep became his consort. She was to give him at least four children, all confusingly named Ahmose: two daughters, Ahmose-Nefertari and Ahmose-Nebta, and two sons. Ahmose the elder died young and it was Ahmose the younger who was to succeed his father. But first there was a blip in the succession. Seqenenre Taa died in battle. His mummy, recovered from the Deir el-Bahari cache, shows horrific head injuries caused by a Hyksos battle axe. Bypassing Ahmose, the

succession passed to Kamose, a man who, although he is often assumed to have been Seqenenre's son, has no known link to the royal family. Whatever his lineage, it is reasonable to assume that Kamose was a warrior of noble birth chosen to continue the struggle against the Hyksos. This he did until, a mere three years later, he too lay dying on a distant battlefield. Kamose was succeeded by Ahmose, the younger son of Seqenenre Taa II and Ahhotep.

Now there was a break in hostilities of almost a decade as Ahhotep raised her son, ruling Egypt on his behalf as regent. As an adult, and king of the unified land, Ahmose was not ashamed to admit the deep debt that he owed to his mother. On a unique stela recovered from Karnak he encouraged his people to revere her as 'one who has accomplished the rites and taken care of Egypt':

She has looked after her Egypt's soldiers, she has guarded Egypt, she has brought back her fugitives and gathered together her deserters, and she has pacified Upper Egypt and expelled her rebels.

If we read this stela literally, and there seems to be no good reason not to, it seems that Ahhotep had been forced to take up arms in defence of her country (Thebes), perhaps in the uncertain days following the death of Kamose. For the first time we have written proof that the queen regent could wield real authority.

Ahhotep's burial

There is little doubt that Ahhotep would have been accorded a splendid burial in the Dra Abu el-Naga royal cemetery on the Theban west bank. However, her tomb is today unknown, and the evidence concerning her burial is to say the least confusing. In 1858 workmen employed by Auguste Mariette to excavate at Dra Abu el-Naga discovered a coffin labelled for a King's Great Wife Ahhotep. King's Great Wife was the title now being used to differentiate the consort from her husband's lesser wives. With the dig director absent in Cairo, the provincial governor took it upon himself to open the coffin. Inside he found a mummy and a collection of golden artifacts. The mummy was stripped, and both body and bandages were thrown away. The grave goods were loaded onto a steamer, destined for the court of the Khedive. Infuriated, Mariette set off to intercept the boat and claim his antiquities. Théodule Devéria, an eyewitness, takes up the tale:

...we saw the boat containing the treasures taken from the pharaonic mummy coming towards us. At the end of half an hour the two boats were alongside each other. After some stormy words, accompanied by rather lively gestures, Mariette promised to one to toss him overboard, to another to roast his brains, to a third to send him to the galleys, and to

a fourth to have him hanged. At last they decided to place the box containing the antiquities on board, against a receipt.[14]

The grave goods included jewelry, an inscribed ceremonial axe made from copper, gold, electrum and wood and decorated with a Minoan-style griffin, a gold dagger and sheath, and three golden flies of valour, the 'medal' used to reward high-ranking Egyptian soldiers. Although some of the items bore the name of Kamose, more bore the name of King Ahmose, suggesting that he might have buried his mother.

Then, in 1881, a large outer coffin belonging to the King's Daughter, King's Sister, King's Great Wife and King's Mother Ahhotep was recovered from the Deir el-Bahari mummy cache. Inside this coffin was found the mummy of the Third Intermediate Period High Priest Pinedjem I, misplaced by the priests who had packed the bodies away. Initially it was assumed that the coffin belonged to Ahhotep II, consort of Amenhotep I. However, Amenhotep's wife never became a King's Mother and the next king, Thutmose I, was adopted into the royal family. More recently it has been accepted that the two coffins probably belong to one and the same Ahhotep (Ahhotep I, mother of Ahmose), although how they got separated remains something of a mystery. A third possibility is that there were indeed two queen Ahhoteps: Ahhotep I, the mother of Ahmose and wife of Seqenenre Taa II and owner of the Deir el-Bahari coffin, and Ahhotep II, a queen of unknown origins who was perhaps married to Kamose, and who owned the Dra Abu el-Naga coffin.

Gold model boat resting on a curious wood and bronze model wheeled vehicle, recovered from the Dra Abu el-Naga tomb of Ahhotep I, and now displayed in Cairo Museum.

THE NEW KINGDOM
1539–1069 BC

DYNASTY 18
1539–1292

Ahmose = = **Ahmose-Nefertari, Ahmose-Nebta**

Amenhotep I = = **Meritamun**

Thutmose I = = **Ahmose**

Thutmose II = = **Hatshepsut**

Hatshepsut

Thutmose III = = **Sitiah, Meritre-Hatshepsut, Nebtu, Manuwai, Manhata, Maruta**

Amenhotep II = = **Tia**

Thutmose IV = = **Nefertari, 'Iaret', Mutemwia**

Amenhotep III = = **Tiy, Sitamun, Isis? Henuttaneb? Gilukhepa, Tadukhepa**

Amenhotep IV/Akhenaten = = **Nefertiti, Kiya**

Smenkhkare = = **Meritaten**

Tutankhamun = = **Ankhesen-amun**

Ay = = **Tiy**

Horemheb = = **Mutnodjmet**

DYNASTY 19
1292–1190

Ramesses I = = **Sitre**

Seti I = = **Tuya**

Ramesses II = = **Henutmire, Nefertari, Isetnofret I, Bintanath I, Meritamun, Nebettawi, Maathornefrure**

Merenptah = = **Isetnofret II, Bintanath II**

Amenmesse = ? = **Baketwernel I**

Seti II = = **Takhat, Tawosret**

Siptah = ?

Tawosret

DYNASTY 20
1190–1069

Sethnakhte = = **Tiy-Merenese**

Ramesses III = = **Iset Ta-Hemdjert, Tiy**

Ramesses IV = ? = **Tentopet**

Ramesses V = = **Henuttawi, Tawerettenru**

Ramesses VI = = **Nubkhesbed, Isis**

Ramesses VII = ?

Ramesses VIII = ?

Ramesses IX = ? = **Baketwernel II**

Ramesses X = ? = **Titi**

Ramesses XI = = **Tentamun**

Names of queens in **bold**
= = known marriage
= ? = possible marriage
= ? queen unknown

SECOND INTERMEDIATE PERIOD ENDS | NEW KINGDOM BEGINS

Ahmose I (**Ahmose-Nefertari** & **Ahmose-Nebta**)
Amenhotep I (**Meritamun**)
Thutmose I (**Ahmose**)
Thutmose II (**Hatshepsut**)
Hatshepsut
Thutmose III (**Sitiah, Meritre-Hatshepsut, Nebtu, Manuwai, Manhata, Maruta**)
Amenhotep II (**Tia**)
Thutmose IV (**Nefertari, 'Iaret' & Mutemwia**)
Amenhotep III (**Tiy, Sitamun, Isis? Henuttaneb? Gilukhepa & Tadukhepa**)
Amenhotep IV/Akhenaten (**Nefertiti & Kiya**)
Smenkhkare (**Meritaten**)
Tutankhamun (**Ankhesenamun**)
Ay (**Tiy**)
Horemheb (**Mutnodjmet**)
Ramesses I (**Sitre**)
Seti I (**Tuya**)

DYNASTY 18   DYNAS

1600   1550   1500   1450   1400   1350   1300

Ahmose-Nefertari

Hatshepsut

Ankhesenamun

Nefertari

QUEENS OF THE EMPIRE
The New Kingdom 1539–1069 BC

As EGYPT BECAME the richest land in the Mediterranean world, Amun of Thebes became the most influential Egyptian god. The Theban kings abandoned the pyramid form, preferring to build hidden rock-cut tombs and highly visible mortuary temples.

Queen consorts maintained a high profile, enjoying a growing collection of secular and religious titles. An expanded range of headdresses ensured that the distinction between the mortal consort and the immortal goddesses, always somewhat blurred, became even less distinct. This coincided with an expansion in the size of the royal harem during the 18th Dynasty.

The unconventional pharaoh Akhenaten brought a temporary halt to stability as he devoted himself to the worship of one solar god, the Aten. His successors restored the old gods, but the dynastic line was failing and the 19th Dynasty dawned with the accession of an ex-general, Ramesses I. His grandson, Ramesses II, was to rule for over 65 years.

International insecurity and population movement followed the death of Ramesses II, and fertile Egypt was a prime target. The accession of the female king Tawosret ended the 19th Dynasty, and the mysterious Sethnakhte founded the 20th Dynasty. A further nine Ramesseses succeeded to the throne, each weaker than his predecessor. The death of Ramesses XI left Egypt once again a divided land.

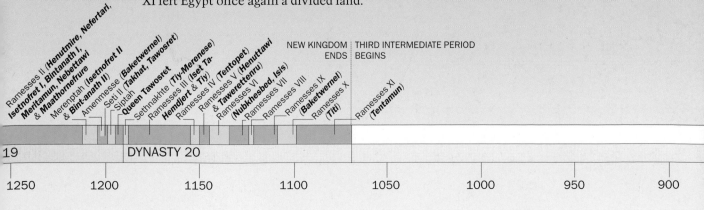

NEW KINGDOM ENDS | THIRD INTERMEDIATE PERIOD BEGINS

Ramesses II (Henutmire, Nefertari, Isetnofret I, Bintanath I, Meritamun, Nebettawi & Maathornefrure) · Merenptah (Isetnofret II & Bint-anath II) · Amenmesse (Baketwernel) · Seti II (Isetnofret II) · Siptah · Queen Tawosret (Takhat, Tawosret) · Sethnakhte (Tiy-Merenese) · Ramesses III (Iset Ta-Hemdjert & Tiy) · Ramesses IV (Tentopet) · Ramesses V (Henuttawi & Tawerettenru) · Ramesses VI (Nubkhesbed, Isis) · Ramesses VII · Ramesses VIII · Ramesses IX (Baketwernel) · Ramesses X (Titi) · Ramesses XI (Tentamun)

19 | DYNASTY 20

1250 — 1200 — 1150 — 1100 — 1050 — 1000 — 950 — 900

DYNASTY 18
1539–1292

Ahmose-Nefertari
Ahmose-Nebta
Meritamun
Ahmose

FAMILY AND TITLES

AHMOSE-NEFERTARI
Husband
  Ahmose
Father
  Seqenenre Taa II
Mother
  Ahhotep I
Son
  Amenhotep I
Daughter
  Meritamen
Titles
  King's Daughter,
  King's Sister, King's
  Great Wife, King's
  Mother, God's Wife,
  Second Prophet of
  Amun
Burial place
  Dra Abu el-Naga,
  Thebes

MERITAMUN
Husband
  Amenhotep I
Father
  Ahmose

Mother
  Ahmose-Nefertari
Titles
  King's Daughter,
  King's Sister, King's
  Great Wife, God's
  Wife
Burial place
  Deir el-Bahari,
  Thebes (TT 358)

AHMOSE
Husband
  Thutmose I
Parents
  Unknown
Daughters
  Hatshepsut,
  Neferubity
Titles
  King's Sister, King's
  Great Wife, King's
  Mother
Burial place
  Thebes

AHMOSE-NEFERTARI AND AHMOSE-NEBTA

Having driven the Hyksos eastwards out of Egypt, King Ahmose first sacked and then rebuilt their capital city, Avaris. His new Delta citadel included a fortified palace whose frescoed walls were decorated with vibrant bull-leaping scenes set against a maze-like background representing the bull-leaping ground. These scenes are so similar to those found on the walls of the contemporary Minoan palace of Knossos, we must conclude that Ahmose employed Minoan artists. Bulls had religious significance in Egypt, where they were associated with the solar cults, but bull-leaping and bull-grasping were purely Minoan rituals. So why had Ahmose – in all other respects a highly traditional Egyptian – chosen to decorate his northern palace in this outlandish foreign style? We have no idea, but some experts have suggested that he may have designed his palace to please a Minoan wife. This idea ties in well with an unexplained title held by the King's Mother Ahhotep, 'Mistress of the Shores of Hau-nebut'. Hau-nebut is an unknown land that may well be Crete. But there is as yet no more concrete evidence to support this theory, and some scholars believe Hau-nebut to have been a more generalized geographical term meaning the countries bordering the Mediterranean Sea.

Ahmose married both his sisters (Ahmose-Nefertari and Ahmose Nebta) and Ahmose-Nefertari became his consort. Even more influential than her redoubtable mother Ahhotep, Ahmose-Nefertari bore a string of titles including the now-standard 'King's Daughter, King's Sister, and King's Great Wife', and the more unusual 'God's Wife of Amun'. The Donation Stela, recovered from the Karnak temple, tells us how Ahmose purchased the 'Second Priesthood of Amun' to endow his wife with a

QUEENS OF THE 18th DYNASTY

Queen
KING
FEMALE KING
Non-royal male
Non-royal female
Princess
* person repeated on same family tree
?
= possible marriage
= marriage
? possible offspring

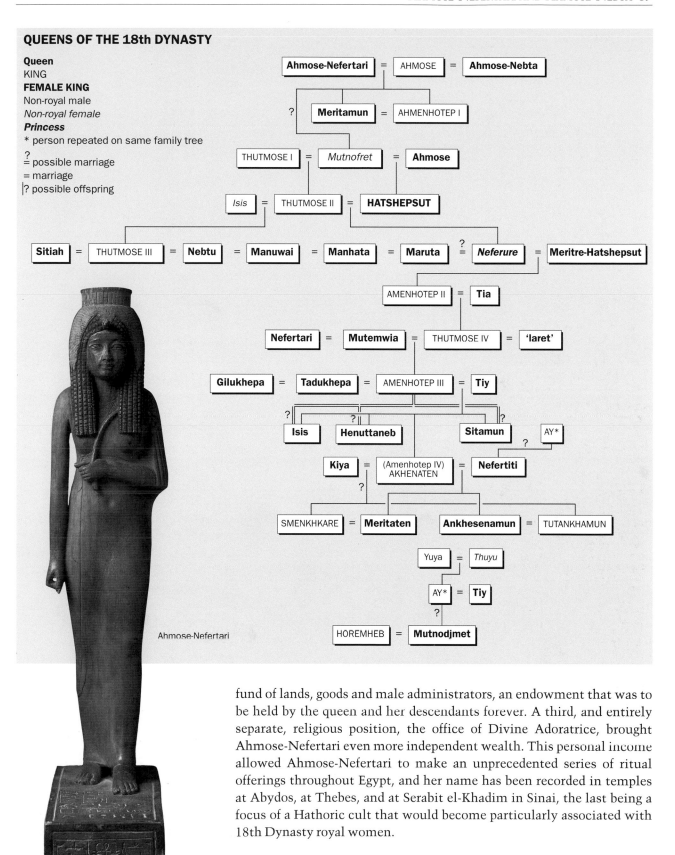

Ahmose-Nefertari

fund of lands, goods and male administrators, an endowment that was to be held by the queen and her descendants forever. A third, and entirely separate, religious position, the office of Divine Adoratrice, brought Ahmose-Nefertari even more independent wealth. This personal income allowed Ahmose-Nefertari to make an unprecedented series of ritual offerings throughout Egypt, and her name has been recorded in temples at Abydos, at Thebes, and at Serabit el-Khadim in Sinai, the last being a focus of a Hathoric cult that would become particularly associated with 18th Dynasty royal women.

Ahmose-Nefertari did not confine her influence to the religious sphere. Texts recovered from the Memphite limestone quarries, and from the Asyut alabaster quarries, record her name alongside that of Ahmose. When the king decided to build the Abydos cenotaph for his grandmother Tetisheri, he discussed his plans with his 'companion' first; his use of the word companion perhaps suggests that Ahmose-Nefertari is to be equated with the goddess Maat, the constant companion of Re and of all Egypt's kings.

Ahmose-Nefertari gave birth to at least four sons and five daughters, five of whom died in infancy or childhood. Following the death of Ahmose she acted as regent for her young son, Amenhotep I. Later, following the death of his childless sister-wife Meritamun, she resumed the role of consort to support her son, playing an active role in the selection of Amenhotep's adopted successor, Thutmose I. Dying during Thutmose's reign, she was buried in the Dra Abu el-Naga cemetery on the Theban west bank. Her mortuary temple stood close by, but is now almost completely destroyed.

Ahmose-Nefertari's mummy, stored in an enormous coffin that also housed the body of the 20th Dynasty king Ramesses III, was recovered from the Deir el-Bahari mummy cache. Unwrapped by Emile Brugsch in September 1885, her badly decomposed body smelt so unpleasant that it was hastily reburied in the museum grounds until the offensive aroma went away. Re-examination of her now odour-free remains has shown that Ahmose-Nefertari died in her 70s, an impressive age even by today's standards. Her thinning hair had been augmented by a series of false plaits that would magically become real hair in the Afterlife, and she shared the family trait of buck teeth already seen in the mummy attributed to her grandmother, Tetisheri. Ahmose-Nefertari's right hand was missing, presumably stolen by ancient thieves in search of jewelry.

Mother and son had become so closely linked that, after their deaths, both were deified as patrons of the state-owned west bank village of Deir el-Medina, the village built to house the workers involved in excavating and decorating the royal tombs in the Valley of the Kings (and later the Valley of the Queens). Here Ahmose-Nefertari, now honoured as a goddess of resurrection, 'Mistress of the Sky' and 'Lady of the West', would be worshipped until the end of the New Kingdom. Often, in this context, she was shown with the black skin that denoted fertility and rebirth rather than decay.

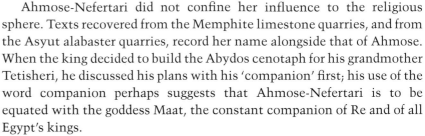

The deified Ahmose-Nefertari whose black skin, denoting the fertility of the land of Egypt, confirms her role as a goddess of resurrection. After death the queen and her son Amenhotep I were revered as gods of the Theban necropolis. From an unknown private Theban tomb, now in the British Museum.

MERITAMUN

Egypt had been blessed with three generations of increasingly influential queens. Now there was a lull as Ahmose-Nefertari's forceful personality completely eclipsed that of her daughter Meritamun. Meritamun took over the position of God's Wife of Amun from her mother, but we know little else about her, beyond the fact that she died young, before she could provide her husband with a living male heir. This failure, humiliating though it may have been for the queen, was not a dynastic disaster; the royal harem existed to cover such an eventuality. However, it seems that there was no suitable son in the harem either and, unlike all his fellow kings, Amenhotep was not inclined to marry again. So, as Ahmose-Nefertari reassumed the vital role of consort, Thutmose I was adopted into the royal family.

Meritamun's mummy, found lying in two cedarwood coffins and a cartonnage outer case in her Deir el-Bahari tomb (TT 358), had been desecrated in antiquity and re-bandaged during the 21st Dynasty. The queen's body shows that although she had died a relatively young woman, she had suffered from both arthritis and scoliosis.

Thutmose I already had at least four sons, Wadjmose, Amenmose, Ramose and Thutmose, the last of whom would eventually succeed his father as Thutmose II. Both Amenmose and Wadjmose survived into their late teens, making their mark on the archaeological record before predeceasing Thutmose I.

MUTNOFRET: FIRST WIFE OF THUTMOSE I

Wadjmose and the little-known Ramose feature in their father's badly damaged Theban funerary chapel where a side-room served as a shrine for the mortuary cults of various family members including the King's Sister Mutnofret, a lady who wears the vulture headdress and uraeus, and whose name is written in a cartouche. It is nowhere spelt out, but it seems that the four sons are the children of Mutnofret, an earlier wife of Thutmose I who must have died before her husband became heir to the throne. In an inscription recovered from Karnak a lady Mutnofret (whom we assume to be identical with the lady from Thutmose's chapel) is described as a King's Daughter. It may therefore be that Mutnofret is a daughter of King Ahmose.

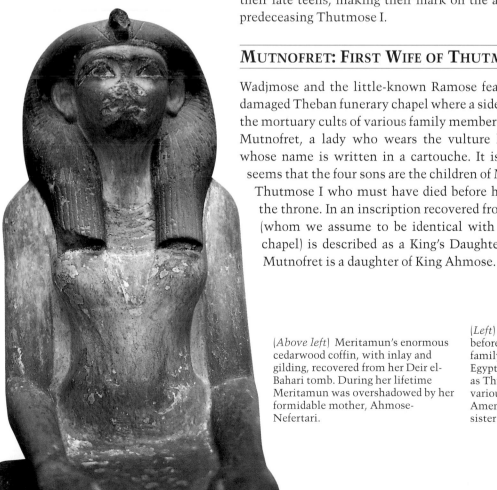

(*Above left*) Meritamun's enormous cedarwood coffin, with inlay and gilding, recovered from her Deir el-Bahari tomb. During her lifetime Meritamun was overshadowed by her formidable mother, Ahmose-Nefertari.

(*Left*) Mutnofret, wife to Thutmose I before he was adopted into the royal family. Mutnofret was never queen of Egypt, but one of her sons was to rule as Thutmose II. Mutnofret has been variously identified as a daughter of Amenhotep I and, more tentatively, a sister of Queen Ahhotep.

AHMOSE

We know that the new king, Thutmose I, was not an immediate member of the royal family, but it seems extremely unlikely that he was not connected in some way to Amenhotep I. Unfortunately, Thutmose's family history is frustratingly opaque. His father goes completely unrecorded – commoner kings being reluctant to emphasize their humble origins – while his mother is simply identified as the King's Mother (but never the King's Daughter or Wife) Seniseneb. As Seniseneb is a relatively common early 18th Dynasty name, it has not been possible to trace this lady's parents.

If we cannot link Thutmose to the royal family, can we link his consort? Again, we face many difficulties. Queen Ahmose's parentage is nowhere recorded and, as we have already seen, Ahmose is another popular New Kingdom name for men and women both within the royal family and in Egypt in general. It has been suggested – on the somewhat dubious grounds that Thutmose must have made a dynastic match to seal his claim to the throne – that his consort might have been either a daughter of Amenhotep I, or a daughter of King Ahmose and Ahmose-Nefertari and therefore a full sister of Amenhotep I. But, while Ahmose claims the title King's Sister, she is never described as a King's Daughter as she surely would have been had she been of royal blood. The obvious implication of her titulary is that she was the sister or half-sister of Thutmose I. Yet incestuous marriages were unknown outside the royal family at this time. If Ahmose was truly the sister-wife of Thutmose, they must have married after Thutmose became heir to Amenhotep I.

Ahmose bore her husband two daughters, Hatshepsut and Neferubity (occasionally referred to as Akhbetneferu). Neferubity appears on the wall of Hatshepsut's Deir el-Bahari mortuary temple wearing a diadem decorated with rosettes, then vanishes; it is assumed that she died young. Ahmose remains in the background throughout her husband's reign, but is featured prominently during her daughter's reign.

Ahhotep, featured on the wall of her daughter's Deir el-Bahari mortuary temple. Hatshepsut's decision to tell the story of her own divine birth – a story that naturally involved Ahhotep having the most intimate of relationships with the god Amun – made the hitherto retiring Ahhotep into a prominent public figure.

The God's Wife of Amun

There had already been at least three Middle Kingdom, non-royal God's Wives (of Amun, Min and Ptah), but from the reign of Ahmose onwards the office, properly funded, would be reserved for royal women and incorporated into their titularies. Ahmose-Nefertari would use this title in preference to any other. Given the rising importance of the cult of Amun at the beginning of the New Kingdom, this is a clear indication of the enhanced status of the queen.

So, what did this important position involve? Unfortunately, we are never told. However, a series of images of early God's Wives, Ahmose-Nefertari included, make it clear that it was more than an honorary position. The God's Wife wore a priestly costume: a short wig, narrow headband and a shift dress occasionally tied at the waist with a girdle. She was allowed the honour of entering the sacred sanctuary to stand before the god himself, and scenes carved on the wall of the 18th Dynasty Red Chapel (built by Hatshepsut within the Karnak temple complex) show the God's Wife being purified in the sacred lake, holding a long-handled fan inscribed with an image of a generalized enemy of Egypt, and carrying a flaming torch. These scenes suggest that she is able to perform the time-honoured rituals guaranteed to destroy foes by fire. In other scenes the God's Wife is present and supportive as the king himself performs the sacred rituals.

It is difficult to escape the conclusion that the role of 'wife' to an unequivocally male god must have had some sort of sexual connotation, as must the even more explicit position of 'God's Hand', a title that was during the 25th and 26th Dynasties joined to that of God's Wife. The latter seems to be an oblique reference to the hand which the creator god Atum used to masturbate when, all alone on the mound of creation, he produced the divine twins Shu and Tefnut. This hand, feminine in the Egyptian language, was closely identified with the goddess Hathor, who is known to have stimulated her father Re the creator god:

After a long while, Hathor, Lady of the southern sycamore, came and stood before her father, the All-Lord. She uncovered her nakedness before him; thereupon the great god laughed at her.[15]

It seems that at least some of the Wife's priestly rituals may have been designed to arouse the god and so encourage him to re-create the world.

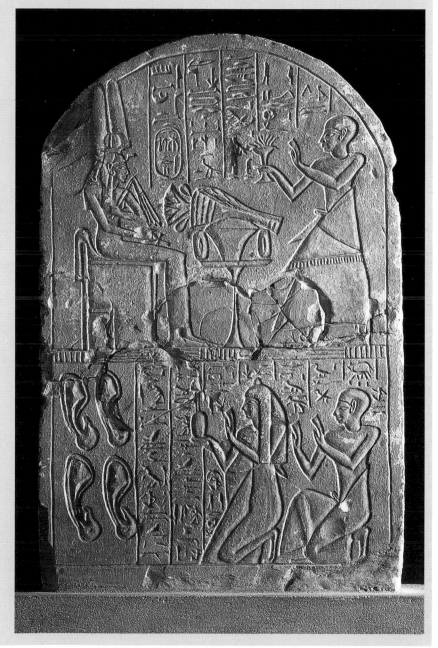

Ahmose-Nefertari, God's Wife of Amun, is petitioned by a family from the workmen's village of Deir el-Medina on this stela belonging to a priest. The large ears illustrated in the lower part of the stela will encourage the goddess to listen. Louvre Museum, Paris.

DYNASTY 18
1539–1292

Hatshepsut

The face of Hatshepsut preserved on one of a series of colossal statues that once decorated her mortuary temple, in which the king takes the form of the god of the afterlife, Osiris.

HATSHEPSUT

HATSHEPSUT	

Throne name
  Maatkare
Husband
  Thutmose II
Father
  Thutmose I
Mother
  Ahmose
Son
  None; stepmother
  to Thutmose III
	Daughter
	  Neferure
	Titles
	  God's Wife of Amun,
	  King's Daughter,
	  King's Sister, King's
	  Great Wife, King
	Burial place
	  Valley of the Kings
	  (KV 20)

HATSHEPSUT

Thutmose II married his half-sister, the King's Daughter, King's Sister and King's Great Wife Hatshepsut who, having inherited the office of God's Wife of Amun from Meritamun, used this as her preferred title. Egypt's new queen started to build a suitable consort's tomb in the remote Wadi Sikkat Taka el-Zeida, on the Theban west bank. Here her quartzite sarcophagus was inscribed with a prayer to the mother goddess Nut:

The King's Daughter, God's Wife, King's Great Wife, Lady of the Two Lands, Hatshepsut, says, 'O my mother Nut, stretch over me so that you may place me amongst the undying stars that are in you, and that I may not die.'

The Wadi Sikkat Taka el-Zeida tomb would be abandoned before the burial shaft could be completed.

Hatshepsut the consort

Hatshepsut bore her brother one daughter, Neferure, but no son. And so, when Thutmose II died unexpectedly after maybe 13 years on the throne, the crown passed to Thutmose III, a son born in the royal harem to the lady Isis. As the new king was still an infant, and as the new King's Mother was not considered sufficiently royal to act as regent, Hatshepsut was called upon to rule on behalf of her stepson. Thutmose III, proud of his mother and perhaps eager to inflate his lineage, would later promote Isis posthumously to the roles of King's Great Wife and God's Wife. We may see Isis on a pillar in Thutmose's tomb (KV 34) where she stands behind her son in a boat. Here she wears a simple sheath dress and tripartite wig but no crown. In contrast, a statue of Isis recovered from Karnak shows her wearing a modius and double uraeus (see p. 14).

His son has risen in his place as King of the Two Lands. He [Thutmose III] ruled on the throne of he who had begotten him. His sister, the God's Wife Hatshepsut, governed the land and the Two Lands were advised by her. Work was done for her and Egypt bowed its head.[16]

For several years Hatshepsut acted as a typical regent, allowing the young Thutmose to take precedence in all activities. But already there were signs that Hatshepsut was not afraid to flout tradition. Her new title, Mistress of the Two Lands, was a clear reference to the king's time-honoured title Lord of the Two Lands. More unusually, she commissioned a pair of obelisks to stand in front of the gateway to the Karnak temple of Amun. Obelisks tall, thin, tapering shafts of hard stone whose pyramid-shaped tops, coated with gold foil, sparkled in the strong Egyptian sunlight – were understood to represent the first rays of light that shone as the world was created. Very difficult to cut and transport, and so difficult to erect that modern scientists have not yet managed to replicate the procedure, they had thitherto been the very expensive gifts of kings to their gods. By the time her obelisks were cut, Hatshepsut too had become a king, and her new titles were engraved with pride on her monuments.

Hatshepsut the king

By year 7 Hatshepsut had been crowned king of Egypt, acquiring in the process a full king's titulary of five royal names – Horus, Powerful-of-Kas; Two Ladies, Flourishing-of-Years; Female Horus of Fine Gold, Divine-of-Diadems; King of Upper and Lower Egypt, Maatkare (Truth is the Soul of Re); Daughter of Re, Khenmet-Amun Hatshepsut (the One who is joined with Amun, the Foremost of Women). Thutmose III was never forgotten. He was scrupulously acknowledged as a co-ruler and the now-joint regnal years continued to be counted from the date of his accession, but Hatshepsut was undeniably the dominant king of Egypt. Only towards the end of Hatshepsut's life would Thutmose acquire anything like equal status with his co-ruler.

We can chart Hatshepsut's journey from conventional consort to king in a series of contrasting images. A stela now housed in Berlin Museum shows us the royal family shortly before Thutmose's death. The young king stands facing the sun god Re. Directly behind him stands his stepmother/mother-in-law Ahmose wearing the vulture headdress and uraeus topped with tall feathers. Hatshepsut stands dutifully behind her mother, her plain sheath dress and simple platform crown emphasizing the fact that here she is very much the junior queen. The modius or platform crown, decorated with flower stalks, was worn by a variety of not particularly prominent New Kingdom royal women. Two years after the death of Thutmose II, images carved at the Semna Temple, Nubia, show

Only the most wealthy, and blessed, of Egypt's rulers were able to raise obelisks. Hatshepsut's Karnak obelisks therefore served as confirmation that her rule was accepted by her divine father, Amun, while providing a link with her obelisk-raising earthly father, Thutmose I.

THE ORACLE

Oracular pronouncements allowed Egypt's deities to speak directly to the people. Normally the cult statues of the gods and goddesses remained hidden in their temples, accessible to only the highest-ranking priests. But as the New Kingdom developed, a growing number of religious festivals allowed them to leave their sanctuaries and process through the crowds as they visited other temples and other gods. And, at certain rest points on these processional journeys, it was possible for the public to approach the deity and ask a specific question. By the 19th Dynasty the wisdom of the oracle was perceived as rivalling the wisdom of the official courts, and aggrieved individuals – those who had been robbed, or were engaged in a dispute – would turn to the oracle for justice.

While the ordinary people consulted lesser, but nevertheless extremely effective oracles such as the deified Amenhotep I, Hatshepsut was able to consult Amun himself. We do not know how Amun communicated his thoughts to his daughter. Lesser oracles 'spoke' by moving (or causing their bearers to move). However, it is possible that some oracles actually spoke. A Ptolemaic bull statue discovered at the Delta site of Kom el-Wist actually contained a bronze speaking tube connected to a nearby chamber!

an adult-looking Thutmose III, sole King of Upper and Lower Egypt and Lord of the Two Lands, receiving the white crown from the ancient Nubian god Dedwen. Finally Hatshepsut's Red Chapel at Karnak shows Hatshepsut and Thutmose III standing together. The two kings are identical in appearance, both wearing the kilt and the blue crown, both carrying a staff and an *ankh*, and both with breastless male bodies. Their cartouches confirm that it is Thutmose who stands behind Hatshepsut in the more junior position.

Hatshepsut offers us no explanation for her unprecedented assumption of power. It seems that there was no opposition to her elevation although, of course, it is very unlikely that any such opposition would have been recorded. We can only guess that it was precipitated by a political or theological crisis requiring a fully adult king. Carved into the walls of her religious monuments Hatshepsut does, however, offer us some justification. Hatshepsut is entitled to claim the throne because she is not only the beloved daughter and intended heir of the revered Thutmose I (the less impressive Thutmose II being conveniently forgotten); she is also the daughter of the great god Amun. And he, via an oracle revealed to Hatshepsut herself, has proclaimed his daughter King of Egypt.

(*Opposite*) Hatshepsut, the dominant ruler, stands in front of the young Thutmose III. Hatshepsut has abandoned any attempt to depict herself as a female pharaoh, and both appear on the walls of the Red Chapel as stereotypical Egyptian kings.

(*Below*) Here Hatshepsut, still experimenting with her image, wears the traditional regalia of an Egyptian king, yet has the face and body of a woman. Metropolitan Museum of Art.

Divine birth

Hatshepsut's semi-divine nature is emphasized on the walls of her mortuary temple, where a cartoon-like sequence of images and a brief accompanying text tell the story of her divine birth. Amun, we learn, has fallen in love with a beautiful queen of Egypt, and has determined to father her child. In one of the few scenes showing a queen communicating directly with a god, we can view Queen Ahmose sitting unchaperoned in her boudoir. Here she is visited by Amun who, for propriety's sake, has disguised himself as her husband. Amun tells Ahmose that she has been chosen to bear his daughter, the future king of Egypt. Then he passes her the *ankh* that symbolizes life, and his potent perfume fills the palace. Meanwhile, in heaven, the ram-headed creator god Khnum crafts both the baby and the baby's soul on his potter's wheel. Nine months later it is time for the birth. The pregnant Ahmose, her baby bump barely visible, is led to the birthing bower by Khnum and the frog-headed midwife Heket. Here, in a scene discreetly left to the imagination, Hatshepsut is born.

Amun is overwhelmed with love for his new daughter. He takes her from Hathor the divine wet nurse, kisses her and speaks:

Come to me in peace, daughter of my loins, beloved Maatkare, thou art the king who takes possession of the diadem on the Throne of Horus of the Living, eternally.[17]

The temple walls show Egypt's new, naked king with an unmistakably male body; her identical and equally naked soul, too, is obviously male. But the new king's names are female, and neither Ahmose nor Amun is in any doubt over the gender of their child. The presentation of Hatshepsut as a male is purely a convention, her response to the artistic dilemma that, three centuries before, saw Sobeknefru don an unhappy mixture of men's and women's clothing. As a queen Hatshepsut had been happy to be portrayed as a conventional woman: slender, pale and passive. But as a king she needed to find an image that would reinforce her new position while distancing her from the consort's role. Towards the beginning of her reign she was depicted either as a conventional woman or as a woman wearing [male] king's clothing. Two seated limestone statues recovered from Deir el-Bahari show her dressed in this hybrid manner. Hatshepsut wears the traditional headcloth and kilt. She has a rounded, feminine, unbearded face and a feminine body with breasts and an indented waist. Soon, however, she evolves into an entirely masculine king, with a man's body, male clothing, male accessories and male ritual actions. It seems that it is the appearance of the king that matters rather than her actual gender; the masculine form of Hatshepsut is happy to alternate between masculine and feminine forms of her titulary.

The courtier Senenmut demonstrates his closeness to the royal family by holding the royal daughter Neferure in a posture more usually associated with women. Cairo Museum.

Princess Neferure

From the time of her coronation onwards, Hatshepsut was careful to behave as an entirely conventional King of Egypt; in consequence, while her story tells us a great deal about the perceived role of the king, it tells us less about the role of the queen than we might have hoped. It does, however, confirm one very important detail: that the queen was an important element of the kingship. Like any other king, Hatshepsut needed a queen to fulfil the feminine aspect of her monarchy, and for this she turned to her daughter Neferure. Most of Egypt's royal children remain hidden in their nurseries throughout their childhoods and, during her father's reign, Neferure had been no exception. But following her mother's coronation, Neferure started to play an unusually prominent role – the queen's role – in public life. Neferure used the titles Lady of Upper and Lower Egypt and Mistress of the Lands and she assumed the office of God's Wife of Amun, a role that Hatshepsut had been forced to abandon as it was incompatible with her kingly status. Neferure, like all other God's Wives before her, adopted this as her preferred title. Scenes carved on the walls of the Red Chapel at Karnak show Neferure as a fully adult woman performing the appropriate rituals.

Neferure's education was clearly a matter of some importance. The young princess was taught first by the courtier Ahmose-Pennekhbet, next by Senenmut, Hatshepsut's most influential advisor, and finally by the administrator Senimen. A series of hard stone statues – highly expensive, produced by the royal workshops – show Neferure and Senenmut together. Neferure has the shaven head and sidelock of youth worn by all Egyptian children. Senenmut, dressed in a heavy striated wig, assumes a typical woman's role by either holding the princess tight, or seating her on his knee and wrapping her body in his cloak. Neferure disappears towards the end of her mother's reign; she appears on a stela at Serabit el-Khadim in Year 11, but is unmentioned in Senenmut's tomb dated to Year 16. The obvious assumption is that she has died and been buried in her tomb which lay near that built for her mother in the remote Wadi Sikkat Taka el-Zeida.

Senenmut

The new king inherited her late brother's courtiers but gradually, as her reign developed, she started to pick new advisors, many of whom, like Senenmut, were men of relatively humble birth. As Hatshepsut well realized, these self-made men had a vested interest in keeping her on the throne: if she fell, they fell with her. Senenmut, Steward of Amun and tutor to Princess Neferure, enjoyed a meteoric rise through the ranks, and this has sparked a great deal of speculation over the precise nature of his relationship with Hatshepsut. They certainly never married – marriage was not an option for a female king, as it would lead to too great a conflict of roles – but could they have been lovers? A crude piece of graffiti scrawled in a Deir el-Bahari

(*Above*) Graffito scrawled in a Deir el-Bahari tomb. The female figure, breastless yet with an obvious pubic triangle and perhaps wearing a king's headdress without a uraeus, has been identified as Hatshepsut. The male figure is said to be Senenmut.

(*Below*) Egypt's queens were invariably depicted as slender beings. The queen of Punt, as a foreigner, need not conform to this artistic ideal, and was instead depicted with multiple rolls of fat. Her husband, who walks before her, is svelte.

tomb, which apparently shows a man having 'doggy-style' intercourse with a woman wearing a royal headdress, cannot be accepted as conclusive proof of anything other than the fact that the ancient Egyptians enjoyed smutty gossip as much as any other people. The fact that Senenmut carved his image into Hatshepsut's mortuary temple – an unprecedented and daring move for a non-royal – combines with the fact that his second tomb encroached upon the Deir el-Bahari precincts to offer a more convincing argument in favour of a close bond between the two. It is difficult to imagine that Senenmut could have ordered these infringements of protocol without Hatshepsut's knowledge and tacit approval.

Policy

The new king set out to maintain *maat* by launching an obvious assault on chaos. Foreigners were to be subdued, the monuments of the ancestors were to be restored, and the whole of Egypt was to be enhanced by a series of ambitious temple-building projects. The subduing of the foreigners was quickly achieved in a token series of military campaigns against the vassals to the south and east. The Deir el-Bahari temple again shows the Nubian god Dedwen, this time leading a series of captive Nubian towns (each depicted as a walled town or fortified cartouche bearing an obviously Nubian head) towards the victorious Hatshepsut.

Next, Hatshepsut turned her attention to trade. There were missions to the Lebanon for wood, increased exploitation of the copper and turquoise mines in Sinai and, most important of all, during Year 9, a successful trading mission to Punt. The real but almost legendary land of Punt was a source of many exotic treasures: precious resins, curious wild

animals, and the ever-desirable ebony, ivory and gold. It was, however, a long way from the safety of Thebes. The exact location of Punt is now lost, but flora and fauna included in the reliefs decorating Hatshepsut's mortuary temple suggest that it was an east African trading centre situated somewhere along the Eritrean/Ethiopian coast. The journey to this distant Utopia involved a long, hot march across 100 miles (160 km) of desert, possibly carrying a dismantled boat, to the Red Sea port of Quseir. This was followed by a sea journey along the coast, an adventure that the Egyptians, always very happy on the calm waters of the Nile, dreaded.

Hatshepsut's envoy Neshy set sail with a small but well-armed army, his precise route undisclosed. After some sharp bargaining with the chief of Punt – the temple walls show a handful of trinkets being exchanged for a wonderful array of goods, but doubtless they exaggerate – he returned home in triumph. Hatshepsut, watching as her ships disgorged their valuable cargos at Thebes, must have been overjoyed. The safe return of her troops proved beyond a shadow of a doubt that her reign was indeed blessed by her divine father. With great perspicacity she promptly donated the best of the goods to Amun, and ordered that the epic voyage be immortalized on the Deir el-Bahari temple walls.

Building projects

Back at home the building projects were proceeding well. It seems likely that Hatshepsut instigated a temple-building project in all of Egypt's major cities, but most of these temples have been lost along with their cities, leaving the Theban monuments to stand as testimony to the prosperity of her reign. We know that there were building works in Nubia, and at Kom Ombo, Hierakonpolis, Elkab, Armant and the island of Elephantine, which received two temples dedicated to local gods. In Middle Egypt, not far from Beni Hassan and the Hatnub quarries, Egypt's first two rock-cut temples were dedicated to the obscure lion-headed goddess Pakhet, 'She who Scratches', a local variant of the goddess Sekhmet, who was herself a variant of Hathor. On one of these temples, known today by its Greek name Speos Artemidos (Grotto of Artemis), Hatshepsut carved a bold statement setting out her policy of rebuilding and restoration:

I have never slumbered as one forgetful, but have made strong what was decayed. I have raised up what was dismembered, even from the first time when the Asiatics were in Avaris of the North Land, with roving hordes in the midst of them overthrowing what had been made; they ruled without Re.... I have banished the abominations of the gods, and the earth has removed their footprints.[18]

In suggesting that she has personally expelled the Hyksos from Egypt, Hatshepsut is being more than economical with the truth; such an outrageous lie can, however, be justified if we take the view, as Hatshepsut herself undoubtedly did, that each of Egypt's kings was a continuation of

The central part of the Great Temple of Amun at Karnak was largely the work of Hatshepsut and her co-regent and successor, Thutmose III.

the kings who had gone before and so fully entitled to claim his deeds for his (or her) own. Her assertion that she is renewing and restoring damaged monuments does appear to be true within the modern meaning of the term. We know, for example, that she repaired the temple of Hathor at the town of Cusae, a town which, situated on the border between the Theban and Hyksos kingdoms, suffered badly during the wars that ended the 17th Dynasty.

The Karnak temple benefited greatly from the new king's generosity. There was another pair of obelisks – this time entirely covered in gold foil – raised to commemorate Hatshepsut's 15-year jubilee, a new bark shrine (the Red Chapel) where Amun's processional boat could rest, a new southern pylon (gateway), a new royal palace and a series of improvements to the processional routes which linked the various temples within the complex. But the most magnificent building she commissioned was a mortuary temple for herself, situated close by the Middle Kingdom tomb of Mentuhotep II in the Deir el-Bahari bay.

THE ROYAL TEMPLE AT DEIR EL-BAHARI

Hatshepsut's most impressive building achievement was her own mortuary temple, situated close by the Middle Kingdom tomb of Mentuhotep II in the Deir el-Bahari bay. Today, as it stands in the arid desert, the tiered temple is undoubtedly an architectural masterpiece, one of the most beautiful buildings in the ancient world. In its heyday it must have been even more spectacular.

Those visitors privileged enough to pass through the gateway in the thick, limestone enclosure wall entered a peaceful, shaded garden complete with plants, trees and pools. The temple itself, a softly gleaming limestone edifice, occupied three ascending terraces set back against the Theban cliff. Its tiered porticoes were linked by a long, open-air stairway running through the centre of the temple towards the dark sanctuary of Amun, cut into the living rock face. The temple was decorated with a series of colossal statues of Hatshepsut in the form of the living Osiris with a white, mummified body and an unbandaged head wearing either the white crown of southern Egypt, or the double crown of the Two Lands. The architect of this masterpiece is generally assumed to be Hatshepsut's favourite, Senenmut.

(Below) Plan illustrating the close proximity of the Middle Kingdom temple-tomb complex of Nebhepetre Mentuhotep II and the New Kingdom mortuary temple of Hatshepsut.

(Below left) Hatshepsut as the mummified Osiris, king of the dead.

(Bottom and opposite) The rising terraces of Hatshepsut's partially restored mortuary temple, as seen by the modern visitor. An aerial view of both temple complexes, nestling side by side in a natural bay in the Theban cliff.

(*Opposite*) The columns in Hatshepsut's Hathor chapel take the form of Hathor-headed sistra (or religious rattles). Hathor, Mistress of Punt and goddess of love, motherhood and drunkenness, was worshipped locally as the goddess of the Deir el-Bahari bay. Many of Egypt's queens demonstrated a devotion to Hathor.

Representations of Egyptian sphinxes with female faces are rare, but Hatshepsut commissioned several sphinxes. Some showed the female pharaoh with a human face and lion's head and body. Others, as here, had a human head and face and a lion's body.

Deir el-Bahari

Deir el-Bahari was a multi-functional temple with a series of shrines and chapels devoted to a variety of gods. The main sanctuary was dedicated to Hatshepsut's divine father, Amun. But there was also a suite of chapels devoted to the royal ancestors; this included a small mortuary or memorial chapel for her earthly father, Thutmose I, and a much larger mortuary chapel for Hatshepsut herself. Here, in front of Hatshepsut's cult statue, the priests could make the daily offerings of food, drink, music and incense that would allow the dead king's soul to live forever. An open-air court dedicated to the worship of the sun god Re-Herakhty balanced the dark and gloomy mortuary chapels, chapels that linked the dead with the cult of Osiris. One level down were the chapels dedicated to the god of embalming, Anubis, and to Hathor, who was not only the goddess of the Deir el-Bahari bay, but also 'Mistress of Punt'. Like many of Egypt's queens, Hatshepsut (now an ex-queen) felt a particular attraction to Hathor's predominantly female cult, and Hathor features prominently in her temple. She is present at Hatshepsut's birth and later, taking the form of a cow, suckles a newborn infant. If Amun can be considered the divine father of the king, it seems that Hathor is now his (or her) mother.

The mortuary temple was one half of Hatshepsut's mortuary provision. Her tomb, the other half, was to be in the Valley of the Kings, the now traditional cemetery for Egypt's kings. The old consort's tomb in the Wadi Sikkat Taka el-Zeida was abandoned, but Hatshepsut (perhaps concerned about her lack of time) did not try to build a replacement. Instead she started to enlarge the tomb (KV 20) which already held her father, until it became the longest and deepest tomb in the Valley. Eventually, or so she hoped, father and daughter would lie side-by-side forever in two

matching yellow quartzite sarcophagi (Thutmose I's sarcophagus, a shade less magnificent than Hatshepsut's own, was actually a second-hand sarcophagus originally prepared for his daughter). The two did indeed lie together for a time, but Thutmose III eventually had his grandfather re-interred in a nest of new coffins placed in a new sarcophagus in a brand new tomb (KV 38).

The end of an era

A single stela, raised at Armant, tells us that Hatshepsut died on the tenth day of the sixth month of the 22nd year of her reign. Finally Thutmose was free to embark on what would be 33 years of highly successful solo rule. First, however, he had to bury his predecessor to consolidate his claim to the throne. Hatshepsut's tomb was looted in antiquity, but included amongst the debris left by the robbers were two vases – family heirlooms? – made for Queen Ahmose-Nefertari. We have Hatshepsut's sarcophagus and her matching canopic chest, and a few fragments of her furniture, but her body has vanished. All that remains is a box recovered from the Deir el-Bahari mummy cache, decorated with Hatshepsut's cartouche and holding mummified tissue identified rather loosely as either a liver or a spleen. We do, however, have several nameless New Kingdom female mummies who might, or might not, be Hatshepsut. Chief amongst these are the 'Elder Lady', a female mummy in her 40s recovered

The goddess Isis, wife of Osiris, was intended to guard the body of Hatshepsut as she lay in her quartzite sarcophagus. Cairo Museum.

(*Above*) Thoth, scribe of the gods, assists in the purification ritual of the dead king. But the subject of the purification – Hatshepsut – has been carefully chiselled away.

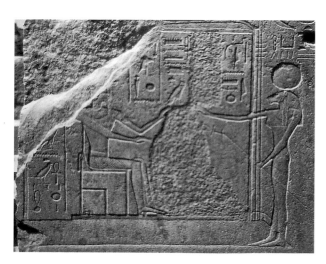

(*Below*) Hatshepsut (now erased) kneels between her father Amun and the goddess Heret-Kau in this scene from the wall of the Red Chapel, Karnak.

from a sealed side-chamber in the tomb of Amenhotep II (KV 35) and an obese female mummy with red-gold hair discovered in the tomb of the royal nurse Sitre (KV 60). Sitre is known to have been Hatshepsut's wet-nurse, and a badly damaged limestone statue shows her sitting with the young Hatshepsut (a miniature adult rather than a child) on her lap.

Erasing Hatshepsut

Towards the end of Thutmose's reign an attempt was made to delete Hatshepsut from the historical record. This elimination was carried out in the most literal way possible. Her cartouches and images were chiselled off the stone walls – leaving very obvious Hatshepsut-shaped gaps in the artwork – and she was excluded from the official history that now ran without any form of co-regency from Thutmose II to Thutmose III. At the Deir el-Bahari temple Hatshepsut's numerous statues were torn down and in many cases smashed or disfigured before being buried in a pit. Over the river at Karnak there was even an attempt to wall up her obelisks. While it is clear that much of this rewriting of history occurred during the later part of Thutmose's reign, it is not clear why it happened.

For many years Egyptologists assumed that it was a *damnatio memoriae*, the deliberate erasure of a person's name, image and memory, which would cause them to

die a second, terrible and permanent death in the afterlife. This appeared to make perfect sense. Thutmose must have been an unwilling co-regent for years. What could be more natural than a wish to destroy the memory of the woman who had so wronged him? But this assessment of the situation is probably too simplistic. It is always dangerous to attempt to psychoanalyse the long dead, but it seems highly unlikely that the determined and focused Thutmose – not only Egypt's most successful general, but an acclaimed athlete, author, historian, botanist and architect – would have brooded for two decades before attempting to revenge himself on his stepmother.

Furthermore the erasure was both sporadic and haphazard, with only the more visible and accessible images of Hatshepsut being removed. Had it been complete – and, given the manpower available, there is no reason why it should not have been – we would not now have so many images of Hatshepsut. It seems either that Thutmose must have died before his act of vengeance was finished, or that he had never intended a total obliteration of her memory at all. In fact, we have no evidence to support the assumption that Thutmose hated or resented Hatshepsut during her lifetime. Had he done so he could surely, as head of the army (a position given to him by Hatshepsut, who was clearly not worried about her co-regent's loyalty), have led a successful coup. It may well be that Thutmose, lacking any sinister motivation, was, towards the end of his life, simply engaged in 'tidying up' his personal history, restoring Hatshepsut to her rightful place as a queen regent rather than a king. By eliminating the more obvious traces of his female co-regent, Thutmose could claim all the achievements of their joint reign for himself.

The erasure of Hatshepsut's name, whatever the reason, allowed her to disappear from Egypt's archaeological and written record. Thus, when 19th-century Egyptologists started to interpret the texts on the Deir el-Bahari temple walls (walls illustrated with not one but two obviously male kings) their translations made no sense. Jean-François Champollion, the French decoder of hieroglyphs, was not alone in feeling deeply confused by the obvious conflict between the words and the pictures:

If I felt somewhat surprised at seeing here, as elsewhere throughout the temple, the renowned Moeris [Thutmose III], adorned with all the insignia of royalty, giving place to this Amenenthe [Hatshepsut], for whose name we may search the royal lists in vain, still more astonished was I to find on reading the inscriptions that wherever they referred to this bearded king in the usual dress of the Pharaohs, nouns and verbs were in the feminine, as though a queen were in question. I found the same peculiarity everywhere.....

Hatshepsut kneels holding a libation vessel as she makes an offering to her father Amun. Red granite statue found in Deir el-Bahari, now in Cairo Museum.

By the late 19th century the truth had been revealed and, despite her masculine appearance, Hatshepsut had been restored to her rightful place as a female king.

DYNASTY 18
1539–1292

Sitiah
Meritre-Hatshepsut
Nebtu
Manuwai
Manhata
Maruta
Tia
Nefertari
'Iaret'
Mutemwia

FROM SITIAH TO MARUTA: THE WIVES OF THUTMOSE III

Given her background as the daughter of two kings and sister to a third, it seems inconceivable that Neferure was not destined to wed her half-brother Thutmose III. Yet just one, highly inconclusive piece of evidence suggests that they did marry. A stela dated to the beginning of Thutmose's solo reign names his consort, 'Sitiah', and describes her as a God's Wife. We know that Sitiah was the first consort of Thutmose III, but there is no other evidence to suggest that she ever bore the title God's Wife. Is it possible that the stela, originally designed to include Neferure as consort, could have been altered after her death to show her replacement?

The office of God's Wife of Amun was to fall into decline during the reign of Thutmose III, and would temporarily die out after the reign of Thutmose IV. This, coinciding with an obvious rejection of the sister-wife as consort which will last until the reign of Smenkhkare, suggests that the royal family may have grown wary of according their sisters and

(*Above right*) Tia, wife of Amenhotep II, wears the vulture headdress and uraeus.

(*Right*) Thutmose III, his wives Sitiah, Meritre-Hatshepsut and Nebtu, and his daughter Nefertiry, watch as the goddess Isis, in the form of a sycamore tree, suckles the young Thutmose. The goddess Hathor is more usually recognized as Mistress of the Sycamore, but the story has been changed to incorporate a reference to Isis, the king's non-royal mother.

Two of three reconstructed headdresses belonging to Thutmose's foreign wives. The lower headdress is decorated with two gazelles which, being the symbolic equivalent of the cobra and the feather, were linked with ideas of creation and rebirth, and with the goddess Hathor. Gazelle crowns, first worn during the Middle Kingdom, were worn by prominent royal women, but never consorts or queens' mothers.

daughters too much power and too much independent wealth. Only the King's Mothers – the women who had enjoyed intercourse with the creator god, and who posed little threat to ruling sons – could be allowed to retain their former position if Hatshepsut's usurpation was not to set a precedent.

A pillar in Thutmose III's tomb in the Valley of the Kings (KV 34) shows the king accompanied by three wives – Sitiah (already deceased), **Meritre-Hatshepsut** and **Nebtu** – plus a dead daughter, Nefertiry. All five stand and watch as a miniature Thutmose is suckled by the tree goddess Isis (a play on the name of the King's Mother Isis). Between them, these three wives produced some 12 children, with Meritre-Hatshepsut, God's Wife, King's Great Wife and King's Mother, almost certainly the mother of Thutmose's heir, Amenhotep II. For a long time Egyptologists believed that Meritre-Hatshepsut must have been the younger daughter of Hatshepsut and Thutmose II, but there was no foundation for this assumption, which was based on nothing more substantial than their shared name. Now it is accepted that Meritre-Hatshepsut was the daughter of the priestess and royal wet-nurse Huy.

Thutmose's Annals, carved into the Karnak Temple, mention that he acquired a bride from Retenu: a chief's daughter who arrived in Egypt with a valuable dowry plus an assortment of attendants, servants and male and female slaves. This anonymous Princess of Retenu was just one of many foreign women – women of widely differing social status – who arrived in Egypt following Thutmose's energetic expansion of the Egyptian empire. We know nothing more about her.

Three foreign wives

The ladies of the harem have until now formed a silent background to our history of Egypt's queens. But an undecorated tomb in the remote Wadi Gabbanat el-Qurud (Valley of the Cemetery of the Ape), not far from the location of Hatshepsut's queenly tomb, has yielded welcome information about three of the foreign wives of Thutmose III. Unfortunately the tomb was discovered by local tomb robbers, and so we have no proper record of its *in situ* contents, although contemporary accounts written by Egyptologists living in Egypt at the time of the discovery (August 1916) agree that there had been three intact burials and a large number of grave goods, including many alabaster storage jars. The wooden parts of the burial and the mummies had rotted away (the tomb was situated in a water course) but the stone and gold survived. By the time of the official excavation in September of the same year, only the objects discarded by the robbers remained. Items from the burial appeared on the antiquities market for several years, and a few eventually made their way into the collections of the Metropolitan Museum of Art, New York.

The names of Thutmose III and Hatshepsut have been found on the grave goods, Hatshepsut being attested both as a consort and a king. These goods include two inlaid wigs or headdresses made from streamers of rosettes suspended from a head plate, and a gazelle crown. The names of the three wives, recovered from their canopic jars, are **Manuwai**, **Manhata** and **Maruta**; these names suggest that all three came from the Syrio/Palestine region, but it is not possible to determine whether they all came from the same state. The fact that at least one of these foreign-born women was entitled to wear the gazelle crown proves that this crown was not, as has often been assumed, the headwear reserved for the eldest royal princess.

We do not know why these three queens were buried together. It may be that they were members of the same birth family; the human heads on their canopic jars suggest that they were not particularly similar in appearance, but this may well be a reflection of the artistic skills of the stoneworkers. It does seem likely that all three died at roughly the same time, but as the bodies have been lost we have no means of knowing exactly how they did die.

TIA	
Husband	*Titles*
Amenhotep II	King's Great Wife,
Parents	God's Wife, King's
Unknown	Mother
Son	*Burial place*
Thutmose IV	Valley of the Kings
	(KV 32)

TIA

Amenhotep II ruled Egypt for almost 30 peaceful years, yet has left evidence for only one named wife. Tia, mother of Thutmose IV, is a lady of uncertain parentage who is known to have usurped some of the later monuments of her mother-in-law, Meritre-Hatshepsut. Tia was eventually buried in the Valley of the Kings; her tomb had yielded some damaged grave goods but no mummy, and no trace of her body has been found elsewhere either.

Tia remained very much in the background during her husband's rule, achieving far greater prominence during her son's reign when she became God's Wife of Amun. A statue recovered from Karnak shows a youthful-looking Tia dressed in a sheath dress, heavy wig, vulture headdress and uraeus, sitting next to Thutmose who wears a king's kilt, wig and uraeus. Mother and son are seated what appears to be an uncomfortable distance apart yet are mutually supportive, each with an arm around the other. This close relationship between Tia and Thutmose is emphasized in a variety of inscriptions, which suggest that Tia is to be regarded as the earthly counterpart of Hathor, Isis and Mut, the mother goddess and wife of Amun. From this time onwards, until the end of the 18th Dynasty, the King's Mother will play an increasingly important role in political and more particularly religious rituals, as successive kings seek to prove their own earthly divinity via their birth stories.

The history of the royal family grows increasingly confused towards the end of Amenhotep's reign, suggesting that there may have been some jostling over the succession. Thutmose IV himself confirms in the Dream Stela that he set between the paws of the Great Sphinx of Giza, that he was not his father's obvious successor, but that he inherited the throne through the direct intervention of the Sphinx god, an ancient form of the sun god. In so doing he established a long-lasting family interest in solar cults.

Tia, wife of Amenhotep II, sits beside her son Thutmose IV, each embracing the other. Statue recovered from Karnak, now displayed in Cairo Museum.

MUTEMWIA	
Husband	*Titles*
Thutmose IV	King's Great Wife,
Parents	King's Mother
Unknown	*Burial place*
Son	Unknown
Amenhotep III	

NEFERTARI, 'IARET' AND MUTEMWIA: THE WIVES OF THUTMOSE IV

Thutmose IV is known to have had at least two principal wives whose names appear alongside his own. His first consort, Nefertari, is featured in several statues recovered from Giza and Luxor. After Nefertari's untimely death Thutmose's sister 'Iaret' (the reading of her name is uncertain, being written simply with the image of a cobra) became queen consort. Thutmose appears to have shared the ritual aspects of the queen-ship between these two ladies and his mother, Tia. A third, less well-known wife was the anonymous daughter of the King of Mitanni; this diplomatic marriage was designed to seal the new peace treaty that allowed Egypt and Mitanni to become allies.

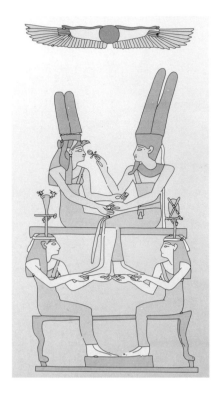

(*Above*) In this redrawn scene, carved on the wall of the Luxor temple, Queen Mutemwia sits on a bed and receives the gift of life from Amun. The bed is supported by the goddesses Selket (left) and Neith (right).

(*Below*) Broken rebus image of Mutemwia, sitting in her boat. Recovered from Karnak and now in the British Museum.

A fourth wife, Mutemwia, mother of the next king, Amenhotep III, did not emerge from the seclusion of the harem until her son came to the throne, suggesting that she was a lady of lesser birth, and therefore of lesser importance, until the day the fates decreed she should become King's Mother. Then, as had been the case with Ahmose (mother of Hatshepsut), her physical relationship with the god Amun was fully exploited in the story of her son's divine birth. Amenhotep had this story carved into the walls of the Luxor temple, a temple dedicated to both Amun and to the celebration of the divine royal soul. Hatshepsut had used her birth story to reinforce her somewhat dubious claim to the throne. Amenhotep, the son of the previous king, can have felt no need to justify his accession. Instead he used his birth-story to reinforce the semi-divine nature of the king of Egypt and, more particularly, his own personal divinity. In a scene copied wholesale from the wall of the Deir el-Bahari temple, we can now see Mutemwia sitting on a bed to receive the attentions of Amun who, for propriety's sake, is disguised as Thutmose IV:

When he had transformed himself into the form of her husband, the King of Upper and Lower Egypt Menkheperure [Thutmose IV].... He found her as she was resting in the beauty of the palace. She awoke upon smelling the perfume of the god and cried out before him. He went to her directly....

Amenhotep may have felt that he owed a particular debt to his mother. Having inherited his throne at no more than 12 years of age, it seems that he must have relied on Mutemwia to protect his interests, although we have no formal record of any regency. He included his mother's statue inside his mortuary temple, and she figures at a smaller (but by no means minute) scale beside the left leg of the Colossi of Memnon, which still stand in their original position outside Amenhotep's now-vanished temple gateway. Accompanying Mutemwia are Amenhotep's consort, Tiy (see next section), and one of his four daughters; it appears that the king was eager to stress his relationship with three generations of royal women.

Today our best-known image of Mutemwia (housed in the British Museum) is a sadly broken statue of a woman sitting on a boat, and protected by the wings of the vulture goddess Mut. This statue is a rebus – a literal representation of the name Mut-m-wia or '[the goddess] Mut in the boat' – and Mutemwia, like her mother-in-law Tia before her, is clearly to be identified with the mother goddess Mut.

DYNASTY 18
1539–1292

Tiy
Sitamun
Isis?
Henuttaneb?
Gilukhepa
Tadukhepa

This broken steatite head recovered from Serabit el-Khadim, Sinai, shows Tiy, consort of Amenhotep III, wearing the double uraeus. Her name is given in a cartouche on her crown. Her strong face hints at a forceful personality. Cairo Museum.

The wedding scarab of Amenhotep III and Tiy (*below*) was designed to ensure that Tiy's children would be considered the legitimate heirs to the throne.

TIY	
Husband	*Titles*
Amenhotep III	King's Great Wife,
Father	Mistress of Upper
Yuya	and Lower Egypt,
Mother	Mistress of the Two
Thuyu	Lands, Lady of the
Sons	Two Lands, King's
Thutmose and	Mother
Amenhotep IV	*Burial place*
(Akhenaten)	Unknown
Daughters	
Sitamun,	
Henuttaneb, Isis,	
Nebetah, Baketaten	

TIY, WIFE OF AMENHOTEP III

By his regnal Year 2 the young Amenhotep III had married a commoner-born wife, Tiy, publishing facts about their union on a series of large commemorative scarabs designed to circulate the happy news throughout the empire:

…Amenhotep ruler of Thebes, given life, and the king's principal wife Tiy, may she live. The name of her father is Yuya and the name of her mother is Thuyu; she is the wife of a mighty king….

This is unusual. Weddings – even royal weddings – were considered to be private affairs, and under normal circumstances the first we know of a new consort is when she appears beside her husband. Here, or so it seems, Amenhotep is stressing that the non-royal Tiy is indeed his consort, to make absolutely sure that everyone will recognize her children as the true heirs to the Egyptian throne.

Tiy may not have been royal, but she was by no means a humble commoner. Her parents, part of the well-established elite whose dynasties ran parallel to the royal family that they served, hailed from Akhmim, a prosperous Upper Egyptian town not far from Abydos. They may even have been linked to the birth family of Queen Mutemwia; this would certainly explain how the young Amenhotep III came to meet his non-royal bride. Yuya was a wealthy landowner, and could boast a string of impressive titles including Overseer of the King's Horses and the more unusual God's Father (King's Father-in-law?). His wife Thuyu, like so many other

upper-class ladies, was active in several religious cults and bore the titles of Singer of Hathor, Singer of Amun and Chief of the Entertainers of both Amun and Min. In addition to Tiy they had a son, Anen, who served as Second Prophet of Amun. There may well have been a second son. Ay's parentage is never formally confirmed, but he inherited many of Yuya's titles to become a prominent minister at the court of Amenhotep III.

The royal parents-in-law

In 1905 Theodore Davis discovered the remarkably well-preserved bodies of Yuya and Thuyu lying in their almost intact tomb in the Valley of the Kings (KV 46). The royal parents-in-law were surrounded by a rich variety of grave goods, and yet Yuya's plentiful burial equipment made absolutely no reference to his relationship with Queen Tiy. Thuyu, in contrast, was happy to record her connection with the royal family, and her title of 'Royal Mother of the Chief Wife of the King' was used repeatedly both on her coffins and on her grave goods. This is interesting: if we did not have the marriage scarabs recording Tiy's parentage, we might be tempted to think that Tiy was not Yuya's daughter. The fact that Tiy's brother, Anen, also neglects to record the fact – vital to historians and, we assume, hardly unimportant to him – that his sister is queen of Egypt, suggests that men did not consider it seemly to boast of their links through female marriages to the royal family. This, of course, has wide-reaching implications for our understanding of the royal family tree. We can never assume, just because an individual does not claim a relationship with the royal family, that such a relationship does not exist.

Given that we are absolutely certain of Tiy's entirely Egyptian parentage, it is surprising that she has been, and continues to be, claimed as either a Syrian or Lebanese princess, or a Nubian beauty. It seems that many early Egyptologists sought to account for Tiy's unusually forceful character and, perhaps, the unusual religious ideas that became apparent towards the end of her husband's reign, by attributing them to the queen's unconventional foreign upbringing. The suggestion that Tiy may have been a blue-eyed pale-skinned Syrian princess is a complete misinterpretation of the archaeological evidence. The suggestion that she may have been of Nubian extraction is more understandable: a bust of Tiy, recovered from the ruins of the harem palace of Medinet Gurob, Faiyum (ancient Mer-Wer), shows the queen with black skin; this piece is, however, carved from ebony and is balanced by other images that depict Tiy as conventionally white. It may be that Yuya was of foreign descent – his name is not a typically Egyptian one – but there is nothing at all to suggest that the family were regarded as anything other than Egyptian or, indeed, that they had anything other than the brown skin and dark hair of the typical Egyptian family.

(*Opposite*) Gilded cartonnage masks from the mummies of Yuya (above) and Thuyu (below), parents of Queen Tiy. The inlaid eyes give the faces a particularly lifelike appearance. Both in Cairo Museum.

(*Below*) An inscribed cosmetic jar decorated in Tiy's favourite colour scheme of yellow and blue. The central and left cartouches name Nebmaatre Amenhotep III; the cartouche on the right is that of the King's Wife Tiy, May She Be Healthy.

Queen of Egypt

Tiy was probably in her early teens at the time of her marriage. She immediately became one of Egypt's most powerful and conspicuous consorts. Completely eclipsing Mutemwia, Tiy was regularly depicted alongside her husband on both public monuments and in private tombs, while her cartouche was linked with his on both official inscriptions and on more personal household furniture, cosmetic equipment and scarabs. Here, on the inscribed faience cosmetic tubes and kohl pots which once graced the royal bedroom, we can see that while Amenhotep favoured an elegant colour scheme of dark blue with a lighter blue inlay, Tiy preferred a more cheerful yellow embellished with blue. At the other end of the scale, a colossal statue, originally included in Amenhotep's mortuary temple and now displayed in Cairo Museum (see overleaf), shows the king and queen seated side by side at an equal size, with three miniature daughters standing by their legs

Amenhotep's long, peaceful and extraordinarily wealthy reign allowed him to fund a nationwide programme of building, arts and crafts. Egypt's painters and sculptors reached new heights of excellence, while glass, jewelry, pottery and faience production all flourished as they never had before. We have many sculptures of Amenhotep and Tiy at various scales and in various guises, but we should almost certainly have more. The blame for the missing artworks can be laid firmly at the door of the 19th Dynasty King Ramesses II. Living a comfortable century after Amenhotep, Ramesses felt no compunction over recycling the monuments and statuary of the illustrious predecessor whose prosperous reign he so admired. Many of our known representations of Ramesses II actually started life as representations of Amenhotep III; it therefore follows that at least some of our images of Ramesses' consort Nefertari may have originated as images of Queen Tiy.

THE GUROB HEAD OF QUEEN TIY

Tiy's numerous portraits, which depict the queen at various stages of her life, show that, although not a conventional beauty, she had a powerful physical presence.

The sculpted head found at Medinet Gurob, carved after Tiy's husband's death, is the portrait of a real, ageing, worldly-wise woman rather than a stereotypically bland, eternally youthful Egyptian queen. Here Tiy has down-turned lips, heavy eyelids shading her slanting, almond-shaped eyes, and deep lines running from her nose to her mouth. In other statuary, images of a younger queen, she has a more youthful, rounded face and her characteristically full lips appear sensual rather than surly.

Curiously, the Gurob head was remodelled in antiquity. Originally Tiy wore the *khat* (bag-like) headdress and a splendid pair of earrings. Over this someone later placed a bobbed round wig, tall plumes and a sun disk headdress. The precise significance of this change in regalia is hard for us to assess, but it seems likely to reflect Tiy's ever-developing role in the royal family.

The Gurob head of Queen Tiy. CAT scans have revealed that the queen originally wore a khat *headdress and a splendid pair of earrings. Berlin Museum.*

Tiy's influence spread beyond Egypt's borders and she played a prominent role in the diplomatic correspondence that linked the Near Eastern states. Here, her reputation as the true power behind the throne would endure beyond Amenhotep's death. A letter of condolence written by King Tushratta of Mitanni soon after Amenhotep's demise assumes (wrongly) that the dowager queen Tiy would be able to influence her son just as she had been able to influence her husband:

...You know that I always showed love to Nimmuaria [Nebmaatre Amenhotep III], your husband, and that Nimmuaria your husband always showed love to me.... I had asked your husband for statues of solid gold.... But now Napkhururiya, your son, has sent plated statues of wood. With gold being as dirt in your son's land, why has your son not given what I asked for?...[19]

Queen Tiy appears at the same scale as her colossal husband, Amenhotep III. Three royal princesses (two badly eroded), far less important than their parents, stand only knee high. Neither Prince Thutmose nor Prince Amenhotep (Amenhotep IV/Akhenaten) appears in the family group. Cairo Museum.

FEMALE SPHINXES

Many of the scenes carved on the Early Dynastic ceremonial palettes – the Narmer Palette included – confirm the association of kingship with raw animal power. By the 4th Dynasty this concept had been formalized in the form of the sphinx. Typified by Khafre's Great Sphinx of Giza, sphinxes were given lion bodies and human (kings') heads or faces. They were associated both with the many forms of the sun god and with the celebration of the king as a living image. Thus it was particularly appropriate that Thutmose IV should have won his crown by rescuing the Great Sphinx from a suffocating blanket of sand.

From Egypt the idea of the sphinx spread both to the Near East and to Greece. Although the Greek sphinx – the malevolent, winged questioner of Oedipus – was female, Egyptian sphinxes were almost invariably male; the popular misconception that the Great Sphinx is female stems from the loss of the Sphinx's beard. Included amongst these male sphinxes, however, are the many sphinxes carved by the female king Hatshepsut.

By the Middle Kingdom queens, too, could be sphinxes, a form of representation that linked them with the solar goddesses Hathor and Tefnut. Hathor we have met many times before. Tefnut is the goddess of moisture, one of the twin children born to the solar creator god Atum on the island of creation; she wears a distinctive flat-topped crown made from sprouting plants. These first female sphinxes were passive observers in scenes primarily involving their kings. The 18th Dynasty Queen Tiy was the first to be shown usurping the role of the king by actively defending her land. A scene in Kheruef's Theban tomb (TT 192) shows Tiy sitting on a throne behind her husband's throne. The queen, slightly smaller than the king, wears the uraeus, modius and tall feathers, and she holds a flywhisk and an *ankh*. The side of her ornate chair, smaller but more richly decorated than her husband's plain box throne, shows the queen taking the form of a human-headed sphinx to trample two bound female prisoners representing the generic female enemies of Egypt.

A second image of Tiy in the form of a human-headed sphinx – this time a winged creature wearing Tefnut's distinctive plant-topped headdress and holding her husband's cartouche – decorates a carnelian bracelet plaque housed in the Metropolitan Museum of Art, New York.

Queen Tiy as a winged sphinx, her headdress derived from that worn by Tefnut, one of the twin children born to the god of creation, Atum.

The only prominent role that Tiy did not play was that of God's Wife of Amun, an unusual omission which suggests that Amun may have been slightly out of favour with the royal family. This perhaps explains why we have so few representations of Tiy recovered from the Karnak temple. Like many of Egypt's earlier queens, Tiy was closely identified with the solar goddesses Maat and Hathor. She became the first queen to include the cow horns and sun disk of Hathor in her tall, feathered crown, and she regularly carried the sistrum or religious rattle that was closely associated with the Hathoric cult. Amenhotep, of course, as high priest of all Egypt's cults, should have been loyal to all the traditional state gods including his dynasty's patron deity, Amun of Thebes. But, as his reign progressed, he developed both a growing interest in Egypt's various solar gods, and a growing interest in his own divinity which had the effect of emphasizing his consort's own divine status. In the Theban tomb of the Queen's Steward Kheruef (TT 192) we can see the king and queen sailing in the evening boat of Re: sailing, and water, were closely connected with the journey of the sun boat across the sky. Back on earth, the barge which sailed on the pleasure lake that, as another series of commemorative scarabs tells us, Amenhotep built for Tiy, was named 'The Sun Disk [Aten] Dazzles', in tribute to the ancient but hitherto insignificant sun god, the Aten.

Tiy the living goddess

Death made Egypt's semi-mortal kings divine. Their consorts and their mothers, too, could acquire divine attributes as they merged with the god Osiris. The dead Ahmose-Nefertari had managed to achieve full divine status, the only one of Egypt's queens to be so honoured before the Ptolemaic Age. Now Amenhotep and Tiy prepared to become fully divine during their own lifetimes. This flouting of theological convention occurred outside Egypt's borders at Soleb in Nubia where, towards the end of his reign, Amenhotep built a temple dedicated to himself as the god 'Amenhotep Lord of Nubia'. A subsidiary temple at nearby Sedeinga celebrated his newly divine consort. Here Tiy, representing Hathor-Tefnut, took the form of a sphinx dressed in Tefnut's tall, plant-topped crown to prowl across the temple pillars.

Back in Egypt, an unusual wooden cosmetic jar shows Tiy in the form of Taweret, the pregnant hippopotamus goddess of childbirth. Taweret and Bes (a dwarf god again identified with childbirth) had always played an important role in popular religion, and the royal bedroom in the Malqata palace, Thebes, was decorated with Bes figures. Tiy's furniture, recovered from the tomb of Yuya and Thuyu, was decorated with images of both Bes and Taweret.

Tiy's children

Tiy provided her husband with six relatively well-documented children: two sons (Thutmose and Amenhotep) and four daughters (Sitamun, Henuttaneb, Isis and Nebetah). There may also have been a fifth daughter. The Amarna tomb of Huya, 'Superintendent of the Royal Harem, Superintendent of the Treasury, Steward in the House of the King's Mother, King's Wife, Tiy', includes two scenes showing Tiy accompanied by a young girl. The girl wears a child's sidelock hairstyle, and is identified as the 'King's Daughter Baketaten' (Handmaiden of the Aten). Neither Baketaten's father nor her mother are named, but her close association with the dowager queen suggests that Tiy is her mother.

Who then is her father? Unfortunately the scenes are undated. As Amarna was not built until the reign of Tiy's son Akhenaten (Amenhotep IV), we know that they must have been carved several years after Amenhotep's death, but how long after? And exactly how old is the princess? Her appearance suggests that she is still a child, maybe as young as four or five years old, so too young to be Amenhotep's daughter. Yet, given the symbolism of Egyptian artistic convention, she may be as old as 14 or 15. This would place her as the daughter of Amenhotep and Tiy, either a previously unknown daughter, or perhaps the otherwise ephemeral Nebetah re-named to fit with the new religious climate. Why does this matter? Because it has been suggested in some less-scholarly publications that Baketaten must have been Tiy's daughter by her son Akhenaten and this suggestion has lingered on in fringe Egyptological literature. There is absolutely no evidence to support this sensational theory, and mother-son incest in the Egyptian royal family remains completely unknown.

SITAMUN	
Husband	*Titles*
Amenhotep III?	King's Great
Father	Daughter, King's
Amenhotep III	Wife, King's Great
Mother	Wife
Tiy	*Burial place*
	Thebes

(*Opposite above*) Tiy's modius crown and double plumes link her with the solar cults. She wears a stunning vulture feather dress (a reminder of Mut, wife of Amun) gathered beneath the breast with a girdle. Louvre Museum.

(*Opposite below*) The artist who imposed Tiy's face on this wooden figure of the hippopotamus goddess Taweret was hinting at Tiy's own divine nature. Turin Museum.

(*Below*) Sitamun's chair, recovered from KV 46 and now in Cairo Museum. The back panel shows the seated Sitamun, in mirror image, wearing the gazelle crown and a lotus headdress reminiscent of Tefnut's crown. An inscription tells us that she is being offered 'gold of the lands of the South'. The arms' inner panels show women offering gold rings, while the outer panels are decorated with images of deities Bes and Taweret.

Sitamun and her sisters

Princess Sitamun, Tiy's eldest daughter, is the most conspicuous of the royal children. Some of her furniture was recovered from the tomb of her grandparents, Yuya and Thuyu. Here, on the back of an ornate chair, we can see the young Sitamun wearing a lotus-blossom crown with two gazelle heads replacing the double uraeus. Sitamun holds both *menit* beads and a sistrum, items which link her with the cult of Hathor. It seems that first-born daughters were now being accorded a special place in a royal hierarchy that was able to tolerate the prominent royal women who could offer feminine support to their father, but which was unable to deal with prominent royal men other than the king. The royal sons, Thutmose and Amenhotep, are completely overshadowed by their sisters. Towards the end of her father's reign Sitamun acquired the title King's Great Wife, although she never took precedence over her still-living mother. If we accept that Sitamun the queen is the same person as Sitamun the princess, the obvious implication is that Sitamun married her father. However, there remains the remote possibility that the marriage was contracted with her brother and heir to the throne, Thutmose.

It would be perfectly logical for Sitamun to have married her brother, and to have retained her position of importance following her husband's untimely death. It makes less immediately obvious sense for her to have married her father during her mother's lifetime, and we must question whether this union (if it did occur) was a true marriage, or a marriage of convenience designed to provide the otherwise unmarriageable Sitamun with rank, a household and source of independent income, while supplying the still-powerful but now-elderly Tiy with a suitable deputy to assist in her many duties. It was already well accepted that a king could take a co-regent to rule beside him; here, perhaps, we are seeing the first instance of a queen taking the feminine equivalent. If, as we suspect, the queen's religious duties included references to her own fertility, the substitution of a younger daughter in some of the religious rituals may have made sound theological sense.

Amenhotep III's long reign – almost 40 years – may have played a part in his decision to promote his daughter during his own lifetime. Father-daughter marriages are not a feature of short reigns. The fact that Sitamun had no known children suggests, perhaps, that their marriage may have been unconsummated, but we must be careful not to fall into the trap of assuming that a true father-daughter marriage would be as distasteful to Amenhotep as it would be to ourselves. There was certainly sound divine precedent for father-daughter unions – the sun god Re was known to have married his daughter Hathor – and this would have formed an attractive model for a king as interested as Amenhotep III in his own solar-based divinity. Now Amenhotep could be supported by both a mother-goddess (Tiy, or Nut) and by a divine daughter-wife (Sitamun, Hathor, Maat or Tefnut). Indeed, there is some evidence to suggest that **Isis** and **Henuttaneb**, too, may have become junior queens since they both write their names in cartouches, although neither uses the title King's Great Wife.

Tiy's final years

One of the last images of Amenhotep's lengthy reign – a painted limestone stela from a domestic shrine – shows the king abandoning all formal, regal poses to adopt a relaxed, almost louche posture; his body swollen and almost feminine in appearance, he sits slumped in his chair before a table piled high with offerings, while Tiy, who is now almost entirely erased from the scene, sits beside him and embraces him. As far as we can tell, Tiy is as fit and alert as ever. This interesting image has misled some observers into suggesting that Amenhotep has regressed into an unfortunate combination of obesity and senility, and that the healthy Tiy is now effectively ruling the empire on her husband's behalf. However, when we view the piece in its wider context we can see that this is merely the tentative beginning of a dramatic change of artistic style which will see the royal family appearing in a series of increasingly informal poses. There is no reason to suppose that Tiy ever ruled Egypt.

Stela recovered from the house of Panehsy. The elderly Amenhotep III sits relaxed – almost slumped – with his queen (now almost entirely vanished) beside him. The informal style of this piece heralds the beginning of Amarna-style art. British Museum.

Tiy outlived her husband by at least eight years. As King Amenhotep IV (later to adopt the name Akhenaten) took the throne, she entered into semi-retirement at the Medinet Gurob palace. Records of her occasional visits to her house at Amarna prove that she was still alive during her son's regnal Year 9, and wine from her estate was being delivered to the royal court during Year 14. Tiy's death goes unrecorded and we do not know where she was buried, although a lock of hair, preserved in a miniature coffin labelled with Tiy's name, was included amongst Tutankhamun's burial equipment. Fragments of Tiy's sarcophagus were recovered inside the ransacked Amarna royal tomb, but other pieces of her burial equipment, including a magnificent gilded shrine, were found in the tomb attributed to King Smenkhkare in the Valley of the Kings (KV 55) and one of her *shabti* figures was retrieved from the tomb of Amenhotep III in the Western Valley, an offshoot of the Valley of the Kings. It seems that Tiy, originally buried at Amarna, may have been re-interred in her

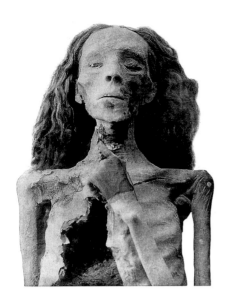

The Elder Lady, recovered from the tomb of Amenhotep II (KV 35) and variously identified as Hatshepsut and Tiy. The mummy is today sealed in the tomb, and is not available for re-examination.

husband's tomb during the reign of Tutankhamun, only to be re-interred again with the other royal mummies at the end of the New Kingdom. If this is the case, Tiy's mummy may have survived in one of the Theban mummy caches.

Archaeologists have looked long and hard for Tiy's body. Theodore Davis, believing that he had identified the mummy – now a skeleton – recovered from the mysterious tomb KV 55, published his most important find as *The Tomb of Queen Tiyi*. However, this skeleton is actually male, and is now generally accepted to be Smenkhkare, brother of Tutankhamun. For many years it was agreed that the Elder Lady, already provisionally identified as Hatshepsut, might be Tiy. This mummy is, however, somewhat younger than we might have expected; given Amenhotep's 37-year reign, Tiy is likely to have been at least 55 years old when she died. As anatomist Grafton Elliot Smith noted, the Elder Lady is remarkable for her luxuriant tresses:

...[The Elder Lady] is a small middle-aged woman with long, brown, wavy, lustrous hair, parted in the centre and falling down on both sides of the head on to the shoulders. Its ends are converted into numerous apparently natural curls. Her teeth are well-worn but otherwise healthy. The sternum is completely ankylosed. She has no grey hair.[20]

The mummy's left arm lies across her chest, her right arm is straight by her side. This is the standard position for 18th Dynasty women in art and sculpture, but is rarely found on mummies.

GILUKHEPA, TADUKHEPA AND OTHER FOREIGN WIVES OF AMENHOTEP III

Amenhotep III ruled over a vast and peaceful empire, which allowed him to fill his treasury with gold and his harem with foreign women, their children and attendants. A series of diplomatic marriages – either marriages contracted between brother kings of almost equivalent status (no one, of course, was as important as the king of Egypt) or between vassals and their Egyptian overlord – plus a tradition of giving women as gifts and seizing women as war booty, led to Amenhotep acquiring many hundreds of wives who were themselves of widely differing status. Little wonder that these women could not live alongside Amenhotep and Tiy in the Malqata palace. Instead they were housed in separate, independent harem palaces, the best known today being the Medinet Gurob palace built by Thutmose III. These were self-contained and self-supporting units that derived their income from their own endowments of land and rents paid by tenant farmers. Here the ladies fell under the protection of a number of male administrators headed by the immensely important Overseer of the Royal Harem and the Inspector of the Harem-Administration. Theirs was not a life of unconfined luxury. While King's Daughters and King's Sisters were treated with the respect the Egyptians

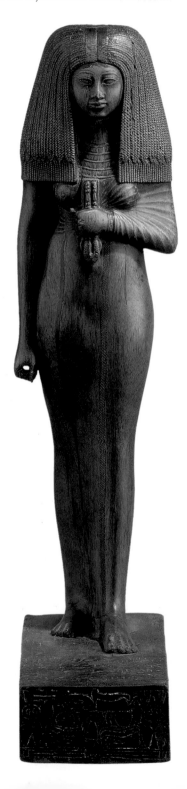

The widowed Queen Tiy spent some time living at the Medinet Gurob harem palace. Several beautiful wooden statues of women have been recovered from this area, probably from tombs dated to the reigns of Amenhotep III and Akhenaten. The statues represent the elite members of the royal harem. Louvre Museum.

felt they deserved, the less important women were expected to work, either supporting their community as cooks, washerwomen, nursemaids, weavers and general servants, or participating in the flourishing textile business that operated out of the harem palaces.

The king's diplomatic marriages were considered to be a very personal bond between Amenhotep and his new fathers-in-law. A change in one of the parties meant that a new relationship had to be sealed with a new marriage and so, as princes inherited their fathers' throne, they too were expected to send a daughter to marry Egypt's long-lived king. The bride would be received with great ceremony and, the bride price and dowry exchanged, the new queen would take up residence in the harem palace where she might well find herself living alongside her aunt, the living evidence of a previous diplomatic bond. To all intents and purposes the harem queens were forgotten by all but their closest relatives. Foreign kings regularly wrote and sent gifts to their sisters, while the royal archives contain one indignant letter from Kadashman-Enlil of Babylon, complaining that Amenhotep had asked for his daughter's hand in marriage even though 'my sister, whom my father gave to you, has been there with you and no one has seen her to know if she is alive or dead'.

The death of the Egyptian king would of course mean that his son, even though he inherited all his father's women, would have to embark on his own series of diplomatic marriages. This was, however, purely one-way traffic. As Amenhotep was forced to explain to Kadashman-Enlil, Egyptian kings simply did not allow their women to marry foreigners. Kadashman-Enlil attempted to argue – he even attempted to secure a non-royal Egyptian bride whom he could pass off as a princess – but to no avail. Amenhotep, the most powerful king in the world, could impose whatever rules he liked. He was to marry two princesses from Syria, two from Babylon, one from Arzawa (Anatolia) and two from Mitanni. The last two are the best known of his harem wives.

Thutmose IV had married a princess of Mitanni, but his death had severed the diplomatic bond. So, in his regnal Year 10, Amenhotep married Gilukhepa, daughter of Shutturna II of Mitanni. Once again a series of commemorative scarabs was issued (in the joint names of Amenhotep and Tiy) to commemorate a royal marriage. This time we learn not only the bride's parentage, but that she arrived in Egypt accompanied by a retinue of some 317 attendants. Eventually Shutturna was succeeded by his son Tushratta, brother of Gilukhepa. Amenhotep was by this time old and sick, but he nevertheless embarked on enthusiastic negotiations for the hand of Tushratta's daughter, Tadukhepa. Tushratta attempted to stipulate that Tadukhepa should become queen consort, although with Tiy still very much alive this was never a realistic proposition. With negotiations successfully concluded – the lavish dowry was to include a chariot and four horses – the bride set off for Egypt. The marriage was to go unconsummated. Amenhotep died just as his new bride arrived, and Tadukhepa remained in Egypt as the wife of the new king, Amenhotep IV.

Nefertiti

(*Right*) An unfinished quartzite head of Nefertiti recovered from Amarna.

(*Left*) Akhenaten at Thebes. The face of his colossal statue, designed to be seen from below, is strikingly long and narrow.

NEFERTITI

Amenhotep III's younger son inherited his throne as Amenhotep IV. Soon after, in tribute to the ancient but somewhat obscure solar god known as the Aten, the new king would change his name to Akhenaten, or 'Living Spirit of the Aten'. Within five years of his succession Akhenaten would radically simplify Egypt's polytheistic religion by abolishing most of the established pantheon and replacing the multitude of deities with one sole god, the Aten. The object of his worship was the bright light of the sun, rather than the sun itself.

Akhenaten's queen, Nefertiti, was not a member of the immediate royal family and her parents are never mentioned although we do know that she had a younger sister, Mutnodjmet, who appears in several Amarna tomb scenes. In consequence, there has been a great deal of speculation over Nefertiti's origins. Although her name, which translates as 'A Beautiful Woman has Come', hints that Nefertiti may have been a foreigner (perhaps even the re-named princess Tadukhepa?), evidence from the unfinished Amarna tomb shared by the official Ay (later king) and his wife – also called Tiy (see p. 139) – indicates that, like her mother-in-law before her, she was a member of the Egyptian elite.

Ay, probable brother of Queen Tiy, was granted a splendid tomb carved into the Amarna cliffs. Here we can watch as both Ay and his wife Tiy receive a reward of golden necklaces from Akhenaten and Nefertiti. The receipt of royal gold was a great honour for any man; for a woman, it was unprecedented. Tiy, 'Favourite of the Good God, Nurse of the King's Great Wife Nefertiti, Nurse of the Goddess, Ornament of the King', was, however, a very important person: she was Nefertiti's wet nurse. Ay had

NEFERTITI	
Full name	Meritaten,
Neferneferuaten-	Meketaten,
Nefertiti (from Year	Ankhesenpaaten
5 of Amenhotep IV's	(Ankhesenamun),
reign)	Neferneferuaten,
Husband	Neferneferure,
Amenhotep IV	Setepenre
(Akhenaten)	*Titles*
Father	King's Great Wife,
Ay?	Lady of the Two
Mother	Lands
Unknown	*Burial place*
Daughters	Unknown

In Ramose's tomb (TT 55) Nefertiti stands behind her husband as he greets his people from the Window of Appearance. The scene is only partially carved, and Nefertiti is hidden from the waist downwards. She is wearing a pleated linen robe, a 'Nubian-style' wig, and a uraeus. This tomb, incompletely decorated when Amenhotep III died, includes both traditional and (as here) Amarna-style art work.

(*Opposite left*) The ageing Nefertiti. A queen defeated by the loss of her beauty, or a powerful wise woman reminiscent of the Gurob head of Nefertiti's mother-in-law, Queen Tiy? This statue was found in the Amarna workshop of the sculptor Thutmose and is now in the Berlin Museum.

(*Opposite right*) Akhenaten or Nefertiti? All too often it is the crown which allows us to distinguish between the two, and here the crown is missing. This curious statue, recovered from Thebes, may be an attempt to depict Akhenaten as a combination of the male and female elements of the god Shu and the goddess Tefnut, twin children of the sun god Atum. Cairo Museum.

inherited many of his titles from Yuya, including that of 'God's Father'. If, as we suspect, this means King's Father-in-law, Ay must be Nefertiti's father. Tiy, however, never uses Thuyu's title of 'Royal Mother of the King's Great Wife', and it is possible that she is Nefertiti's stepmother rather than her birth mother.

Images of Nefertiti

One of the earliest representations of Nefertiti comes from the Theban tomb of the vizier Ramose (TT 55). Here we see a slender young woman dressed in a long, pleated linen robe with sleeves. Nefertiti wears a uraeus and a Nubian-style wig, a curly layered bob cut at an angle leaving the nape of the neck exposed. This style of wig will from now on be reserved for women close to the king. Nefertiti is happy to wear a variety of crowns: either the single or double uraeus (itself often wearing a solar disk with cow horns) with either the double feathers, or the double feathers plus sun disk and cow horns, which link the queen with the cults of Re and Hathor. However, she avoids the vulture headdress that, due to its connection with the goddess Mut, wife of Amun, may not have been acceptable in the new solar-centred religious climate. Eventually Nefertiti develops her own unique crown, a tall, straight-edged, flat-topped blue helmet-shaped headdress whose colour reminds us of the blue war-crown worn by kings, and whose shape is reminiscent of the sprouting crown worn by the solar goddess Tefnut (see box overleaf).

Nefertiti's stereotypical appearance is about to undergo a startling change, a change started by the king himself. By his regnal Year 5, Akhenaten's hitherto conventional statuary and portraits show a bizarre range of features. He now has a narrow head emphasized by his false beard and long, thin neck. His face has narrow eyes, a pronounced jaw, lengthy nose, hollow cheeks and thick, sensuous lips. His upper body has an under-developed musculature that serves to highlight his wide hips, feminine breasts, narrow waist and protruding stomach. There has been some speculation that Akhenaten may have suffered from a feminizing medical condition, but no known condition entirely fits his symptoms, and it seems far more likely that these images are intended to symbolize the king's new role as the earthly representative of the asexual creator god, the Aten.

As Akhenaten evolves, so does his court. The once gamine Nefertiti suddenly acquires a classic pear shape: a rounded abdomen, large hips, thick thighs and pronounced buttocks. Little attention is paid to her breasts, but her rounded stomach – evidence that she has already borne several children – is highlighted by a single curved line at the base of the abdomen, and the whole effect is emphasized by her transparent, pleated clothing that leaves nothing to the imagination. Queen Tiy, who has also

borne six or seven children, and who is considerably older than Nefertiti, has two lines to emphasize her drooping abdomen. To modern eyes these flabby stomachs are unappealing; to Akhenaten, intent on stressing the fertility of his womenfolk, they are clearly not.

Suddenly it becomes very difficult to distinguish between Nefertiti and Akhenaten, particularly as the two often wear similar garments. One unfinished, damaged colossal statue recovered from Thebes has provoked intense debate. The statue is naked, has no obvious genitals, and is inscribed with the cartouches of the Aten. Is this Akhenaten, and if so why does he have no genitals? Or is it Nefertiti, and if so, why is she assuming the role of a king? This confusion between genders is made worse by the Amarna convention of showing royal women with the red-brown skin hitherto reserved for men.

Following the move to the new capital city, Amarna, Nefertiti's face becomes rounded, developing a square jaw, prominent cheekbones and straighter lips. At the same time her body assumes a less-exaggeratedly feminine shape. By now Nefertiti has changed her name to reflect her religious beliefs. She is now officially Neferneferuaten-Nefertiti:

THE BERLIN HEAD OF NEFERTITI

The sculptor Thutmose had a studio in a southern Amarna suburb. Here he worked on heads and limbs for inclusion in composite statues of the royal family. When, some time during the reign of Tutankhamun, Thutmose decided to leave Amarna he abandoned over 50 examples of his unwanted and unfinished work. A plastered, painted limestone bust of Nefertiti was left sitting on a shelf in a storeroom. Eventually, as the shelf collapsed, it toppled forward and fell to the ground.

Nefertiti's bust was rediscovered by a local workman employed by the German excavator Ludwig Borchardt on 6 December 1912. The bust shows Nefertiti in a flat-topped blue crown decorated with golden ribbons, whose red, blue and green inlays reflect the colours in her bead collar. There is no hair visible under the crown, and it seems that Nefertiti has shaved her head. The queen's starkly symmetrical face has a pink-brown skin, deeper red-brown smiling lips, and delicately arched black eyebrows. The tips of her ears and the top edge of her crown have been slightly damaged, and the uraeus on the front of the crown has snapped off.

Nefertiti's kohl-rimmed right eye is inlaid with rock crystal and has a black pupil. Her left eyeball is missing and, as the socket shows no trace of glue, is unlikely to have been in place when the head was discarded. It is doubtful that the bust is simply unfinished. Nor is it likely – as some commentators have suggested – that the eye would have been gouged out in an attack on the memory of the dead queen. It may perhaps be that the bust was an artist's teaching aid, the eye socket being deliberately left vacant to allow apprentices to study inlay techniques.

Following the division of the finds at the end of the excavation season, the head was taken to Berlin and presented to Dr James Simon, the financial sponsor of Borchardt's expedition. In 1920 the bust was donated to the Berlin Museum, and in 1924 it went on public display. Today Thutmose's masterpiece is one of the best-known and best-loved pieces of sculpture in the world.

(Above) The moment of discovery for excavator Ludwig Borchardt and his team on 6 December 1912. Nefertiti's bust is unearthed amongst the ruins of the workshop of ancient Egyptian sculptor Thutmose at Amarna.

(Left) Despite repeated requests for its return to Egypt, the painted, plastered limestone bust of Nefertiti remains one of the highlights of the Berlin Museum collection. Its discoverer, Ludwig Borchardt, searched in vain for the missing left eye.

'Beautiful are the Beauties of the Aten. A Beautiful Woman has Come'. Within her cartouche the writing of the god's name Aten is reversed so that it faces the determinative sign indicating Nefertiti's queenly status; this transposition is a great honour allowing the queen's image to face the name of her god. Occasionally Nefertiti's name is written in two cartouches, so that at first glance it resembles that of a king. At Thebes the two cartouches contain her shorter name and her longer name, while at Amarna each of the double cartouches holds her longer name.

A new religion

To celebrate his jubilee Akhenaten built a series of sun temples dedicated to the Aten. To the east of the Karnak temple complex, the impressive *Gempaaten* (The Sun Disk is Found) temple and its subsidiary temple *Hwt-Benben* (Mansion of the *Benben* Stone[21]) dominated the skyline. Both of these temples were destroyed in antiquity, but re-used blocks originally from the *Hwt-Benben* show Nefertiti performing the king's role of priest assisted by her eldest daughter, the 'King's Bodily Daughter whom he Loves, Meritaten, Born of the Great King's Wife whom he Loves, Mistress of the Two Lands, Nefertiti, May she Live'. Meritaten stands behind her mother, assuming a typical queenly role. Nefertiti, of course, is a queen rather than a king; in her husband's presence she will always take the subsidiary religious position. But when, in his absence, she performs a male or kingly role (that of offering to the gods) Nefertiti needs a female supporter to make the ritual complete.

Nefertiti's role in the new religion is in many ways a natural evolution of the prominent position previously allocated to Queen Tiy. Royal divinity, once reserved for the dead, has become a living, if unspoken,

Computer reconstruction of the Small Temple of the Aten at Amarna, showing the three sets of gleaming white pylons and the many offering tables open to the light of the sun. The central city can be seen in the background.

In a scene carved on a limestone slab, Akhenaten offers to the Aten. Behind him stand Nefertiti and two of their daughters who wear the sidelock of youth, but who resemble their mother in body shape. Akhenaten regularly featured his growing band of daughters on his monuments, but made no reference to any son. Cairo Museum.

Gold stirrup ring featuring Akhenaten and Nefertiti as Shu and Tefnut, children of the sun god. Akhenaten holds the feather of Maat, Nefertiti wears the double plumes. Cairo Museum.

reality at the Amarna court. But it is not necessarily a personal divinity like that enjoyed by Ahmose-Nefertari. The asexual Aten requires both male- and female-based rituals and Nefertiti, as the consort of the semi-divine son of the creator god, is required to serve as an emblem of divine fertility. Together the royal couple can be regarded as the living representatives of the twins Shu and Tefnut in the divine triad formed by the creator god (the Aten) and his children. Nefertiti is also the mother figure in the lesser triad formed by the king, queen and their children. She is the only mortal, Akhenaten apart, who can receive life from the rays of the Aten.

Now as the king and his queen prayed before the Aten, the people of Amarna prayed before Akhenaten and Nefertiti. The houses and gardens of the Amarna elite included stone statues depicting the royal family, while their tomb walls showed the royal family at work and play. The most elaborate private tomb was that allocated to Ay and Tiy and here, as we might expect, Nefertiti featured prominently. These scenes are very different in composition from scenes that have gone before. The Aten is a disembodied being – he has to hang high in the sky above the royal family. This allows the king to become the most important standing figure. Meanwhile the queen, for the sake of symmetry and as a sign of her increased power, is allowed to stand facing her husband rather than behind or beside him.

Nefertiti's political role

If Nefertiti's increasingly important religious role is obvious, her political significance is less easy to ascertain. To a large extent this is, anyway, very much an artificial, modern division; the Egyptians themselves would have drawn no distinction between secular and sacred matters, and many of the overtly political rituals – the smiting of Egypt's enemies, for example, first seen in the carving on the Narmer Palette – were derived from the king's religious duty to maintain *maat*. Curiously, and unlike Queen Tiy, Nefertiti is not mentioned in the diplomatic correspondence recovered from the remains of the Amarna royal archives (the Amarna Letters). Yet she often appears at true scale beside her husband, while her title, Lady of the Two Lands, a title which has been used by earlier New Kingdom queens but never directly in front of the cartouche, emphasizes her role as the feminine counterpart of the king, Lord of the Two Lands.

Blocks recovered from both Karnak and Hermopolis Magna (the latter having come originally from Amarna) show Akhenaten's boat decorated with traditional smiting images. The king stands beneath the rays of the sun disk, his right arm raised to deliver a fatal blow, and Nefertiti stands passively behind him. But parallel scenes on Nefertiti's boat show the queen herself striding forward to execute a female enemy with the sword that she wields in her right hand. Behind Nefertiti stands the passive Meritaten, once again assuming the queen's role. Again, this is very much a logical development of the earlier scenes showing Queen Tiy assuming the form of a sphinx to trample Egypt's female enemies. Whether or not Akhenaten and Nefertiti were actually called upon to dispatch token enemies is unclear – but there is no good reason to believe that they did not.

A very different Amarna scene carved on a private devotional stela of unknown provenance now housed in Berlin Museum shows Nefertiti, Akhenaten and three of their children seated together, apparently informally, in a tent or bower. But here we have a slight confusion of roles. While Nefertiti sits on what is obviously the more regal chair (but remember the image of Queen Tiy occupying a decorated chair while her husband sits on a simple box throne), Akhenaten holds the eldest and therefore most important princess. A similar but not identical private stela in Cairo Museum shows both king and queen sitting on regal

(*Right*) In this fragmented wall painting from the King's House, Amarna, princesses Neferneferuaten and Neferneferure sit at their mother's feet. Nefertiti has vanished, but the sash of her dress can still be seen. The two princesses display the characteristic egg-shaped heads found on all Amarna royal children. Ashmolean Museum, Oxford.

(*Opposite above*) On this block recovered from Hermopolis Magna, Nefertiti's boat may be identified by the carved heads on the end of the steering oars. It includes a central cabin and a small kiosk decorated with an image of Nefertiti, dressed in her distinctive crown, raising her right arm to smite a female foe.

(*Opposite below*) This devotional stela, recovered from a private Amarna house, has sparked a great deal of controversy. Akhenaten holds the oldest and most important princess, Meritaten, but sits on a simple stool. Facing him, Nefertiti holds Meketaten and Ankhesenpaaten, and sits on a stool decorated with the symbol of the Two Lands. Is this simply an artistic error? Or is Nefertiti as politically powerful as her husband?

chairs. In both these stelae Nefertiti wears her favourite blue crown, but other Amarna scenes show her dressed in a variety of wigs and crowns including a close-fitting rounded cap, and the *khat* headcloth, a bag-like headdress usually reserved for kings but also worn by Tiy and the goddesses Isis and Nephthys. In the tomb of Panehsy both Akhenaten and Nefertiti wear a *khat* headcloth plus an ornate *atef* crown, a crown more usually associated with the cult of Osiris. The *atef* was a sophisticated headdress incorporating ostrich feathers, ram and bull horns, a solar disk and numerous uraei. Here Akhenaten's crown is even larger and more complex than that worn by his wife. The only other woman known to have worn any form of *atef* is King Hatshepsut.

This evidence of increased political and religious power has led to suggestions that Nefertiti may have acted as Akhenaten's co-regent and, maybe, following his death as sole king of Egypt. Could Nefertiti have acted as king? In theory, yes – Akhenaten was free to choose a co-regent – but the choice of a wife would have been an astonishing one. While Nefertiti was undeniably a powerful woman, we have absolutely no proof to support claims that she was ever more than a queen consort.

Nefertiti's children

Nefertiti bore six daughters, the elder three (Meritaten, Meketaten and Ankhesenpaaten) being born at Thebes, the younger three (Neferneferuaten, Neferneferure and Setepenre) at Amarna. Given the increasingly strong emphasis placed on the father-female (mother, wife or daughter) bond, we have to ask whether she could have also borne one or more sons. Whether a son could have gone entirely unrecorded in such a well-

Calcite *shabti* prepared for the burial of Nefertiti. The two fragments of the *shabti* are now housed in the Louvre and Brooklyn Museum. The head has been reconstructed. The figure carries a royal crook and flail and is inscribed for 'the Chief Wife of the King, Nefertiti'.

documented family is hard to assess, although Akhenaten himself had been 'invisible' until his accession. However, the appearance of a second highly favoured wife, Kiya, suggests that perhaps Nefertiti failed in this aspect of her queenship.

All six daughters were alive during the great festival which marked Akhenaten's regnal Year 12, but Meketaten, Neferneferuaten, Neferne-ferure and Setepenre died soon after, as did Queen Tiy. Nefertiti herself vanished soon after Meketaten's death. The obvious inference is that she too died, perhaps of some infectious disease that was attacking the Amarna community. But the only evidence for her burial in the Amarna royal tomb is a single broken *shabti* figure inscribed with her name and this, of course, could have been inscribed many years before her death. This sudden disappearance of a queen who has become so familiar to us is unsettling, and it is not surprising that it has sparked many theories based on the premise that Nefertiti did not die, but went on to rule Egypt first as a co-regent then as a king in her own right, using the name Smenkhkare. The recent identification of the unmistakably male body of Smenkhkare in Theban tomb KV 55 [22] has meant that these theories need substantial revision.

It seems highly unlikely that Akhenaten would have buried Nefertiti anywhere other than at Amarna, the site where he himself intended to be buried for all time. But there is no reason why her body could not have been moved after the abandonment of the city. In consequence, archaeologists have looked long and hard for Nefertiti at Thebes. Until recently a leading contender was the 'Younger Lady' discovered lying beside the Elder Lady and a young prince in the tomb of Amenhotep II. But the apparent age of this mummy – a female in her early twenties – suggests that she is simply too young to be Nefertiti.

An unfinished sculptor's model, recovered from the Amarna North Palace, showing a princess eating a whole roasted duck.

FOOD

With the old religious themes banned, the Amarna artists turned to the royal family for inspiration. We have more images of Nefertiti behaving in a natural fashion than we have of any other queen. At Amarna we can see Nefertiti riding in a chariot, kissing her husband, and tucking into a hearty meal.

Egypt was blessed with abundant natural resources. The annual Nile flood allowed the farmers to grow grain, fruit and vegetables. There were fish in the river, birds in the marshes, cattle in the Delta fields and pigs, sheep and goats in the villages. While poorer Egyptians would have relied on a fairly monotonous diet of bread, fish and vegetables, the royal family enjoyed the best of everything.

The widespread availability of fresh food meant that there was little need for Egypt's cooks to develop complicated recipes or spicy sauces. Meats were grilled, roasted or boiled and many vegetables were eaten raw. It was the sheer variety of foodstuffs on offer that stimulated the tastebuds. Little wonder that the scribes warned against greed:

When you sit down to eat in company, shun the foods you love. Restraint only needs a moment's effort, whereas gluttony is base and is reproved. A cup of water will quench your thirst and a mouthful of herbs will strengthen your heart....[23]

DYNASTY 18
1539–1292

Kiya
Meritaten
Ankhesenamun
Tiy
Mutnodjmet

(*Below*) One of the two 'harem buildings' depicted in the Amarna tomb of Ay. The women are musicians, and have an assortment of lyres, harps and lutes.

(*Above*) The head of Kiya, altered after her death to represent Princess Meritaten. Kiya's Nubian-style wig has been transformed into an unusually thick sidelock hairstyle. Limestone relief recovered from Hermopolis Magna.

KIYA	
Husband	daughter –
Akhenaten	Meritaten the
(Amenhotep IV)	Younger and/or
Parents	Ankhesenpaaten
Unknown	the Younger?
Children	*Titles*
Smenkhkare?,	Great Beloved Wife
Tutankhamun?	*Burial place*
At least one	Amarna?

KIYA

The scenes of daily life carved in the Amarna tomb of Ay allows us to glimpse behind the closed gates of Akhenaten's harem. Here we see groups of women housed in two buildings whose doors are guarded, or perhaps protected, by men. Most of the women are either making music or dancing, and the walls of their rooms are hung with an assortment of musical instruments. The women in the upper rooms have strange, un-Egyptian-looking hairstyles and this, taken in conjunction with the unusual skirt worn by one of the women, has led to the suggestion that they may be Syrian musicians, perhaps part of the large retinue which accompanied Tadukhepa of Mitanni to Egypt.

We have already met Akhenaten's favourite secondary queen, Kiya, 'Wife and Great Beloved of the King of Upper and Lower Egypt Living in Truth, Lord of the Two Lands Neferkheperure Waenre [Akhenaten], the perfect child of the living Aten'. Kiya is yet another royal bride of uncertain origins, and her unusual name – which is either foreign, or perhaps a contraction of a lengthier Egyptian name – has led to suggestions that she might be one of Akhenaten's distinguished foreign brides, perhaps even Tadukhepa herself. Kiya never became a King's Great Wife (maybe, as a foreigner, she was ineligible for the role?) and she never wore the uraeus, but she was nevertheless allowed to play a part in the rituals of Aten worship and she did bear the king at least one anonymous daughter.

One of a set of four canopic jars recovered from tomb KV 55 (one now housed in the Metropolitan Museum of Art, three in Cairo Museum). The jars were originally carved for Kiya. The heads are not necessarily the original stoppers, and have been variously identified as Tiy, Kiya or Meritaten.

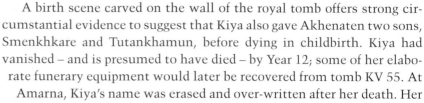

(*Below*) Relief showing a royal couple, usually identified as Meritaten and her husband and half-brother Smenkhkare (but occasionally identified as Akhenaten and Nefertiti). The piece is of unconfirmed provenance, but is believed to have come from a private Amarna house. The queen is offering a bouquet to her husband.

A birth scene carved on the wall of the royal tomb offers strong circumstantial evidence to suggest that Kiya also gave Akhenaten two sons, Smenkhkare and Tutankhamun, before dying in childbirth. Kiya had vanished – and is presumed to have died – by Year 12; some of her elaborate funerary equipment would later be recovered from tomb KV 55. At Amarna, Kiya's name was erased and over-written after her death. Her mummy has never been found.

MERITATEN

Meritaten had always been a prominent figure at the Amarna court. Closely associated with her mother, we have already seen her serving as Nefertiti's deputy in the Theban *Hwt-Benben* when she can have been no more than ten years of age. In other scenes she is associated with her father. Akhenaten holds or stands by Meritaten while Nefertiti cares for her younger sisters. With the disappearance of Tiy, Nefertiti and Kiya, Meritaten became a King's Great Wife, her name now written in a cartouche. Her fame spread quickly beyond Egypt's borders, encouraging the King of Babylon to send her presents. Meanwhile, back home, in the Amarna solar temple complex known as *Maru Aten*, Meritaten's name was carved over that of the dead Kiya, while Kiya's many Amarna images were converted into Meritaten, her adult Nubian wig being transformed into an elaborate sidelock of youth.

For a long time Egyptologists believed that Meritaten must have married her father. Now, with Smenkhkare recognized as a real, male heir to the throne, it seems clear that she married her half-brother as he became co-regent to his father Akhenaten. The Amarna tomb of Meryre II provides us with a glimpse of the new royal couple. On the south and east walls of the main chamber we see Akhenaten, Nefertiti and their daughters; these walls were clearly carved before death tore the original Amarna family apart. The unfinished image on the north wall shows a king and queen standing beneath the rays of the Aten. The figures of the royal couple look like Akhenaten and Nefertiti but their recorded cartouches belong to 'King of Upper and Lower Egypt, Ankhkeprure son of Re, Smenkhkare' and the 'King's Great Wife Meritaten'. Unfortunately the king's cartouche has since been hacked off the wall by thieves and is now lost.

Two unexplained princesses, Meritaten the Younger and Ankhesenpaaten the Younger, who appear at this time may well be daughters born to Meritaten and Smenkhkare (alternatively, they may be daughters born to Kiya and Akhenaten). But when Smenkhkare died after the briefest of reigns, most if not all of which had been spent ruling alongside his father Akhenaten, he left no male heir. After a possible brief and ill-documented period of rule by the otherwise

MERITATEN	
Husband Smenkhkare *Father* Akhenaten (Amenhotep IV) *Mother* Nefertiti *Children* None known	*Titles* King's Bodily Daughter, King's Great Wife *Burial place* Unknown

unknown female king Neferneferuaten (Meritaten?), Smenkhkare was succeeded by his young brother Tutankhaten (re-named Tutankhamun) and his sister-consort, Ankhesenpaaten (Ankhesenamun). Meritaten, displaced by her sister, vanished; her body has never been found.

ANKHESENAMUN

The newly re-named Tutankhamun and his consort Ankhesenamun abandoned Amarna and returned the court to Thebes. The traditional gods were reinstated and the old temples re-opened as Tutankhamun set about restoring *maat* to his land.

Ankhesenamun had appeared in several Amarna art scenes as a naked little girl with a deliberately elongated egg-shaped head, the egg being a potent symbol of creation. Now, her head restored to normal proportions, she became a vigorous queen in the tradition of her mother and grandmother. She appears on many of Tutankhamun's public monuments including the Luxor temple, and on more private items recovered from his tomb where she takes the role of the goddess Maat to support her husband. A statue of the goddess Mut, recovered from the Luxor temple, has Ankhesenamun's calm face.

The back panel of the 'Golden Throne', one of six chairs recovered from Tutankhamun's tomb (KV 62). Standing in a floral pavilion, Ankhesenamun anoints her husband with perfume, while above them shines the Aten. The throne, which was altered in antiquity, gives both forms of the king's name – Tutankhaten and Tutankhamun.

One of the two mummified female children – one a foetus of five months' gestation, and the other a baby who died at or soon after birth – recovered from the Treasury in Tutankhamun's tomb. It is generally assumed that these are the daughters of Tutankhamun and his only known wife, Ankhesenamun. Department of Anatomy, Cairo University.

ANKHESENAMUN	
Formerly known as Ankhesenpaaten *Husband* Tutankhamun *Father* Akhenaten (Amenhotep IV) *Mother* Nefertiti *Children* Two foetuses found	in Tutankhamun's tomb *Titles* King's Bodily Daughter, King's Great Wife, Lady of the Two Lands *Burial place* Thebes

It is generally assumed that Ankhesenamun was the mother of the two stillborn daughters whose tiny mummified bodies, each cocooned in a double anthropoid coffin, were found in a box in Tutankhamun's tomb. There were no other children of the marriage, and so no obvious male heir to the throne. As a precaution, the teenage Tutankhamun adopted the elderly Ay, his probable step-grandfather, as his heir. And so when tragedy struck and Tutankhamun died unexpectedly, the throne passed to the man presumed to be Nefertiti's elderly father. Suggestions that Ay consolidated his claim to the throne by marrying the widowed Ankhesenamun are now known to be based on a single piece of doubtful evidence: a ring bezel displaying the cartouches of Ankhesenamun and Ay. Certainly there is no record of Ankhesenamun playing any part in Ay's reign.

Suggestions that either Ankhesenamun or anyone else may have facilitated her husband's death are equally unsupported. Ankhesenamun, childless and the last of her family line, had more to lose through his death than any other member of his court. The obvious physical damage to the king's body – damage to the legs, chest and head – are not diagnostic, but indicate that he may have died as the result of an accident, perhaps while chariot-racing or boating. Recent CAT scans performed by Zahi Hawass, head of Egypt's Supreme Council of Antiquities, have found no evidence to suggest that Tutankhamun was murdered, and conclude that some of the broken bones that had given rise to rumours of foul play had in fact occurred during Howard Carter's 1922 discovery and removal of the body from its coffin.

A curious correspondence

The death of her husband should have caused Ankhesenamun to retire to the harem. But there is evidence to suggest that she was not prepared to give up her position without a fight. A copy of a cuneiform letter written at this time and recovered from the Anatolian Hittite capital, Boghaskoy, tells a remarkable tale. A widowed queen of Egypt has written to the Hittite king Suppiluliumas, pleading for a husband:

My husband has died. I do not have a son. But, they say, you have many sons. If you would give me one of your sons he would become my husband. I shall never pick out a servant of mine and make him my husband.... He will be my husband and King of Egypt.[24]

Suppiluliumas was highly suspicious, and rightly so. Everyone knew that Egyptian princesses did not marry outside their own family. Marriage to a foreigner was unheard of; no pharaoh would willingly run the risk of Egypt falling into foreign hands. Furthermore, widowed queens never remarried. He was, however, strongly tempted. The promise of the throne of Egypt – still, despite years of neglect during the Amarna period, the most powerful and prestigious throne in the world – was a prize not to be missed. An ambassador was sent to Egypt to investigate, and eventually a prince, Zannanza, was dispatched to marry the queen. The would-be pharaoh was ambushed and killed as he reached the Egyptian border, and relations between Egypt and the Hittites plunged to an all-time low.

The name of the letter writer is given as 'Dahamenzu', a phonetic version of the standard queen's title *ta set neferu* (King's Wife). There are only four son-less and widowed queens who could possibly have written a letter at this time: Nefertiti, Kiya, Meritaten and Ankhesenamun. Nefertiti and Kiya, however, had almost certainly predeceased Akhenaten. Meritaten may or may not have survived Smenkhkare, but her son-less husband did leave a younger brother to inherit the throne. Only Ankhesenamun fits the lonely profile of the letter writer.

Of course, we have to consider the possibility that the letter was not written by a queen of Egypt at all. The irresistible offer of the Egyptian throne may have been the bait necessary to lure the Hittite prince into an elaborate Egyptian trap. Indeed, the letter may not even have originated in Egypt; there is no known Egyptian record of these curious events. But if the letter is genuine, we must assume that Ankhesenamun was troubled by the ascent of either Ay (who ruled for a mere 3–4 years) or the next king, Horemheb. We do not see Ankhesenamun again, and her body has never been discovered.

TIY, WIFE OF AY

Ay, already over 60 years of age, took the throne as 'God's father Ay, divine ruler of Thebes, beloved of Amun' with Nefertiti's old nurse/stepmother Tiy (not to be confused with Amenhotep III's chief wife of that name) as his consort. This could never be anything other than the briefest of reigns, an immediate response to a dynastic crisis that would grant sufficient time to search for a new king. We have several images of Tiy during her residence at Amarna, but know little of her life as queen. Ay was eventually buried, not in the splendid Amarna tomb that has provided us with so much information about daily life at the Amarna court, but in a relatively simple unfinished tomb in the Western Valley (WV 23).

TIY	
Husband	*Titles*
Ay	Nurse of the Great
Parents	King's Wife, King's
Unknown	Great Wife, Lady of
Son	the Two Lands,
Nakhtmin?	Mistress of Upper
Daughters	and Lower Egypt
Stepdaughters	*Burial place*
Nefertiti and	Thebes
Mutnodjmet?	

The God's Father Ay and his wife Tiy receive gold collars from Akhenaten and Nefertiti. Scene from the Amarna tomb of Ay (no. 25). Ay and Tiy would eventually be buried in the Western Valley (WV 23), an offshoot of the Valley of the Kings.

Here on the tomb walls we may see Tiy accompanying her husband. The tomb was robbed in antiquity, but scattered fragments of female human bone found in and around the tomb may represent the last remains of Queen Tiy.

MUTNODJMET

MUTNODJMET	
Husband	Great Wife, King's
Horemheb	Great Wife,
Father	Mistress of Upper
Ay?	and Lower Egypt,
Mother	Lady of the Two
Unknown	Lands
Children	*Burial place*
None known	Saqqara tomb of
Titles	Horemheb
Sister of the King's	

General Horemheb, a soldier of obscure origins, followed Ay on the throne. Horemheb continued the reconstruction of Egypt that had started under Tutankhamun. It was during his 28-year reign that the *Hwt-Benben* (the temple to the sun god built by Akhenaten) was dismantled and used as filling in a new gateway – the Second Pylon – to the Karnak temple. It is a curious irony that Horemheb's demolition of the temple actually saved it for posterity. Inside Horemheb's gateway the blocks were carefully reassembled to make up partial scenes, but at least two scenes were reconstructed upside-down. Furthermore, Nefertiti's image was defaced, while many of the hands at the tip of the Aten's rays were slashed. Whether this was part of the official policy to erase all traces of the Amarna heresy, a private vendetta against Nefertiti, or maybe a spot of independent and ultimately hidden vandalism on the part of Horemheb's masons, is not clear. Today many of the blocks have been retrieved from the Pylon, allowing computer reconstruction of the vanished temple.

Horemheb's first wife, Amenia, had died before he came to the throne. His second wife, Mutnodjmet, is likely (but not proven) to have been Nefertiti's younger sister. We last saw Mutnodjmet, clearly labelled as the 'Sister of the King's Great Wife', on the walls of the elite Amarna tombs. The young Mutnodjmet did not play any active role in Aten worship but she was nevertheless an important court figure. Curiously, and inexplicably, she was often shown accompanied by two dwarves.

Mutnodjmet disappeared from the Amarna scenes before Nefernefer-uaten was born. She re-emerged from obscurity as a queen consort and God's Wife of Amun. Like all the women of her birth family, she proved to be a powerful queen. She sat beside her husband on his coronation statue, and a scene on the side of his throne shows her as a winged human-headed sphinx wearing the tall flat-topped plant crown associated with Tefnut and Queen Tiy. She was also featured in the inscriptions of the Luxor temple, inscriptions which she had usurped from her niece, Ankhesenamun. Mutnodjmet died some time during her husband's regnal Year 14–15 and was probably buried, as Amenia may have been before her, in his Saqqara tomb. Female human remains recovered from the tomb are assumed to belong to Mutnodjmet; these had been buried with the body of a newborn baby or foetus, suggesting that the middle-aged queen may have died attempting to provide her husband with an heir.

With Mutnodjmet and her baby died the 18th Dynasty. The line of remarkable queens from Akhmim had ended.

(*Opposite above*) Mutnodjmet, sister of Nefertiti, stands behind the immediate royal family, slightly taller than her nieces yet, like them, dressed in flowing pleated garments, sandals and the sidelock hairstyle which tells us she is a child.

(*Opposite*) Mutnodjmet sits beside Horemheb on his coronation statue recovered from Karnak. It has been speculated that the commoner Horemheb married the last remaining member of the Amarna royal family to reinforce his claim to the throne of Egypt. The side of the sculpture shows Mutnodjmet as a winged sphinx. The rear of the statue tells the story of Horemheb's rise to power. Turin Museum.

DYNASTY 19
1292–1190

Sitre
Tuya
Henutmire
Nefertari
Isetnofret I
Bintanath I
Meritamun
Nebettawi
Maathornefrure

Nefertari, consort of Ramesses II, as she appears on the wall of her vibrantly painted tomb in the Valley of the Queens.

SITRE	
Husband	King's Great Wife,
Ramesses I	Mistress of Upper
(Paramessu)	and Lower Egypt,
Parents	Lady of the Two
Unknown	Lands, King's
Children	Mother
Seti I	*Burial place*
Titles	Valley of the Queens
God's Wife,	(QV 38)

SITRE

Ramesses I, the first king of the 19th Dynasty, was the former vizier Paramessu, an able courtier with a successful military career behind him. Married for many years to the lady Sitre, he already had an adult son, Seti, and a grandson, Ramesses, who could continue his dynastic line. This instant royal family may be, in part, why the childless Horemheb selected the elderly Ramesses as his heir. He can have had no realistic hope that his successor would rule for any length of time – in fact Ramesses would serve as king for a mere two years – but he knew that the succession would be secure. And this, for an Egypt still suffering the after-effects of the Amarna Period, was a very important matter.

The age of the powerful queen consorts had ended. The queens of the 19th Dynasty are consistently overshadowed by their husbands, and Sitre's only known monument is her unfinished tomb in the Valley of the Queens (QV 38). Although used sporadically during the 18th Dynasty, *Ta set neferu* or 'the Place of Beauties' was now to be developed as the main cemetery of the more important Ramesside royal wives and their children. Effectively, it had become an annex of the nearby Valley of the Kings. It is therefore curious that, while the Valley of the Kings has yielded several royal mummy caches, the Valley of the Queens has so far provided very few human remains. This may be, of course, because all the burials were robbed and their mummies destroyed in antiquity. But it holds out the tantalizing prospect of a so-far undiscovered queens' mummy cache hidden somewhere in the Valley.

QUEENS OF THE 19th DYNASTY

Queen
KING
FEMALE KING
Other royal male
?
= possible marriage
= marriage
|? possible offspring

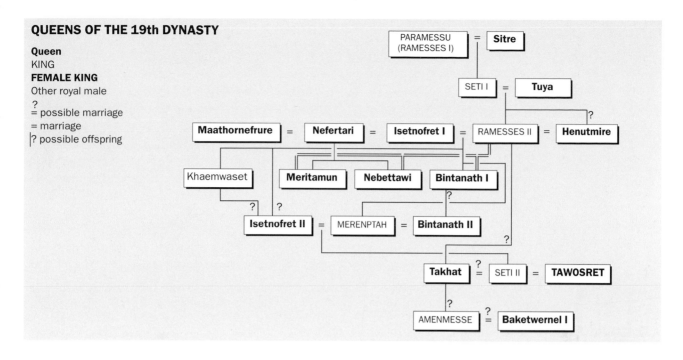

(Genealogical chart)

PARAMESSU (RAMESSES I) = **Sitre**

SETI I = **Tuya**

Maathornefrure = **Nefertari** = **Isetnofret I** = RAMESSES II = **Henutmire** ?

Khaemwaset   **Meritamun**   **Nebettawi**   **Bintanath I**
?
?   ?

Isetnofret II = MERENPTAH = **Bintanath II**
?

Takhat ? = SETI II = **TAWOSRET**
?

AMENMESSE ? = **Baketwernel I**

TUYA	
Also known as	*Daughters*
Mut-Tuya	Tia, Henutmire?
Husband	*Titles*
Seti I	King's Wife, King's
Father	Mother, God's Wife
Raia	*Burial place*
Mother	Valley of the Queens
Ruia	(QV 80)
Son	
Ramesses II	

Ruia (left) and Raia, parents of Tuya, as depicted on a block at Medinet Habu. The queen's parents came from a similar upper-class military background to the king's own.

TUYA AND HENUTMIRE

Seti had married Tuya (also known as Mut-Tuya) before his father became king. Tuya was, like Seti himself, a member of Egypt's military elite, the daughter of the Lieutenant of Chariotry Raia and his wife Ruia. Seti and Tuya were to have at least two children: a daughter named Tia and a son named Ramesses after his grandfather. There is likely to have been a third, much younger child born after Seti became heir to the throne. The parentage of the mysterious Princess Henutmire is never specified, but her appearance on a statue of Tuya (now housed in the Vatican Museum, Rome) suggests a close relationship to the queen. Tia, who was born a commoner, married Tjia son of Amenwahsu. She played no formal part in her brother's reign, and was eventually buried with her husband in the Saqqara cemetery. Her 'sister' Henutmire, born a princess

Tuya, widow of Seti I and mother of Ramesses II. This above life-size statue was taken to Rome by the emperor Caligula, who used it to decorate the Gardens of Sallust. Today it is displayed in the Vatican Museum.

(if not the daughter of Seti and Tuya, she must have been their grand-daughter), married Ramesses II. We know little of her time as queen beyond the fact that she was eventually buried in the Valley of the Queens (QV 75).

Tuya, who had remained very much in the background during Seti's 13-year reign, was to enjoy a brief burst of celebrity as King's Mother at the court of Ramesses II. Nevertheless, she remains an enigma, a queen who had reverted to the traditional role of offering passive support to her menfolk. Her Vatican statue depicts the widowed Tuya as a bland, conventionally ageless woman. Gone are the wrinkles and imperfections that make Queen Tiy such an authoritative and attractive figure. Tuya was featured twice at a small scale alongside other royal women on the façade of Ramesses' Abu Simbel temple in Nubia, and at a much larger scale in the Ramesseum, Ramesses' Theban mortuary temple. Here she sat, preserved in stone, beside the much larger statue of her son in the first courtyard, and here she rattled her sistra (the Hathoric sistrum having replaced the female sphinx as a royal emblem) alongside the King's Great Wife Nefertari on the wall of the hypostyle hall. A double shrine to the north of the hypostyle hall was dedicated to Seti and Tuya, while a cult chapel in the first court was dedicated to Tuya herself. Here she was identified with the local goddess Hathor, Mistress of the West.

A divine birth

Why did Tuya figure so prominently in her son's reign? Ramesses II, denied royal parents, had decided to follow the precedent set by Hatshepsut and his great hero Amenhotep III, and develop a birth legend that would reaffirm his right to rule while highlighting his own personal divinity. And this, of course, involved elevating his mother to a semi-divine status as one who had enjoyed intercourse with a god. The story of Ramesses' conception and birth, heavily 'borrowed' from Hatshepsut (Ramesses would have been very familiar with her story, as he usurped blocks from her Deir el-Bahari temple to build his own mortuary temple), was displayed most appropriately on the walls of Tuya's now destroyed chapel in the Ramesseum. One crucial block from the chapel wall has survived. Once again we are invited to watch as a queen of Egypt sits on a bed facing the great god Amun who is disguised as Seti I, and whose potent perfume is filling the palace. The sadly broken text explains that the queen is 'The Mother of the God, Mut..., the Mother of the King, Tuya...'. Meanwhile, across the river in the Karnak temple, we can see the unborn Ramesses being moulded on the potter's wheel of Khnum the creator, and the infant Ramesses being suckled by a goddess.

At Abu Simbel and at Karnak, the Blessing of Ptah upon Ramesses II, a lengthy text dating to Ramesses' Year 35, tells a subtly different birth story. Here the creator god Ptah of Memphis is the divine father and, as Ptah has the power to make life via the spoken word, Tuya's role in events has been much reduced:

Words spoken by Ptah-Tatonen, he of the tall plumes and sharp horns, who begot the gods:

I am your father, who begot you as a god to act as King of South and North Egypt on my seat. I decree for you the lands that I created, their rulers carry their revenue to you....[25]

Tuya died soon after Year 22 and was buried in a large tomb in the Valley of the Queens (QV 80). Here she was given the simplified name Tuya. The Mut element of her name, a name which connected her with the vulture goddess wife of Amun, may well have been an earthly title used to reinforce her role as divine wife and mother. Her tomb was looted in antiquity, but it has yielded the lid of a canopic jar carved in the queen's image.

NEFERTARI

Ramesses II, like his father and grandfather before him, had been born a commoner. With his father's elevation his life underwent a profound change. While still a teenager he was officially proclaimed First King's Son, a position of great honour that brought with it a harem full of beautiful women. Ramesses clearly appreciated his good fortune:

In this scene from her tomb Nefertari, first and best-attested consort of Ramesses II, wears the vulture headdress, modius, double plumes and sun disk, and is led by the goddess Isis.

It was Menmaatre [Seti I] who nurtured me, and the All-Lord himself advanced me when I was a child until I could start to rule.... He equipped me with private attendants and with female attendants who resembled the great beauties of the palace. Throughout the land he selected women for me...harem women and female companions.[26]

This harem was only the beginning. Throughout his reign Ramesses continued to add to his collection of wives, both foreigners and Egyptians, until he could boast some 100 children surviving infancy (a conservative estimate; some observers have put the number of royal children at over 150) with daughters and sons in roughly equal numbers. Breaking with convention, Ramesses displayed and named his numerous offspring – the children of lesser wives shown alongside children born to consorts – walking in procession on the walls of his various temples. However, it is the children (the daughters in particular) born to his two principal wives Nefertari and Isetnofret I, who play a prominent role in his reign. With the exception of Suterery, mother of Ramesses-Siptah, who appears in a relief alongside her son, his minor wives go unrecorded while the lives of his less significant children are more or less unrecorded.

Ramesses was to rule Egypt for 66 years, outliving most of his wives, many of his children and even some of his grandchildren in the process. Because of this extreme longevity, he is associated with more queen consorts than any other Egyptian king. However, none of his wives attained the high political and religious profile of the Amarna women.

His first, and best attested, consort is Nefertari, whom he married

NEFERTARI	
Husband	Nebettawi,
Ramesses II	Nefertari?
Parents	*Titles*
Unknown	God's Wife, King's
Sons	Wife, Mistress of
Amenhirwenemef,	Upper and Lower
Prehirwenemef,	Egypt, Lady of the
Seti, Merire the	Two Lands
Elder, Meriatum	*Burial place*
Daughters	Valley of the Queens
Baketmut,	(QV 66)
Meritamun,	

before becoming king. Nefertari's parentage is never disclosed although, as she never uses the title King's Daughter, we know that she was not born a princess. It may be that she was a member of Ay's wider family; the discovery of a glazed knob (possibly the head of a walking stick, or the fastener from a wooden box) decorated with Ay's cartouche in her tomb lends some support to this theory. However, she is probably too young to have been Ay's daughter – a sister to queens Nefertiti and Mutnodjmet – as Ramesses reigned 20 years after Ay's death.

Nefertari produced Ramesses' first-born son and heir, Amenhirwenemef, before Seti I's death. More children followed: Ramesses' third son Prehirwenemef, his ninth son Seti, his eleventh son Merire the Elder, and his sixteenth son Meriatum. Several of these sons served as crown prince, but all predeceased their long-lived father. Nefertari's daughters included the ephemeral Baketmut, and Meritamun and Nebettawi who would eventually take their mother's place as queen. Princess Nefertari's name suggests that she, too, may have been the daughter of Queen Nefertari.

Nefertari spent at least 20 years appearing alongside her husband as a dutiful, beautiful, but entirely passive wife. As such, she is a frustrating subject for any biographer. She supports Ramesses on all appropriate ceremonial occasions, and may well have accompanied him on his military campaigns. During the Year 5 battle of Kadesh the royal family (Nefertari and her children included?) came dangerously close to being captured by the Hittites. Many years later, with the Hittites and the Egyptians reconciled, Nefertari was to correspond with the formidable Pudukhepa, queen of the Hittites. This seems somewhat out of character. It appears that Pudukhepa, who played a more prominent role in state affairs than her Egyptian counterpart, wrote first, and that Nefertari had to reply for the sake of politeness. Her stilted letters, however, reveal little of interest and nothing at all of her character.

Thus says Naptera [Nefertari], the Great Queen of Egypt, to Pudukhepa, the Great Queen of Hatti, my sister:

All goes well with me, your sister, and all goes well with my country. May all go well with you too, my sister, and with your country may all go well also. I have noted that you, my sister, have written to enquire after my well-being. And that you have written to me about the new relationship of good peace and brotherhood in which the Great King of Egypt now stands with his brother the Great King of Hatti.[27]

The temples of Abu Simbel

As his reign progressed Ramesses, seemingly immortal in a land where 40 years of age was considered old, grew increasingly interested in his own personal divinity. Like Amenhotep III before him, he stopped short of announcing his divine nature in Egypt, but was quite happy to become a fully-fledged deity in the provinces. Again, the masons picked up their hammers and twin temples started to rise in Nubia. The larger temple,

(*Opposite*) Nefertari stands before her colossal husband in the peristyle court of the Luxor temple.

(*Right*) The façade of Abu Simbel's Lesser Temple is decorated with four colossal images of Ramesses II, two of Nefertari, and smaller-scale images of their children. Nefertari wears the cow horns and carries the sistrum which associate her with Hathor, the goddess of the temple.

(*Below*) The more important members of the royal family appear between the seated colossi on the façade of the Great Temple of Abu Simbel (see opposite), in groups of three. From left to right, facing the temple, they are: Nebettawi, Isetnofret II, Bintanath I; Tuya, Prince Amenhirwenemef, Nefertari; Nefertari, Prince Ramesses, Baketmut; Meritamun, Nefertari II, Tuya. Here we see Bintanath I and Tuya.

the Great Temple of Abu Simbel, was officially dedicated to the gods Re-Herakhty, Amun and Ptah, but actually celebrated Ramesses himself. The companion Lesser Temple, in every respect a subsidiary temple designed to support the Great Temple, celebrated Nefertari's almost-divine role as consort to a fully divine being.

The façade of the Great Temple is dominated by four colossal seated figures of Ramesses. But supporting each colossus, and represented at a much smaller scale, stand the more important female members of his immediate family arranged in groups of three, one on each side of each colossus and one in front. Only two men, the eldest sons of Ramesses' two principal wives, are included in this family group which includes the King's Mother Tuya, Queen Nefertari, and daughters born to both Queen Nefertari and Queen Isetnofret I.

To the north of the Great Temple, The Lesser Temple – officially dedicated to Hathor of Ibshek (a local form of Hathor) – was decorated with four colossal standing images of Ramesses and two of Nefertari, wearing the Hathoric cow horns, solar disk and tall feathers and carrying the sistrum (see p. 7). Alongside Ramesses and Nefertari, again at a much

(*Left*) The Great Temple of Abu Simbel, decorated with four colossal seated figures of Ramesses II. Above the doorway stands the smaller figure of Re-Herakhty, the goddess Maat by his left leg and the hieroglyphic sign for *user* by his right, so that the image forms a rebus '*user-maat-re*', the name of Ramesses himself.

(*Opposite*) Nefertari stands between the goddesses Hathor (in front of the queen) and Isis (behind her). All three wear the uraeus, modius, solar disk and cow horns that link them with the solar cults. Nefertari also wears the double plumes.

(*Below*) The columns in the first hall of the Lesser Temple decorated with Hathor heads. New Kingdom queens often felt a strong devotion to Hathor. Here she is being worshipped in the form of the local goddess Hathor of Ibshek.

smaller scale, stand their children. Just in case anyone is in any doubt, the temple facade proclaims: 'Ramesses II has made a temple, excavated in the mountain, of eternal workmanship...for the Chief Queen Nefertari Beloved of Mut...Nefertari...for whom the sun shines.' Inside the temple there are scenes of temple ritual and, alongside the traditional slaying scenes, more female-orientated images of the goddesses Hathor and Isis. The columns in the first hall are topped with Hathor heads, while the niche at the back of the sanctuary contains an image of Hathor the divine cow, protector of the king. Here on the sanctuary walls we can see Ramesses offering to the deified Ramesses and Nefertari.

The Abu Simbel temples were inaugurated during Year 24, although they would not be fully completed until some time after Year 35. A stela endowed by the viceroy Hekanakht shows the royal family as they attend the dedication ceremony. We can see a seated Nefertari dressed in full queenly regalia and, on a separate register, her eldest daughter Meritamun accompanying Ramesses as his queen. No explanation is offered, but it seems that Meritamun is deputizing for her mother; whether this is because Nefertari is ill, or because Meritamun is now routinely serving as her mother's deputy (as Sitamun had previously deputized for Queen Tiy) is unclear. Nefertari is absent from Ramesses' jubilee celebrations of Year 30, and is presumably dead.

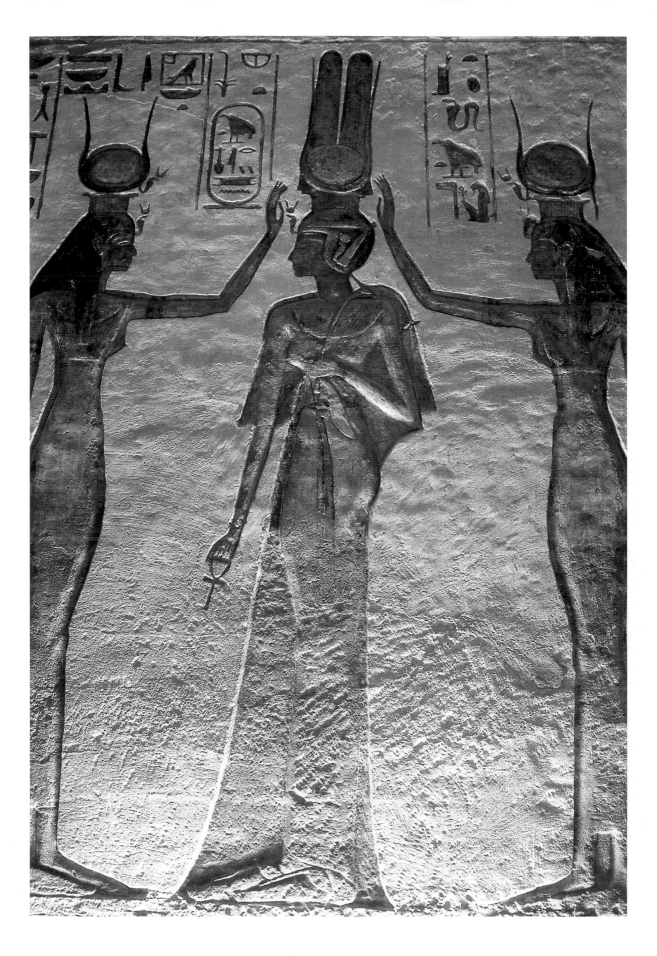

NEFERTARI'S PAINTED TOMB

Nefertari's own longevity had allowed Ramesses to make adequate provision for her burial. She was to be interred in one of the largest tombs in the Valley of the Queens (QV 66). Her tomb was looted in antiquity, subsequently lost, and rediscovered in 1904 by the Italian Egyptologist Ernesto Schiaparelli. All that now remains of the queen's once impressive burial are the glazed knob inscribed for King Ay, some wooden *shabti* figures, many pottery fragments, a box lid, a small wooden *djed* pillar (symbolizing stability), splinters from a gilded coffin, a gold bracelet fragment, part of a sarcophagus lid, a pair of woven sandals and a pair of mummified knees – presumably Nefertari's – which are now housed in Turin Museum.

Nefertari's tomb is today justly famous for its painted plaster decoration which, once sadly deteriorated, has recently been restored to its former brilliance by a team of international conservationists headed by the J. Paul Getty Museum. Beneath the dramatic ceiling – a deep blue night sky glittering with many hundreds of golden stars – the tomb walls and columns tell the story of Nefertari's spiritual and physical journey from death to a perpetual afterlife in the company of her fellow gods. The antechamber presents the beginning of the tale. Here in various colourful scenes we see Nefertari as a bandaged and masked mummy lying on a bier, Nefertari as a beautiful woman playing an invisible opponent at *senet* (a board game with religious significance), and Nefertari being greeted by Hathor and Isis who, in their solar disks, cow horns and patterned dresses, look confusingly alike, and confusingly like Nefertari.

The goddess Maat stretches her feathered wings wide to protect the dead queen as she makes her way down the steps leading into the pillared burial chamber. Here, in the darkest and most private region of the tomb, we see representations of five of the twelve gateways leading to the Kingdom of Osiris. Nefertari will have to name each gate and each of its three divine gate-keepers before she can reach her own resurrection. Fortunately, spells from the Book of the Dead – including the answers to the many riddles – are provided to help the queen on her travels. The queen's pink granite sarcophagus (now represented by fragments of sarcophagus lid in Turin Museum) is the centre of the funerary ritual, the womb from which the queen will eventually be reborn. The outcome of Nefertari's perilous journey is never in doubt. A red-wrapped Nefertari, her living face exposed, stands triumphant in a small room opening off the burial chamber.

(Opposite) Nefertari's burial chamber, looking to the southeast. The far wall shows three of the divine gatekeepers sitting in their caverns. The pillars are painted with representations of the djed pillar – the backbone of Osiris which represents resurrection.

(Left) Nefertari plays a game of senet against an invisible opponent. The movement of her pieces across the board symbolizes her own journey towards the afterlife.

(Below) On the east wall of the stairway Nefertari wears a white linen dress, beaded collar, bracelets, earrings, vulture headdress and modius crown as she brings offerings to the goddesses Hathor (shown), Selket and Maat. The opposite wall shows the queen offering to Isis, Nephthys and Maat.

ISETNOFRET I	
Husband	*Titles*
Ramesses II	King's Great Wife,
Parents	Lady of the Two
Unknown	Lands
Sons	*Burial place*
Ramesses,	Valley of the
Khaemwaset,	Queens?
Merenptah	
Daughters	
Bintanath I,	
Isetnofret II?	

Gebel Silsila image showing the family of Isetnofret I. Ramesses II is worshipping the god Ptah. Behind him stand Isetnofret I and Bintanath I, below him are princes Ramesses and Merenptah, and before him stands Prince Khaemwaset. Only Bintanath and Merenptah would outlive their father.

ISETNOFRET I

With Nefertari dead and buried, Ramesses had to appoint a new consort to fulfil the feminine aspects of his reign. For many years Egyptologists believed that he turned to his most prominent secondary queen, Isetnofret, mother of some of his favourite children. However, there is little concrete evidence to prove that Isetnofret outlived Nefertari. Judging from her children's birth dates, which are interwoven with the birth dates of Nefertari's children, Isetnofret must have married Ramesses at roughly the same time that he married Nefertari. As a secondary wife she remained very much in the background; as we would expect, Isetnofret is absent from the façade of the Abu Simbel temple although her daughters are present. After Nefertari's death Isetnofret features on a small number of monuments alongside the king. She appears as queen consort with Ramesses and their children on stelae erected at Aswan (Years 24–30) and in the Gebel Silsila rock temple (Years 33–34).

However, these images were erected not by Ramesses, but by Isetnofret's son, Khaemwaset, and may well have been carved after her death. Khaemwaset would not be the first Egyptian to revise (and improve) his personal history by promoting his dead mother. While the Aswan stela shows Isetnofret holding a floral sceptre and a papyrus or lotus, the Gebel Silsila stela shows her holding the *ankh* of life. This suggests that she may have been dead by Year 34; indeed, she may even have predeceased Nefertari. All that we can state with any degree of certainty is that she was definitely alive for the birth of her son Merenptah.

We do not know where Isetnofret was buried. It seems highly likely that she, too, would have been granted a splendid painted tomb in the Valley of the Queens, although a 19th Dynasty ostracon recovered by Howard Carter hints that she may instead have been buried in the nearby Valley of the Kings, as it gives measurements 'from the tomb in preparation of Isetnofret to the tomb of Meriatum 200 cubits, from the end of the Water of the Sky to the tomb of Isetnofret 445 cubits'.[28] Unfortunately this tomb has not yet been discovered, and there is no proof that this lady is the same Isetnofret who married Ramesses II.

Isetnofret bore at least four children: princes Ramesses, Khaemwaset and Merenptah, and Ramesses' first and most beloved daughter, Bintanath. Again, Princess Isetnofret's name suggests that she may also have been a daughter

PERSONAL NAMES

Babies were named by their mother immediately after birth to ensure that every child, no matter how short-lived, had a name to be remembered by.

All but the shortest of Egypt's personal names had meanings. We have already met Nefertiti 'A Beautiful Woman has Come'; her very specific name may be compared with Neferwaty 'The Beautiful One is Unique', Neferteni 'The Beautiful One is for Me', Aneksi 'She Belongs to Me' and Senetenpu 'She is Our Sister'. Other children were named after their parents, grandparents, favoured deities, or members of the royal family.

Bintanath's unusual Canaanite name translates as 'Daughter of the [Canaanite] Goddess Anath'. Could Isetnofret's choice of an exotic foreign name for her daughter indicate that she was a foreign bride? We have no information at all about Isetnofret's birth family, but her daughter's name may well be a red herring. None of her other children had foreign names, although at least two of Ramesses' other children did: Meheranath 'Child of Anath', and Astarteherwenemef 'Astarte is on his Right'. The cults of the foreign goddesses Anath and Astarte enjoyed a surge in popularity during the reign of Ramesses II.

of Queen Isetnofret. Curiously, although Nefertari is clearly senior on all occasions to Isetnofret, their children are classed as equals. When Ramesses ranks his children on his temple walls it is gender and birth order, rather than mother's status, that dictates the line-up. All the sons of his two wives were considered to be potential future kings, and the title of Crown Prince passed from brother to half-brother in order of birth. Eventually Merenptah, son of Isetnofret and 13th son of Ramesses, would inherit his father's throne.

BINTANATH I

With both Nefertari and Isetnofret dead by Year 34, Ramesses II had to choose yet another consort. This time, following the precedent established by Amenhotep III, he married at least three of his daughters, Bintanath, Meritamun and Nebettawi, plus his 'sister' Henutmire.

Bintanath, eldest daughter of Isetnofret and Ramesses, was the first to become her father's consort. We can see her assuming the role of queen in a late-dating carving on one of the pillars in the great hall of Ramesses' Abu Simbel temple, and at Aswan where she stands alongside her mother and her brothers Ramesses, Khaemwaset and Merenptah.

Now we find our first and only instance of a child apparently born to a queen who is married to her father. A fully-grown woman who is clearly labelled Bodily King's Daughter appears beside Bintanath on the wall of the latter's tomb in the Valley of the Kings (QV 71). Bintanath wears a vulture headdress and modius, and her name is written in a cartouche. Her daughter has a simple lotus flower on her head, and no name. The daughter's title is a vague and confusing one, and her paternity remains unclear. She may indeed be the daughter of Ramesses II. But she may also, with equal validity, be his granddaughter, born to Bintanath and an

Bintanath I and her daughter, the 'King's Bodily Daughter', an anonymous woman who wears a lotus flower rather than a crown. The paternity of this daughter has caused intense scholarly debate.

(*Opposite*) Bintanath stands before her colossal husband-father Ramesses II in the first court of the Karnak temple. Colossal statues were more than simple decoration. Each figure was understood to be an intermediary between mortals and the gods. The statues developed their own cults and their own priesthoods, and people of all classes dedicated stelae to the colossi.

(*Below*) Meritamun, 'the White Queen', discovered near the Ramesseum. The queen wears an ornate wig, double uraeus, and a modius decorated with multiple uraei. (See frontispiece for frontal view.)

otherwise undistinguished husband, possibly before Bintanath became queen. If the latter were the case, it would suggest that Bintanath and her sisters were queen consorts in name only. Bintanath outlived her father, dying during the reign of her brother Merenptah.

MERITAMUN

We have already encountered Meritamun, Ramesses' fourth daughter born to Nefertari, deputizing for her mother at the consecration of the Abu Simbel temple. Meritamun died during father's reign, and was buried in the Valley of the Queens (QV 68).

We have a series of remarkable statues of Meritamun. One, a beautiful, painted limestone statue showing an anonymous but stereotypically young New Kingdom queen wearing a tripartite wig topped by a modius with multiple uraei (it is generally assumed that the double plumes which would have towered above the modius have broken away), was recovered from the vicinity of the Ramesseum by Flinders Petrie in 1896. This piece, universally known as the 'White Queen', was only identified as Meritamun when, almost a century later in 1981, a strikingly similar but much larger named statue was recovered from the ruins of the Ramesside Akhmim temple. The 42-ft (13-m) high painted limestone colossus wears a modius with multiple uraei and double plumes.

A second colossal statue of Meritamun has recently been discovered in the temple of Bast at the Delta site of Bubastis. This colossus, carved from granite, shows the queen wearing a heavy wig and vulture headdress.

NEBETTAWI

Nebettawi, Ramesses' fifth daughter also born to Nefertari, succeeded Meritamun as consort. She too was buried in the Valley of the Queens (QV 60).

MAATHORNEFRURE	
Husband	*Children*
Ramesses II	One daughter
Father	*Titles*
Hattusilis III, king of	King's Great Wife
the Hittites	*Burial place*
Mother	Gurob?
Pudukhepa	

MAATHORNEFRURE

The early years of Ramesses' reign had been devoted to strengthening his empire and consolidating Egypt's sphere of influence further afield. Year 5 had been the year of the celebrated battle of Kadesh: the Egyptian troops led by the valiant Ramesses himself, pitted against the massed armies of the Near East led by the Hittite king Muwatallis. Ramesses claimed a great victory at Kadesh – but then so did Muwatallis. In fact there was no great victory and no real winner, and the situation in the Near East remained more or less unchanged.

In Year 21 the Egyptians and the Hittites signed a peace treaty and Ramesses, uxorious as ever, sought to cement his new friendship by marrying another beautiful young bride, the eldest daughter of the new Hittite king Hattusilis. Negotiations proceeded slowly, but eventually the extravagant bride price and equally extravagant dowry were agreed, and the princess was anointed with oil to seal the marriage. The bride, accompanied by her mother Pudukhepa, travelled overland to southern

THE WOMEN OF DEIR EL-MEDINA

The workmen who hollowed out the tombs in the Valleys of the Kings and Queens lived with their families in the purpose-built workmen's village of Deir el-Medina. Deir el-Medina was a village of small, stone-built terraced houses defined by a thick mud-brick wall that allowed government officials to control and if necessary search those entering and leaving. It was occupied for almost five centuries, housing approximately 120 families, or 1,200 people.

The village contained an unusually high proportion of skilled and educated people. This education extended to the women, at least some of whom were able to read and write. Papyrus was extremely expensive, but the local stone offered an ideal substitute that could be picked up anywhere, written on and then discarded. This allowed the villagers to record the most mundane details of daily life, and has provided archaeologists with the personal letters, shopping and laundry lists that are missing from Egypt's other domestic sites.

Deir el-Medina was an isolated, tight-knit community where everyone knew everyone else's business. Naturally, it was a hotbed of gossip. Paneb was one of the biggest scandal makers. Not only had he been caught desecrating royal tombs, he had been accused of sexual offences against the women of the village:

…Paneb slept with the villager Tuy, when she was married to the workman Kenna, with the villager Hunro when she was living with Pendua, and again with the villager Hunro when she was with Hesysenebef. His own son said this. And after he had slept with Hunro he slept with her daughter, Webkhet. What's more his son, Apahte, slept with Webkhet too….[29]

There is no suggestion that Paneb forced himself on any of these women. But, in a village where the workmen regularly left their families unprotected as they spent the working week living in temporary huts close by the royal tombs, adultery was seen as a grave social offence. No wonder someone wrote a letter of complaint to the Theban vizier.

Ramesside ostracon recovered from Deir el-Medina and now housed in Turin Museum. A scantily dressed dancing girl performs a flip.

(*Above*) The Hittite bride Maathornefrure and her father Hattusilis, featured at Abu Simbel.

(*Below*) The badly damaged image of Egypt's new queen stands beside her own cartouche on a colossus of Ramesses II.

Syria where she was transferred into the care of the Egyptian authorities. Ramesses, eagerly waiting in his new Delta capital, Per-Ramesse, feared that the unseasonable bad weather might delay her arrival. His frantic prayers to the storm god Seth were answered, the weather turned mild, and the new bride finally reached her groom.

A stela giving details of Ramesses' Hittite marriage was carved at the southern end of the terrace fronting the façade of the Great Temple of Abu Simbel, where it served as a companion piece to the story of Ramesses' divine birth. Here, in a highly imaginative account that contrasts markedly with the recovered diplomatic correspondence, Ramesses boasts that his new bride was effectively given as war booty:

…The great prince of Hatti said to his soldiers and courtiers, 'Look. Our land has been devastated [by the Egyptians].… Let us strip ourselves of all our possessions and with my eldest daughter in front of them, let us carry peace offerings to the Good God [Ramesses].…

It is unlikely that the proud Hattusilis would have recognized this version of events! We can see the new bride, entirely Egyptian in appearance, dressed in a loose robe, vulture headdress and modius as she stands beside her father who wears an un-Egyptian-looking headdress. As the stela tells us, Ramesses found her to be 'beautiful in the heart of his majesty, and he loved her more than anything'. She was given a suitable new Egyptian name, Maathornefrure (the One who sees Horus, the Visible Splendour of Re) and, most unusually (and perhaps due to her father's insistence), the title of queen consort, although Bintanath and her half-sisters, first Meritamun and then Nebettawi, continued to perform this most important and most Egyptian of roles. Maathornefrure lived for a time at Per-Ramesse before retiring to the Medinet Gurob harem palace. Here Flinders Petrie recovered her papyrus laundry list which detailed rolls of cloth '28 cubits 4 palms' long and '4 cubits' wide. The new queen gave birth to a daughter – disappointing her father, who had hoped that his grandson would one day rule Egypt – then disappeared. We must assume that Maathornefrure died young.

A second Hittite bride

Ten years after his first Hittite marriage Ramesses successfully negotiated a marriage with a second daughter of Hattusilis. The name of this second bride went unrecorded, and we know nothing of her married life in Egypt. But this may not have been the end of the king's marital adventures. A solitary stela recovered from Kesweh, 16 miles (25 km) to the south of Damascus, and dated to the summer of his Year 56, confirms an unusual level of Egyptian activity in this area. We do not know why the stela was erected, but it is just possible that a third Hittite bride, this time a daughter of Tudkhalia IV, was perhaps travelling southwards to her wedding.

DYNASTY 19
1292–1190

Isetnofret II

Bintanath II

Baketwernel I

Takhat

Tawosret

ISETNOFRET II	
Husband	*Daughter*
Merenptah	Isetnofret
Father	*Titles*
either Ramesses II	King's Great Wife
(with Isetnofret I) or	*Burial place*
Khaemwaset	Thebes
Son	
Seti-Merenptah	
(Seti II)	

ISETNOFRET II

Eventually Merenptah, some 60 years old, succeeded his father. Merenptah was married to Isetnofret II. For a long time it was assumed that this lady was his slightly older sister, the sixth daughter of Ramesses II born to Isetnofret I. However, there are many Isetnofrets in the Rammesside royal family, and it may be that she is in fact Merenptah's niece, the daughter of his brother Khaemwaset. This would explain why the new Queen Isetnofret never uses the title King's Daughter. The queen bore her husband at least two children: a daughter, Isetnofret, and a son, Seti-Merenptah.

BINTANATH II

The 'Royal Daughter, Royal Sister, Great Royal Wife Bintanath' appears on a statue of Merenptah erected in front of the gateway to the Luxor temple. Some Egyptologists have read this as proof that Bintanath, daughter of Ramesses II, married her brother after her father's death. However, given her age – at least 60 at the time of Merenptah's succession – and the fact that Bintanath was effectively Merenptah's stepmother as well as his sister, this seems unlikely. Second marriages were very common amongst non-royal Egyptians, but with the possible exception of the Old Kingdom Hetepheres II, there is no recorded instance of a widowed queen remarrying. It seems far more reasonable to suggest that this queen may be Bintanath II, the anonymous daughter shown in Bintanath I's tomb. Alternatively, it may be that a statue originally belonging to Ramesses has been usurped by his son Merenptah.

BAKETWERNEL I

Seti-Merenptah, son of Isetnofret II, 'Heir of the Two Lands, Generalissimo and Senior Prince', had clearly been intended to inherit his father's crown. But something went badly wrong and, after ten years on the throne, Merenptah was most unexpectedly succeeded by the unknown and totally unexplained King Amenmesse.

At this point we are entering a very muddled period, made worse by deliberate attempts to re-write history by erasing the names of kings and queens from their monuments. Lacking any details of Amenmesse's paternity, we can only assume that he was a member of the royal family, perhaps a son born to Merenptah by a secondary queen, a son born to Seti-Merenptah, or maybe a young son or grandson of Ramesses II. He may well be identical with the viceroy of Nubia, Messuy, who served under Merenptah.

Amenmesse was to share his Valley of the Kings tomb (KV 10) with two ladies: Takhat (assumed to be the King's Mother Takhat, see next entry) and the King's Great Wife Baketwernel I. It is generally thought that Baketwernel was Amenmesse's consort although their precise relationship is never explained, and there is a strong possibility that she may have been a late 20th Dynasty tomb usurper, possibly the identically named wife of Ramesses IX.[30]

The unfinished KV 10, originally decorated with carved scenes taken from the Litany of Re and the Book of the Dead, was partially redecorated with painted plaster reliefs showing Takhat (in the well room) and Baketwernel (first pillared hall) offering to a variety of gods. Unfortunately most of the plaster has now fallen off the walls, and only one damaged relief survives to show Baketwernel dressed in a sheath dress, shawl, beaded collar, short wig and uraeus, in the company of the gods Anubis and Horus. The tomb has been known and open for many hundreds of years; it is therefore not surprising that it has yielded few grave goods and its history is correspondingly difficult to reconstruct. Not everyone who decorated

Baketwernel I – queen of Amenmesse, or Ramesses IX? – in an ill-preserved image on the wall of Amenmesse's tomb (KV 10).

a tomb was eventually buried in it. However, fragments of Takhat's smashed canopic jars and granite sarcophagus lid (itself usurped from the burial of an earlier King's Daughter and King's Wife Anuketemheb) suggest that she at least was buried in the tomb.

TAKHAT

Amenmesse's mother Takhat has her own mystery. A statue still in place at Karnak originally showed King Amenmesse, although, as the statue was usurped in antiquity, it now bears the name of Seti II. On the back pillar of the statue is carved the smaller-scale image of the 'King's Daughter and King's Wife' Takhat. Takhat wears a flimsy robe, bobbed wig and uraeus. Her inscription, too, has been altered in antiquity; her original title, King's Mother, is still visible under the carving of King's Wife. A second statue, now housed in Cairo Museum, also describes Takhat as the wife of Seti II. Here, however, her inscription has not been altered.[31]

It may be that we are looking at two entirely separate Queen Takhats. If not, this evidence, somewhat perversely, would suggest that Takhat was wife to Seti II, and mother to his predecessor Amenmesse. It may therefore be that she is the Princess Takhat recorded amongst the offspring of Ramesses II. How had Amenmesse managed to snatch the crown from his putative father Seti-Merenptah? It may simply be that the elderly Seti-Merenptah was away from the court when his father died, and did not manage to return within the 70-day embalming period. Amenmesse may then have claimed the throne which, tradition decreed, fell to the heir who buried the previous king. An alternative suggestion – stemming from the fact that all the evidence for Amenmesse's reign comes from southern Egypt – is that Seti-Merenptah did indeed succeed as Seti II, only to be displaced in southern Egypt by the usurper (his son?) Amenmesse. Four years later, with Amenmesse dead, Seti II then reclaimed his entire land.

FAMILY AND TITLES	
TAKHAT	**TAWOSRET**
Husband	*Throne name*
Seti II?	Sitre-Meritamun
Father	*Husband*
Ramesses II?	Seti II
Son	*Children*
Amenmesse	Possibly one
Titles	daughter;
King's Daughter,	stepmother to
King's Great Wife,	Siptah
King's Mother	*Titles*
Burial place	King's Great Wife,
Valley of the Kings	Mistress of Upper
(KV 10)	and Lower Egypt,
	Lady of the Two
	Lands, God's Wife,
	King
	Burial place
	Valley of the Kings
	(KV 14)

Tawosret

Seti II, undisputed master of the whole of Egypt, was to rule for six undistinguished years with Tawosret as his consort. Then, since his intended heir was already dead, the throne passed to a hitherto-unknown young man. Ramesses-Siptah's parentage is never stated, but he is likely to have been either a son of Seti II born to a secondary queen (perhaps the foreign-born Sutailja), or perhaps a son of the now-disgraced Amenmesse. By Year 3 the young king had changed his name to Merenptah-Siptah; today he is known simply as Siptah.

Siptah, still a minor and possibly ill – his mummy reveals that he had a twisted leg indicative of cerebral palsy – needed a regent. His mother being ineligible for the role (because she was already dead? Or of inferior birth? Or a foreigner?), Seti's consort Tawosret took up the reigns of power on her young stepson's behalf. Here we have yet another prominent lady of unknown parentage who does not claim the title King's Daughter, but who may have been born a member of the wider royal family. A small cache of 19th Dynasty jewelry recovered from the 'Golden Tomb', actually a pit in the Valley of the Kings (KV 56), links the names of Tawosret and her husband Seti II. Decorated silver bracelets from the same tomb show the queen pouring a drink – a scene symbolizing fertility and rebirth – for her seated husband. Originally it was believed that this cache represented the sorry remains of Tawosret's own burial equipment, salvaged at the time that her tomb was usurped by Sethnakhte. It may, however, represent the badly decayed burial of a young daughter of Tawosret and Seti II.

Chancellor Bay

Initially Tawosret was supported in her regency by the 'Chancellor of the Whole Land' Bay, a man whose unusual name implies that he may have been of Syrian descent. Bay's precise role is never made clear, but his claim to have 'established the King on his Father's Throne' indicates that he may have played a crucial role in installing and maintaining the young Siptah – and Tawosret – as king. Bay was depicted both with Siptah (standing behind his throne, an unusual honour for a non-royal) and with Tawosret (standing on the doorjamb of the Amada temple, opposite the queen). For four years Bay was the dominant figure in Egyptian politics; then, like Senenmut before him, he vanished. An ostracon refers to Bay's execution in Year 5 of Siptah. His death left Tawosret sole regent of Egypt.

King Tawosret

Siptah has left no record of any queen consort although this does not mean, of course, that he did not marry. Presumably, with Tawosret effectively ruling on his behalf, he – or perhaps she – did not feel the need for another powerful female figure. Tawosret herself could continue to perform the consort's role. Siptah's death at just 20 years of age left Egypt

(*Opposite*) Queen Takhat standing on the left side of the back pillar of a statue of her son Amenmesse at Karnak. The statue was subsequently usurped by her husband Seti II.

without an obvious heir. Now Tawosret stepped forward, apparently unopposed, to become a fully-fledged female king: 'Daughter of Re, Lady of Ta-merit, Tawosret chosen of Mut'.

Superficially the circumstances of her ascent – the lack of a son, the young stepson, and the prominent male supporter – recall the circumstances of Hatshepsut's elevation some 250 years earlier. But while Hatshepsut had inherited a flourishing kingdom with a stable political infrastructure, Tawosret faced a rapidly escalating political crisis. Her assumption of royal power may itself be read as a symptom of the malaise that was affecting the once-vigorous 19th Dynasty. The royal family had grown feeble and, as we have already seen, was plagued with infighting – the fecund Ramesses II had left far too many descendants, each with an equally weak claim to the throne. The empire, once an unfailing source of revenue, was starting to dwindle. There was inflation, occasional food shortages, and sporadic civil unrest on the Theban west bank, where the necropolis workmen were prone to down tools at the merest whiff of political weakness. Meanwhile, on the western border, various Libyan tribes were threatening the security of the Nile Delta.

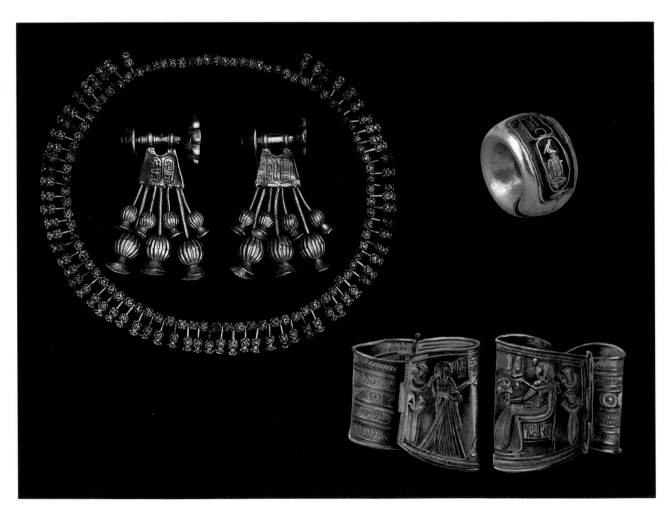

Jewelry recovered from KV 56, the 'Golden Tomb', discovered by Edward Ayrton in 1908. The gold beads and earrings are inscribed with the name of Seti II. The silver bracelets, illustrated by Harold Jones, are inscribed with the names of Seti II and Tawosret, and in a scene symbolizing rejuvenation, show the queen pouring a drink for her husband. The single gold earring shows Tawosret's cartouche surmounted by ostrich feathers. The cartouche is strangely positioned so that the hieroglyphs would be upside down when the earrings were worn.

Tawosret's burial chamber (KV 14) included scenes from the Book of Gates and the Book of Caverns, and an astronomical ceiling. Here, in the final scene from the Book of Caverns, we see the course of the sun god as a beetle, solar disk and ram-headed bird.

A brief reign

Tawosret's reign lasted a mere two years, and had little impact on the archaeological record. She continued Siptah's regnal years (allowing later historians to completely overlook her reign), her full regal titulary goes unrecorded, and her only substantial monuments are the unfinished mortuary temple that stood to the south of the Ramesseum, and her Valley of the Kings tomb. Her temple, originally excavated by Petrie, is currently being re-excavated by the University of Arizona under the direction of Richard H. Wilkinson. It is becoming apparent that Petrie's excavations were only partial, and that the temple was more developed than previously believed. KV 14 has a complicated history. Started during the reign of Seti II, it may well have been designed to house both king and queen. The tomb was then extended during Tawosret's regency and extended again during her solo reign. It was, however, unfinished at her death. Sethnakhte, first king of the 20th Dynasty, usurped the tomb and extended it to become one of the longest in the Valley. He removed Tawosret's burial (now unknown), and re-buried Seti II in tomb KV 15.

Siptah, re-labelled as Seti II, offers to the god of the earth, Geb. Tawosret stands behind her stepson/husband wearing the double plumes, modius and solar disk of a conventional New Kingdom queen.

(*Below*) 'Unknown Woman D', found in a broken coffin lid bearing the name Sethnakhte in the tomb of Amenhotep II. The mummy was believed to be that of Sethnakhte until its true gender was revealed by an autopsy in 1905.

Tawosret's stone sarcophagus was later reused in a 20th Dynasty burial. Sethnakhte's own burial was looted, and the tomb was reused during the Third Intermediate Period.

The decorated walls of Tawosret's tomb tell the abbreviated history of her career. The first passageways show her as a royal wife and regent. Here she stands behind Siptah as he offers to the god Geb. The fact that the young king's name has been erased and replaced by that of Seti II suggests that Tawosret preferred to be associated with her husband rather than her weaker stepson. This alteration has provoked speculation that Tawosret may have married her young stepson in order to consolidate her hold on the throne; there is, however, no further evidence to support such an assumption. Deeper in her tomb Tawosret appears as an unmistakable king of Egypt.

Tawosret's mummy has never been found, although some experts believe that an anonymous female mummy, 'Unknown Woman D', recovered from the Amenhotep II cache, may be the missing queen. The mummy was autopsied in Cairo in 1905 by the anatomist Grafton Elliot Smith, with Howard Carter assisting. Stripping away the bandages, and removing the carefully tied headscarf that covered the mummy's abundant hair, Smith discovered:

…an extremely emaciated woman with apparently complete atrophy (?senile) of the breasts. Her hair is well preserved and has been made into a series of sharply-rolled curls, of the variety distinguished by modern ladies by the name 'Empire'. She had a prominent, narrow, high-bridged 'Ramesside' nose; but the pressure of the bandages has distorted the cartilaginous part and marred its beauty. She had a straight line of brow, and a long hanging jaw. The packing of the mouth has given the lips a pouting expression and further disturbed the natural profile of the face.[32]

This body is today housed in Cairo Museum.

Tawosret vanishes with an abruptness that again makes us suspicious. Had she died a natural death in office? Or had she been deposed by her successor, the mysterious Sethnakhte? His Elephantine stela drops heavy hints that he did indeed depose his predecessor. Her disappearance marks the end of the 19th Dynasty. The historian Manetho preserved her memory as 'King Thuoris, who in Homer is called Polybus, husband of Alcandara, and in whose time Troy was taken'.

DYNASTY 20
1190–1069

Tiy-Merenese
Iset Ta-Hemdjert
Tiy
Tentopet
Henuttawi
Tawerettenru
Nubkhesbed
Isis
Baketwernel II
Titi
Tentamun

(*Right*) Iset Ta-Hemdjert as she appears on a statue originally commissioned by Ramesses IV but usurped by his brother Ramesses VI (Luxor Museum). The two kings may have been full brothers, their reigns separated by that of Ramesses V, son of Ramesses IV.

TIY-MERENESE

The 20th Dynasty was founded by the obscure Sethnakhte, possible son or grandson of Ramesses II, and usurper of Tawosret's tomb. He reigned for a mere two years and left no substantial monuments. Little is known about his consort Tiy-Merenese, mother of Ramesses III.

ISET TA-HEMDJERT

Ramesses III modelled his reign on that of the now-legendary Ramesses II (no known relation), even choosing the same names and titles for his sons. Ramesses III, however, was living in difficult times. Egypt's borders were once again under threat, not only from the Libyans, but also from the piratical Sea Peoples who were terrorizing the eastern Mediterranean, forcing the closure of the trade routes that for many centuries had united the international community. Ramesses was forced to spend the first third of his reign defending his land, an expensive and energy-sapping business.

The next 22 years were more peaceful. Temporarily secure, Ramesses was able to develop an ambitious building programme whose scope was limited only by his lack of funds. Egypt, like many other Mediterranean countries, was heading slowly but surely into economic failure. A series of poor harvests led to food shortages and high inflation, and this in turn led to civil unrest in the Theban necropolis. The bureaucracy, for many centuries the envy of the Mediterranean world, had grown unwieldy, demotivated and corrupt, while the increasingly powerful semi-autonomous priesthood of Amun was starting to challenge the king's divine authority to rule.

ISET TA-HEMDJERT	
Husband Ramesses III	*Titles* King's Great Wife, King's Mother, God's Wife
Mother Hemdjert or Hebnerdjent	
Sons Ramesses IV?, Ramesses VI	*Burial place* Valley of the Queens (QV 51)

Ramesses III, following the example set by Ramesses II, developed a large harem that provided him with at least ten sons. We can see some of his wives, unnamed, on the walls of the Migdol Gate leading into his Theban mortuary temple complex of Medinet Habu, the site of one of his harem palaces. The King's Great Wife featured at Medinet Habu also goes unnamed, her cartouches a curious blank, but she is likely to be Iset Ta-Hemdjert, mother of Ramesses VI and daughter of the foreign-sounding lady Hemdjert or Hebnerdjent. Iset appeared on a statue of Ramesses III in the temple of Mut at Karnak and, during her son's reign, on a scene from Deir el-Bakhit (Dra Abu el-Naga) commemorating the installation of her granddaughter, another Iset, as God's Wife of Amun. She was eventually buried in the Valley of the Queens (QV 51).

QUEEN TIY AND THE HAREM PLOT

Harem life was comfortable but dull. There was only one escape route for an ambitious woman: she had to become the next King's Mother. Her son had to become king of Egypt before one of his half-brothers succeeded to the throne and he became displaced from the succession. Usually the throne passed to the son of the consort, but this was not invariably the case; not all consorts produced sons, and there was always a chance that a favourite son born to a more junior wife might succeed his father. We have no contemporary account of harem life, and can only guess at the amount of scheming and manipulation designed to bring a lesser son to his father's notice.

We do know, however, that at least one of Ramesses' secondary queens was not prepared to leave things to chance. A collection of contemporary court papers preserves the details of a plot masterminded from the 'harem of the accompanying' by the secondary queen Tiy, and supported by a number of courtiers close to the king. Ramesses was to be killed, the people were to rebel, and the throne was to pass to Tiy's otherwise insignificant son, a youth named as Pentaweret. The name Pentaweret translates as 'The [male] One of the [female] Great One', the female Great One presumably being his mother, Tiy. This was almost certainly not the prince's real name. Records of criminal trials tended to replace 'good' Egyptian names – names incorporating the name of a god, for example – with more appropriate descriptive 'bad' names, and this is likely to be the New Kingdom equivalent of the Old Kingdom Queen 'Great of Sceptre' whom we met in the Pepi I harem case.

The unthinkable crime

Regicide should, of course, have been the unthinkable crime. Ramesses III was untouchable, a semi-divine being, the only mortal capable of maintaining the *maat* that was so crucial for Egypt's survival. The assassination of such an important individual was not only an act of treason, but also a dangerous act of heresy that threatened the whole world. His wife, however, did not see things that way.

(*Above*) The Medinet Habu mortuary complex of Ramesses III was almost certainly modelled on the less well-preserved Ramesseum built by the king's great role model, Ramesses II. The extensive complex included the king's own mortuary temple (which itself included a series of suites and chapels dedicated to Egypt's gods) plus a palace, harem, administrative offices and warehouses.

(*Opposite above*) The two Windows of Appearance in the Migdol Gate of the Medinet Habu temple complex, an entrance which takes the form of a fortified Syrian gateway, or *migdol*. Here Ramesses III would stand to communicate with his people and here, perhaps, he died.

(*Opposite below*) The Migdol Gate displays several unusual scenes of Ramesses III in intimate circumstances with unnamed women. Here the seated king caresses an anonymous lady.

(*Right*) The hieroglyphic determinative for 'putting to the wood'. Death by impaling meant a painful and sometimes lingering death.

The first assassination attempt relied on magic alone, an entirely logical approach for a people who believed in the supernatural. Remote killing was an accepted part of Egyptian ritual, and everyone knew that the king's symbolic smiting of a token foe on a Theban temple wall would cause vast numbers of the enemy to weaken, if not actually drop down dead, many miles away. And so a group of conspirators decided to use a combination of wax figurines and potent spells to murder their king. Fortunately for Ramesses, they were caught before any damage could be inflicted. Two contemporary and near-identical documents – Papyrus Rollin and Papyrus Lee – are, like so many Egyptian texts, infuriatingly vague, but they do give us a good idea of the sequence of events. Here Papyrus Rollin takes up the tale:

It happened because writings were made for enchanting, for banishing and confusing. Because some gods and some men were made of wax.... He was examined and substance was found to every allegation and every crime.... These were offences that merited death.... And when he understood that the offences that he had committed were worthy of death, he brought death upon himself.[33]

Naturally, such a heinous crime deserved the ultimate sentence. In ancient Egypt this meant a painful death either by impaling on a sharp wooden stake pushed through the torso, or by burning. It is not surprising that the offender chose instead to commit suicide, and equally unsurprising that the palace officials, wary of a harem scandal, allowed it.

The next plan was, to modern eyes at least, far more practical. The king was to be killed as he celebrated a religious festival at his Medinet Habu mortuary temple at Thebes. It is tempting to assume that the king

The strikingly lifelike unwrapped head of Ramesses III served as the inspiration behind the appearance of Boris Karloff's character in *The Mummy*. The king's body, protected by hardened resin-impregnated bandages, has never been unwrapped and it has not been possible to determine how the king died. Cairo Museum.

was to be killed in the most intimate and unguarded environs of the Medinet Habu harem palace. We know that the plot went ahead, and we know that it ultimately failed, as the conspirators were arrested and Ramesses III was succeeded by his intended heir Ramesses IV. What we don't know, most crucially, is whether Ramesses survived the assassination attempt. His mummy, recovered from the Deir el-Bahari cache, remains partially wrapped and therefore unautopsied. It shows no immediately obvious wounds, but as we do not know what weapons were used, we do not know what sort of injuries we should be looking for. Poison or smothering, of course, need leave no obvious mark. Contemporary accounts of the trial of the conspirators are less helpful than we might have hoped. The Turin Judicial Papyrus implies that Ramesses himself presided over the court, but this may be a literary conceit similar to that which saw the definitely dead 12th Dynasty king Amenemhat I writing to tell his son about his own death.

The trial

Initially the legal proceedings went much as expected. Three separate trials saw 38 people condemned to death, either by their own hands or by execution:

The great enemy Pabakkamun ['The Blind Servant'; presumably a distortion of Pabekenamun, 'The Servant of Amun'], sometime Chief of the Chamber. He was brought in because he had been plotting with Tiy and the women of the harem. He had made common cause with them. He had carried their words outside to their mothers and their brothers who were there, saying, 'Arouse the people and incite hostility so as to make rebellion against their lord.' And they set him in the presence of the great officials of the Court of Examination. They examined his crimes and found him guilty. And his crimes took hold of him, and the officials who examined him caused his punishment to befall him....

Wives of the men of the harem gateway, who had colluded with the men who plotted these matters, were placed before the officials of the Court of Examination. They found them guilty, and caused their punishment to befall them. They were six women....

Pentaweret was found guilty of plotting with his mother, and was allowed to kill himself. Tiy presumably suffered the same fate, although we have no record of her trial and sentence. Then things took a most unexpected turn, as some of the trial judges and court officials were themselves arrested and charged with gross misconduct with the ladies of the harem. This, again, was a highly serious offence. Only one judge was found not guilty. The rest received suitably severe punishments that would allow them to survive as a dire warning to others:

Persons who were punished by the amputating of their noses and ears because they had ignored the good instructions given to them. The women had gone. They had followed them to the place where they were and revelled with them.... Their crime caught up with them....

From Tentopet to Tentamun: The Wives of the Later Ramesside Kings

Ramesses III was followed by eight further kings called Ramesses, a mixture of fathers, sons, brothers, uncles and nephews whose brief reigns occasionally overlapped. Their rule saw Egypt plunge deeper into economic decline, and royal authority slowly but surely restricted to the north of the country. We know little about these kings, and even less about their wives.

Ramesses IV was almost certainly married to his sister **Tentopet**, owner of a tomb in the Valley of the Queens (QV 74). Ramesses V had two known queens, **Henuttawi** and **Tawerettenru**, but no children; his successor Ramesses VI was married to **Nubkhesbed**, mother of Ramesses VII and **Isis**, God's Wife of Amun. Ramesses VII had at least one son but the name of his consort goes unrecorded; Ramesses VIII, too, has no recorded queen. Ramesses IX has no confirmed wife but may have been married to the mysterious **Baketwernel II** (who, alternatively, as we have seen, may have been the consort of Amenmesse). Ramesses X was perhaps married to **Titi**, who was buried in the Valley of the Queens (QV 52). Ramesses XI, the last of the Ramessides, was married to **Tentamun**.

The death of Ramesses XI left Egypt again split in two. This time the division was an amicable one. In the north Smendes, founder of the 21st Dynasty, ruled from the Delta city of Tanis. In the south the powerful High Priest of Amun, Herihor, and his descendants ruled from Thebes.

SEXUAL ETIQUETTE

Keep your wife from power, restrain her.... In this way you will make her stay in your house.

Beware the woman who is a stranger, who is not known in her town. Do not stare at her as she passes by and do not have intercourse with her.

He who makes love to a woman who has a husband will be killed on her doorstep. [34]

The Egyptians had neither a civil nor a religious wedding ceremony: men and women who wished to be recognized as a couple simply moved in together. This seemingly casual approach to matrimony, combined with the acceptance of both incest and polygamy, has led many observers to assume that dynastic Egypt was a land of sexual licence and loose morals. Nothing could be further from the truth.

Both incest and polygamy were, until the Graeco-Roman period, restricted to the royal family. While liaisons between single consenting adults were considered matters of little importance to the wider community, a married couple were expected to observe certain moral rules. The wife was expected to remain faithful to her husband, who could then be sure that her children were his own. The husband, in turn, was expected to stay clear of other men's wives although, with prostitutes an ever-present temptation, he was not necessarily expected to remain faithful.

Adultery was a moral outrage that would be dealt with by the individuals or families concerned. A 20th Dynasty letter recovered from the close-knit workmen's community of Deir el-Medina, a town where everyone knew everyone else's business, illustrates how this worked. The letter records the misadventures of Nesamenemope, who for many months has been sleeping with a woman who is not his wife. Naturally enough, Nesamenemope's wife's family do not approve of this arrangement. One night they rouse the entire village, and march to the woman's house. 'We are going to beat her, and her family too!' A steward is able to hold back the crowd, and he sends a message to the couple. If they are to continue their affair, Nesamenemope must divorce his wife and set her free to marry another.

THE THIRD INTERMEDIATE PERIOD
1069–657 BC

High Priests of Amun (Thebes)

Piankh = = **Nodjmet**

Herihor = = **Nodjmet** (again)

Pinedjem I = = **Henttawy**

Pinedjem II = = **Nesikhonsu, Isetemkheb III**

Psusennes 'III' = ?

DYNASTY 21 (Tanis)
1069–945

Smendes = = **Tentamun**

Amenemnisu = ?

Psusennes I = = **Mutnodjmet, Wiay**

Amenemope = ?

Osorkon the Elder (Osochor) = ?

Siamun = ?

Psusennes II = ?

DYNASTY 22
945–715

Shoshenq I = = **Karomama I, Penreshnes**

Osorkon I = = **Maatkare, Tashedkhonsu**

Names of queens in **bold**
= = known marriage
= ? = possible marriage
= ? queen unknown

Shoshenq II = = **Nesitanebetashru**

Takelot I = = **Kapes**

Osorkon II = = **Isetemkheb IV, Djedmutesankh, Karomama II**

Shoshenq III = = **Tadibast, Tentamenopet, Djedbastiusankh**

Shoshenq IV = ?

Pimay = ?

Shoshenq V = ?

Pedubast II = ?

Osorkon IV = ?

DYNASTY 23
830–715

A line of Libyan kings ruling parallel to the 22nd Dynasty

DYNASTY 24
730–715

Tefnakht = ?

Bakenrenef (Bocchoris) = ?

DYNASTY 25 (Nubia)
800–657

Piye = = **Tabiry, Abar, Khensa, Peksater**

Shabaka = = **Qalhata**

Shebitku = = **Arty**

Taharqa = = **Atakhebasken, Tabekenamun, Naparaye, Takahatamun**

Tantamani = = **Piankharty**

THE LATE PERIOD
664–332

DYNASTY 26 (Sais)
664–525

Psamtik I = = **Mehytenweskhet**

Necho II = = **Khedebneithirbinet I**

Psamtik II = = **Takhuit**

Apries = ?

Amasis = = **Nakhtubasterau, Tentkheta**

Psamtik III = ?

DYNASTY 27 (Persia)
525–404

Egypt, ruled by Persian kings, is effectively without a queen

DYNASTY 28
404–399

Amyrtaeus = ?

DYNASTY 29
399–380

Nefarud (Nepherites) I = ?

Psammuthis = ?

Hakor = ?

Nefarud (Nepherites) II = ?

DYNASTY 30
380–343

Nectanebo I = ?

Teos = ?

Nectanebo II = = **Khedebneithirbinet II**

DYNASTY 31 (Persia)
343–332

Egypt ruled by Persian kings

NEW KINGDOM ENDS | THIRD INTERMEDIATE PERIOD BEGINS

Smendes (**Tentamun**)
Amenemnisu
Psusennes I (**Mutnodjmet, Wiay**)
Amenemope
Osorkon the Elder
Siamun
Psusennes II
Shoshenq I (**Karomama I, Penreshnes**)
Osorkon I (**Maatkare, Tashedkhonsu**)
Shoshenq II (**Nesitanebetashru**)
Takelot I (**Kapes**)
Osorkon II (**Isetemkheb IV, Djedmutesankh, Karomama II**)
Shoshenq III (**Tadibast, Tentamenopet, Djedbastiusankh**)
Shoshenq IV
Pimay
Shoshenq V
Piye (**Tabiry, Abar, Khensa, Peksater**) (Dyn. 25)
Pedubast II
Osorkon IV
Tefnakht (Dyn. 24)
Bakenrenef (Dyn. 24)

DYNASTY 21 | DYNASTY 22 | DYN. 23 | DYN. 24

1100   1050   1000   950   900   850   800   750   700

Nodjmet

Karomama II

Khedebneithirbinet I

WEAKENED ROYAL POWER
The Third Intermediate Period 1069–657 BC
The Late Period 664–332 BC

WHILE SMENDES CLAIMED sovereignty over the whole of Egypt, the High Priests of Amun effectively ruled southern Egypt from Thebes. At the end of the 21st Dynasty the northern throne passed to a king of Libyan extraction. A reduction in the status of the High Priest of Amun allowed Egypt to become a united land, but gradually the country started to fragment. The 23rd and 24th Dynasties were lines of local rulers contemporary with the late 22nd and early 25th Dynasties.

The Nubian kings seized their chance. Piye marched northwards and was crowned king of Egypt. Throughout the subsequent 25th Dynasty Thebes regained much of her old status, but the High Priest of Amun was now junior to the God's Wife. An Assyrian invasion saw the end of Nubian rule. With his daughter adopted as heiress to the God's Wife, Egypt's next king, Psamtik I, was able to reunite Egypt. His Saite descendants achieved a century-long renaissance of Egypt's cultural heritage.

In 525 Cambyses invaded and Egypt endured over a century of Persian rule punctuated with brief periods of independence: the 28th Dynasty had one king, the 29th Dynasty four. The 30th Dynasty proved more durable, with the former general Nakhtnebef defeating a combined Persian-Greek invasion. The 31st Dynasty, the Second Persian Period, lasted a mere decade. When, in 332, Alexander the Great claimed Egypt, his arrival was greeted with a feeling of relief.

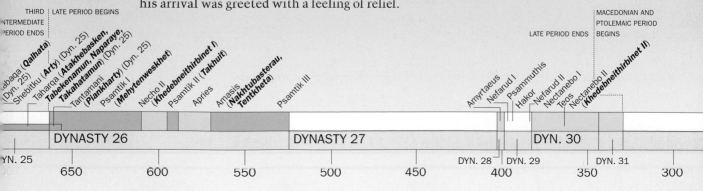

High Priests of Amun (Thebes) 1069–945	Nodjmet Henttawy	 Isetemkheb I Tentnabekhnenu Nesikhonsu  Isetemkheb III
DYNASTY 21 (Tanis) 1069–945	Tentamun  Mutnodjmet Wiay	
DYNASTY 22 945–715	 Karomama I Penreshnes Maatkare Tashedkhonsu Nesitanebetashru Kapes	Isetemkheb IV Djedmutesankh  Karomama II Tadibast Tentamenopet Djedbastiusankh
DYNASTIES 23 & 24 830–715	No known queens	
DYNASTY 25 (Nubian) 800–657	Tabiry Abar Khensa Peksater Qalhata	Arty Atakhebasken Tabekenamun Naparaye Takahatamun Piankharty
DYNASTY 26 (Saite) 664–525	Mehytenweskhet Khedebneithirbinet I Takhuit Nakhtubasterau Tentkheta	
DYNASTIES 27–29 525–380	No known queens	
DYNASTY 30 380–343	Khedebneithirbinet II	

FAMILY AND TITLES	
NODJMET	**HENTTAWY**
Husbands	*Husband*
Piankh, Herihor	Pinedjem I
Father	*Father*
Amenhotep High	Ramesses XI?
Priest of Amun?	*Sons*
Mother	Psusennes I,
Herere	Masaharta,
Sons	Menkheperre
At least four,	*Daughters*
including Pinedjem I	Maatkare,
Daughters	Mutnodjmet?
Up to five	*Titles*
Titles	King's Daughter,
Chief of the Harem	Daughter of the
of Amun, King's	King's Great Wife,
Great Wife, Lady of	King's Wife, Lady of
the Two Lands,	the Two Lands,
King's Mother	King's Mother, Chief
Burial place	of the Harem of
Thebes	Amun
	Burial place
	Thebes

FROM NODJMET TO ISETEMKHEB III: THE WOMEN OF THE THEBAN COURT

The northern kings and the southern warrior-priests co-existed on good terms, their cordial relationship cemented by a series of diplomatic marriages that made them one extended family. This constant intermarrying, combined with the repeated use of the same female names – we have up to six near-contemporary Henttawys, for example – makes the relationships between the two royal houses very difficult to disentangle. The women of these marriages are known by name, but in most cases that is all. Only two, Nodjmet and Henttawy wife of Pinedjem I, have left sufficient information to allow us to partially reconstruct their lives.

General Piankh had married a lady named **Nodjmet**, daughter of the lady Herere and, perhaps, the High Priest of Amun Amenhotep. Nodjmet bore Piankh four sons, including the future High Priest Pinedjem I. Her high political status is confirmed in a letter, addressed to her by her husband, which asks her to supervise an inquiry (and, if necessary, an execution) into the behaviour of two corrupt policemen.

A short time later a lady named Nodjmet married Herihor, High Priest of Amun. If we are not looking at two Nodjmets – and the evidence is by no means clear in this respect – it seems that the widowed Nodjmet must have married her husband's successor. The temple of Khonsu at Karnak, a temple where Herihor appears as a king, shows us Herihor's children, an impressive 19 named sons and 5 daughters, but does not confirm that these children were all born to 'Queen' Nodjmet. Indeed, as the presentation of the children is clearly modelled on the New Kingdom presentations of the children of Ramesses II and III, it seems reasonable to speculate that Herihor has not only acquired royal titles, but a royal harem too.

Technically Nodjmet was never a queen of Egypt. But the Theban court, a secure 400 miles (643 km) up-river from the royal court of Tanis, was happy to develop its own royal family. In the forecourt of the Khonsu temple, Nodjmet is accorded the title King's Great Wife. A beautifully illustrated Book of the Dead, prepared for the joint burial of Herihor and Nodjmet, was recovered from the Deir el-Bahari mummy cache; here Nodjmet, her name written in a cartouche, is more fully described as 'King's Wife, Kings Mother of the Lord of the Two Lands, God's Mother of Khonsu-the-Child, Chief of the Harem of Amun, Chief Noblewoman, Lady of the Two Lands, Nodjmet'.

Nodjmet outlived Herihor by some five years. Neither Herihor's body nor his tomb have been discovered, but Nodjmet's mummy, two coffins and canopic chest were included in the Deir el-Bahari cache. Like all subsequent 21st Dynasty mummies, Nodjmet had been stuffed and padded to give her limbs a realistic roundness. Her face has artificial eyes, padded cheeks, false eyebrows made of human hair and a braided brown

Nodjmet, partially unwrapped by Gaston Maspero in 1886 and subsequently re-examined by Grafton Elliot Smith in 1906. The queen had been stuffed with sawdust and her limbs and wrinkled face padded so that, as Smith noted, 'the lower part of the face has become almost circular'. Cairo Museum.

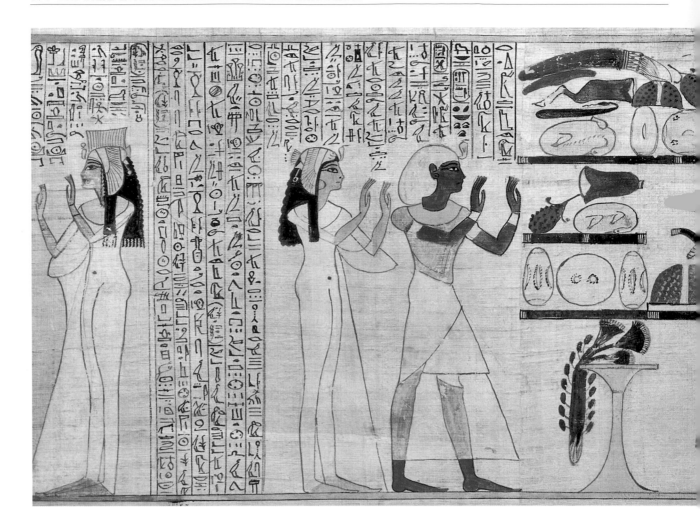

wig covering her own scanty grey hair. The result is a startlingly life-like and, in spite of the queen's many obvious wrinkles, youthful appearance.

Pinedjem I, son of Piankh, succeeded his stepfather Herihor as High Priest of Amun. From this point onwards the High Priesthood would be regarded as an hereditary position and would pass from father to son – confirmation, if any were needed, that the Theban priests considered themselves a quasi-royal dynasty. On the grounds that some of her children and grandchildren bore names compounded with 'Ramesses', it has been suggested that the King's Daughter, King's Wife, King's Mother **Henttawy**, wife of Pinedjem I, may have been a sister or even a daughter of Ramesses XI. Pinedjem is also known to have had at least two secondary queens, **Isetemkheb I** and **Tentnabekhenu**, but nothing is known of their origins.

Henttawy's children were destined for greatness. One of her sons was to rule Egypt from Tanis as Psusennes I, while two others, Masaharta and Menkheperre, 'ruled' as successive High Priests of Amun at Thebes. Meanwhile Henttawy's daughter, Maatkare, served as Divine Adoratrice and God's Wife of Amun, a title which had apparently died out (we have a

(*Above*) Nodjmet and her husband Herihor depicted on the Book of the Dead papyrus found with Nodjmet's mummy. To the right of the tables of offerings we can see a weighing of the heart scene, the goddess Isis, the four sons of Horus, and the god of the dead, Osiris, seated on a throne.

gap in our knowledge at this point) in the mid 18th Dynasty, only to be revived during the 19th. The original God's Wives had been queens of Egypt, but from the 20th Dynasty reign of Ramesses VI onwards, the title was born exclusively by celibate princesses.

(*Right*) Fluted gold jar from the tomb of Psusennes I at Tanis. The king's name and titles are inscribed in two cartouches on the neck, beside two others. Cairo Museum.

THE BURIAL OF MAATKARE

Maatkare, daughter of Pinedjem I and Henttawy, was a celibate God's Wife of Amun. It was therefore interpreted as clear evidence of an ancient scandal when Maatkare's coffin, recovered with her mother's from the Deir el-Bahari cache, was found to include a small mummified body, tentatively identified as the infant Princess Mutemhat (actually Maatkare's prenomen). The idea that Maatkare must have died in childbirth clearly influenced the anatomists who examined her body:

Makeri's [Maatkare's] breasts were enormously enlarged, probably because she was lactating…. The skin of the abdomen was loose and somewhat puckered. Taken in conjunction with the large size of the breasts, these facts support M. Maspero's hypothesis that Makeri died in childbirth or soon after giving birth to the baby princess buried with her.[35]

In more modern times X-ray analysis has confirmed that the bundle identified as a 'baby princess' is in fact the mummified remains of Maatkare's pet baboon. It seems that the loose skin and enlarged breasts may have been the result of the vigorous over-stuffing employed by the undertakers.

The stuffed and moulded body of Maatkare, her wrappings torn open by modern tomb robbers. Cairo Museum.

Henttawy. Her face, overstuffed at the embalmers, burst in antiquity to reveal the packing beneath. This damage has recently been repaired. Cairo Museum.

Henttawy's mummy was recovered from the Deir el-Bahari cache. Her face had been stuffed to give a youthful appearance; the opposite result was obtained, however, when her over-packed cheeks burst open. Curiously, Henttawy's wig was made of black fibre rather than human hair.

The two wives of Pinedjem II, Nesikhonsu and Isetemkheb III, both predeceased their husband and were buried in his family tomb in the cliff behind Deir el-Bahari. Soon after, this tomb would be used to house the cache of royal mummies. **Nesikhonsu**'s mummy is a splendid example of the 21st Dynasty embalmer's art; padded, but not over-padded, it retains a lifelike appearance. **Isetemkheb**'s mummy reveals that she suffered from arthritis and, like many others, bad teeth.

TENTAMUN, MUTNODJMET AND WIAY: QUEENS OF THE 21ST DYNASTY AT TANIS

Herere, mother of Nodjmet of Thebes, bears the title 'King's Mother' to an unnamed king, suggesting that she may also have been the mother of Smendes (or Nesibanebdjed I), who may therefore have been the son of the Theban High Priest Amenhotep.

Smendes' 26-year rule has left remarkably little archaeological or written evidence and it is difficult to reconstruct the intricacies of his reign. However, both he and his wife, **Tentamun**, are featured in the fictional Report of Wenamun. This adventure story tells us how, during the reign of Ramesses XI, the eponymous hero was sent by Herihor of Thebes to buy cedarwood for the sacred boat of Amun. The first leg of his journey saw Wenamun sailing to the northern city of Tanis (modern San el-Hagar):

I arrived in Tanis, home to Smendes and his wife Tentamun. I handed over the letter from Amun, King of the Gods, and it was read out to them. The royal couple graciously agreed to do as the god had asked. I stayed in Tanis until the fourth month of summer. Then Smendes and Tentamun waved me off in the care of the Syrian ship's captain Mengebet. On the first day of the first month of the inundation I sailed down to the great Syrian Sea.[36]

At the time of Wenamun's visit Ramesses XI ruled Egypt from Per-Ramesse, and Smendes was merely an influential local governor. Soon after, following the death of Ramesses XI, Smendes succeeded to the throne with Tentamun as his consort and Tanis as his capital. The fact that Tentamun is specifically included in Wenamun's story suggests that she was, even before her husband's coronation, a woman of considerable importance. If she were, as many suspect, a younger daughter of Ramesses XI, her husband's otherwise inexplicable rise from obscurity to kingship would be explained.

Smendes was succeeded by Amenemnisu, a short-lived and ill-documented king of unknown parentage (although there is speculation that he might have been either the son of Smendes or another son of the fertile Herihor) and with no documented wife. Amenemnisu was in turn succeeded by Psusennes I.

The Tanis tomb of Psusennes I included a burial chamber for Queen **Mutnodjmet** although, as her tomb was usurped by her husband's successor Amenemope, it is not certain that she was ever buried there. Mutnodjmet's name, however, is closely associated with that of Psusennes on objects from his intact burial. We therefore know that she claims the titles King's Daughter, King's Great Wife and a King's Sister, but never King's Mother. This suggests that she may have been the daughter of Henttawy and Pinedjem I of Thebes, and a sister-consort to Psusennes. A secondary queen of Psusennes, the otherwise unknown

The burial complex of Psusennes I (Tomb III) at Tanis, discovered by Pierre Montet on 17 March 1939 but largely ignored by the world's press, who were preoccupied with the impending war. While Psusennes' burial lay undisturbed, Mutnodjmet's neighbouring chamber was usurped by Psusennes' successor, King Amenemope, for his own burial.

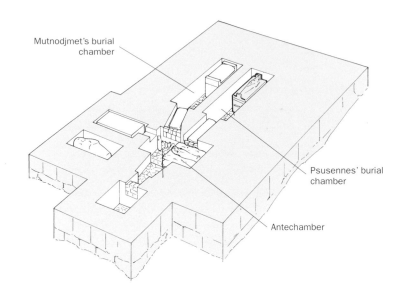

Mutnodjmet's burial chamber

Psusennes' burial chamber

Antechamber

(*Below*) The Delta city of Tanis (modern San el-Hagar), capital of the 21st Dynasty kings. Tanis was embellished with artifacts and monuments taken from other, more ancient sites, including Per-Ramesse, the Delta city built by Ramesses II. The kings of Tanis were buried in the precincts of the Mut temple.

Flower-shaped drinking bowl from the tomb of a senior official at Tanis, the petals made alternately of gold and electrum. One of the petals bears the names of Psusennes I and his wife Mutnodjmet, above signs interpreted as a wish for life, prosperity and health. Cairo Museum.

Wiay, bore the King's Daughter Isetemkheb, wife of the Theban High Priest of Amun Menkheperre, and mother of the future High Priest Pinedjem II.

THE QUEENS OF THE LATE 21ST DYNASTY

We have no confirmation of the parentage of Amenemope, successor of Psusennes I, and the name of Amenemope's wife goes unrecorded.

Egypt's next king, Osorkon the Elder, was a man of Libyan extraction, born to the lady Mehytenweskhet. We know little of the new king's family, and even less about his successor Siamun, although we do know that during his reign the centuries-old ban on Egyptian princesses marrying foreigners was lifted, as we now find a King's Daughter marrying Hadad, Crown Prince of Edom. At roughly the same time another princess, daughter of an anonymous pharaoh, became one of the many wives of the Jewish king Solomon who, as the Bible tells us, 'had seven hundred wives of royal birth and three hundred concubines and his wives led him astray'.[37]

The final king of the dynasty, Psusennes II, has no recorded queen.

FROM KAROMAMA I TO DJEDBASTIUSANKH: THE 22ND (LIBYAN) DYNASTY

Shoshenq I, first king of the 22nd Dynasty, was a king of Libyan extraction but not, as many popular accounts suggest, a pure-blooded, primitive Libyan nomad freshly arrived from the desert. Shoshenq belonged to one of the many prosperous Delta families with a mingled Libyan/Egyptian heritage, and was in fact the nephew of the 21st Dynasty king Osorkon the Elder. Shoshenq moved the Egyptian capital to his Delta hometown, Bubastis, and united his land by appointing his son to the position of High Priest of Amun.

Lion-headed gold aegis of Osorkon IV, last king of the 22nd Dynasty. Osorkon's wife goes unrecorded. Cairo Museum.

Once again we enter an ill-documented realm of confused genealogies and shadowy queen consorts. We know that Shoshenq's consort, **Karomama I**, bore his successor Osorkon I. A secondary queen, **Penreshnes**, bore a second son, Nimlot, while two other royal children are of undocumented maternity. Osorkon I took as his consort **Maatkare** (not to be confused with the God's Wife of Amun of the same name), daughter of Psusennes II. Their son Shoshenq II was married to **Nesitanebetashru,** mother of the High Priest of Amun and self-proclaimed king Harsiese. The succession then passed back to Takelot I, the son of Osorkon I and the secondary queen **Tashedkhonsu**. Takelot was married to **Kapes**, and their son succeeded to the throne as Osorkon II. Blessed with three principal wives (**Isetemkheb IV**, **Djedmutesankh** and his sister-wife **Karomama II**), Osorkon II had many children and yet his successor, Shoshenq III, is not definitely proven to have been his son.

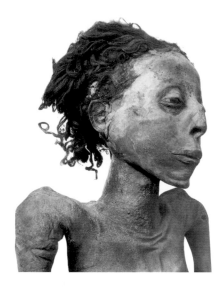

The reign of Osorkon II had seen the fragmentation of the temporary unity achieved by Shoshenq I. Once again Thebes was threatening independence, as the High Priests of Amun started to assume royal prerogatives. The reigns of Shoshenq III (amongst whose wives were **Tadibast**, **Tentamenopet** and **Djedbastiusankh**), Shoshenq IV, Pimay, Shoshenq V and Pedubast II saw a rapid contraction of royal power until the final king of the 22nd Dynasty, Osorkon IV, was forced to submit to the Nubian invader, Piye.

THE 23RD AND 24TH DYNASTIES

While some scholars regard the kings of the 23rd Dynasty as true Thebans, others classify them as a parallel line of Libyan kings originating at the Delta site of Leontopolis.

At the same time, less significant local dynasties were springing up in

(*Above*) Nesitanebetashru's mummy, unwrapped by Gaston Maspero in 1886. The queen's face is extremely well preserved, and is light yellow in colour with brown patches of discolouration. Her brown hair is a short, wavy bob. Cairo Museum.

(*Right*) Osorkon II and his sister-wife Karomama II; scene from the entrance to Osorkon's jubilee hall in the Bubastis temple. Karomama is also mentioned on two scarabs, and on a stela held by a statue of Osorkon II at Tanis. British Museum.

other major cities, including Hermopolis Magna and Herakleopolis. The 24th Dynasty was a short-lived coalition of the northern independent kings, based at Sais. Only two 24th Dynasty kings are known, Tefnakht and Bakenrenef, and nothing is known of their queens.

FROM TABIRY TO PIANKHARTY: THE 25TH (NUBIAN) DYNASTY

With Egypt a divided and disorganized land, Piye marched north to challenge the 24th Dynasty coalition of northern kings. Piye's first victory was at Thebes, where he insisted that the current God's Wife of Amun, Shepenwepet I (daughter of Osorkon III), adopt his sister Amenirdis I as her successor. Piye then completed his conquest of Egypt. However, he did not feel the need to live in his new land and, allowing the northern alliance of vassal kings to govern on his behalf, he returned home to Napata (Gebel Barkal). Successive Nubian kings (Shabaka, Shebitku, Taharqa and Tantamani) ruled Egypt from Memphis until, inevitably, the arrival of the fiercely militaristic Assyrians forced them back into Nubia.

Each of the Nubian kings aspired to rule as an entirely typical pharaoh, adopting the cartouches, titularies and dress of their Egyptian predecessors and demonstrating an impressive devotion to the cult of the god Amun. There was only one obvious difference: scorning the traditional Memphite cemeteries the Nubian rulers preferred to be buried in the Napata cemetery, under sharp, steep-sided pyramids. We may therefore assume that the new kings regarded the role of the King's Great Wife as an important one; an assumption that is supported by the discovery of a stela raised by Atlanersa, successor to Tantamani, which details his female ancestry rather than his male lineage. Unfortunately we have little evidence concerning the role allotted to Egypt's new queens and

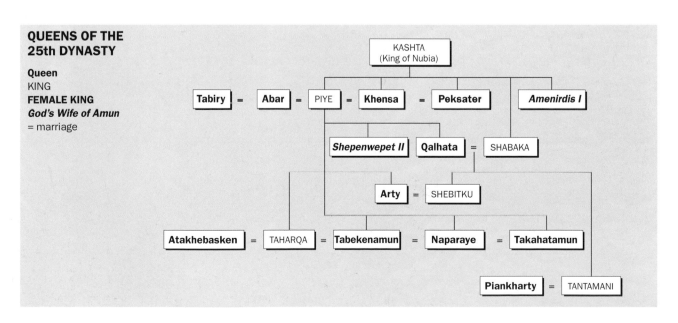

QUEENS OF THE 25th DYNASTY

Queen
KING
FEMALE KING
God's Wife of Amun
= marriage

The God's Wife of Amun Amenirdis I, daughter of Kashta of Nubia, and sister of Piye king of Egypt. Amenirdis has assumed the double-plumed headdress formerly reserved for queens and goddesses. British Museum.

once again we find a faceless list of names. Piye had as many as four principal wives: **Tabiry**, daughter of his Nubian predecessor Alara, **Abar**, and his sisters **Khensa** and **Peksater**. He was succeeded by his brother Shabaka, husband of **Qalhata**, who in turn was succeeded by his son Shebitku, husband of **Arty**, daughter of Piye. Taharqa, another son of Piye, then took the throne with **Atakhebasken**, **Tabekenamun**, **Naparaye** and **Takahatamun** as his queens. Finally the throne passed to Tantamani, son of Shabaka and Qalhata, and husband of **Piankharty**.

The God's Wives of Amun

The Nubian kings made astute use of the increasingly important role of God's Wife of Amun. The God's Wives had enjoyed a massive increase in status, and were now considered capable of performing temple rituals – making offerings, pouring libations and conducting foundation ceremonies – that had once been reserved for kings. As an acknowledgment of this increased status, they routinely wore queenly crowns and wrote their names in royal cartouches. Their role, ostensibly a religious one connected with the stimulation of the creator god (see box p. 93), had become almost entirely political. Remaining loyal to their birth families, they were expected to curtail the power of the Theban High Priests. Effectively they ruled Thebes on behalf of their fathers.

The God's Wives proved more durable than his High Priests, many of whom are now forgotten. Amenirdis I served as God's Wife through the reigns of Piye, Shabaka and Shebitku, and was eventually buried alongside Shepenwepet I in a tomb-chapel at Medinet Habu. An inscription above the doorway records the building of Amenirdis' tomb:

(*Right*) Statue of the cat-headed goddess Bastet, now in the Louvre. The name of Piye's wife Khensa is inscribed on the back pillar. Khensa was buried in the Nubian cemetery of El-Kurru (Tomb KU 4).

(Above) Shepenwepet II, daughter of Piye, stands before the god Atum on the wall of her Medinet Habu funerary chapel.

(Below) Shepenwepet II takes the form of a sphinx to offer a ram-headed jar to the god Amun. Recovered from the sacred lake in the Karnak Temple and now housed in Berlin Museum.

O you living who walk upon this earth and pass by this Ka house which Shepenwepet built…for Amenirdis, deceased: as you love your children and would bequeath them your possessions…as your wives perform rituals for Hathor, Lady of the West…please [pray for Amenirdis].

Her successor and niece Shepenwepet II, daughter of Piye, served as God's Wife under the remaining Nubian kings and, having survived the sacking of Thebes during the Assyrian invasion, died during the reign of the Saite king Psamtik I.

THE 26TH (SAITE) DYNASTY

Although we know their names, the lives of the Saite queens are shrouded in mystery and we know far more about their long-lived daughters, the God's Wives of Amun.

Next in line to Shepenwepet II was her niece and adopted successor Amenirdis II, daughter of Taharqa; it seems, however, that Amenirdis was persuaded (or maybe paid?) to pass the office immediately on to her adopted successor Nitocris I Shepenwepet III, daughter of the Saite king Psamtik I. A red granite stela carved to celebrate the adoption of Nitocris and erected, naturally enough, in the temple of Amun at Karnak (and now housed in Cairo Museum), allows us a glimpse of the young princess as she leaves Sais for Thebes:

I [Psamtik] have given to him [Amun] my daughter to be a God's Wife, and have endowed her better than those who were before her. Surely he will be gratified with her worship, and protect the land of he that gave her to him….

Year 9, 1st month of winter, day 28: Departure from the King's private apartments by his eldest daughter clad in fine linen and adorned with new turquoise. Her attendants about her were many in number, while marshals cleared her way. They set

The black greywacke sarcophagus lid of Ankhnesneferibre recovered from Deir el-Medina, where it had been reused. The God's Wife of Amun wears a queen's plumed crown and carries a royal crook and flail. She is surrounded by texts from the Book of the Dead. The underside of the sarcophagus lid shows the naked figure of the sky goddess Nut, stretched over the deceased. British Museum.

forth happily to the quay in order to head southwards for the Theban province. The ships around her were in great numbers, the crews consisted of mighty men, all being laden up to their gunwales with every good thing of the palace....[38]

The stela goes on to give details of Nitocris' 'dowry': her extensive estate, her household (including male administrators and high-born female priestesses who were also expected to remain celibate) and her income, which included a daily ration of 600 *deben* of bread, almost 6 litres of milk, cakes and herbs. In addition, each month she was to receive 3 oxen, 5 geese, 10 litres of beer and yet more bread. The well-nourished and extremely wealthy Nitocris was to reign as God's Wife for almost 70 years. She was buried in the tomb of her adoptive grandmother, Shepenwepet II, to which was added extra shrines and burial places for Nitocris and her mother, Queen Mehytenweskhet (see below). Today Nitocris' sarcophagus, which was re-used during the Ptolemaic Period, is displayed in Cairo Museum.

Year 4 of Wahibre [Apries], 4th month of summer, day 4: the God's Wife Nitocris, the justified, was raised up to heaven, being united with the sun's disk, the divine flesh being merged with him who made it.[39]

Since Nitocris' chosen successor, her niece Shepenwepet, had predeceased her, the office fell to her great-niece Ankhnesneferibre, daughter of Psamtik II. An adoption stela, raised at Karnak, confirms the details of this succession, and tells us that Ankhnesneferibre also bore the title of High Priest of Amun. Ankhnesneferibre reigned as God's Wife for over 60 years and was eventually buried at Medinet Habu. Again her black greywacke sarcophagus was re-used during the Ptolemaic Period; today it is displayed in the British Museum where, on the coffin lid, we may see Ankhnesneferibre lying peaceful in death.

Ankhnesneferibre had chosen her successor, Nitocris II, daughter of the Saite king Ahmose II and another High Priest of Amun, but the Persian invasion put an end to the office of God's Wife of Amun.

Regarding the Saite queens themselves, our information is scanty. **Mehytenweskhet**, daughter of the vizier Harsiese and wife of Psamtik I, was the mother of the God's Wife Nitocris and the next king, Necho II. The King's Wife, King's Mother **Khedebneithirbinet I** was the wife of Necho II and mother of Psamtik II. **Takhuit** was the wife of Psamtik II and mother of his successor, Apries (Wahibre) and the God's Wife Ankhnesneferibre. Takhuit was buried at Athribis; her tomb was discovered in 1950.

The sarcophagus lid of Khedebneith-irbinet I, wife of the 26th Dynasty king Necho II. Reportedly recovered from Sebennytos and now housed in the Kunsthistorisches Museum, Vienna.

Apries' wife goes unrecorded. **Nakhtubasterau** and **Tentkheta** are the two known wives of the usurper Amasis (Ahmose II) while Herodotus, who is happy to pad out his more factual narrative with risqué stories to stimulate his readers' flagging interest, tells an amusing, and doubtless entirely fictional, story involving a third wife, Ladice:

Amasis, having contracted a friendship and an alliance with the Cyrenaeans, resolved to take a wife from that country, either as a sign of his friendly feeling, or out of a desire to have a Greek woman. He married a Cyrenaean woman named Ladice.... But when Amasis lay with Ladice he was unable to have intercourse with her. Astonished – for this did not happen when he lay with other women – Amasis said to Ladice 'O woman, you must have used charms against me. Now nothing can prevent you from perishing by the most cruel death meted out to any woman.' Ladice, finding that Amasis was not at all swayed by her denial, made a vow to the goddess Venus that if Amasis should have intercourse with her that night (for this was the only time she had left) she would send a statue of the goddess to Cyrene. Immediately after she had taken this vow Amasis had intercourse with her; and from that time forward, whenever he came to her, he was able to function correctly. After this, he became extremely fond of her.[40]

The queen of the final Saite king, Psamtik III, goes unrecorded.

THE PERSIAN QUEENS OF EGYPT (27TH AND 31ST DYNASTIES)

Egypt's Persian rulers presented themselves as traditional pharaohs, but ruled their new land from afar. Only Cambyses and his immediate successor, Darius I, bothered to visit their new acquisition. Although each of the Persian kings was married – Cambyses adopting Egyptian custom and marrying two of his sisters – their wives played no part in Egyptian life. To all intents and purposes, Egypt was without a queen throughout the 27th and 31st Dynasties, the two periods of Persian rule.

THE LAST NATIVE KINGS (28TH–30TH DYNASTIES)

Amyrtaeus, sole ruler of the 28th Dynasty, has no known consort, and the following 29th Dynasty is a confused period. We know the names of four kings – Nefarud (Nepherites) I, Psammuthis, Hakor and Nefarud II – but understand nothing of their domestic lives.

The 30th Dynasty is better documented, but offers little information concerning the near-invisible royal women. We know that Nefarud II was deposed by Nectanebo I (Nakhtnebef), a king with no recorded consort. His son and successor, Teos (Djedhor), also lacks a named queen. The final native-born king of Egypt, Nectanebo II (Nakhthorheb) was married to **Khedebneithirbinet II**, daughter of his uncle Teos.

THE MACEDONIAN AND PTOLEMAIC PERIODS
332–30 BC

Alexander III (the Great) = = **Roxane, Stateira, Parysatis, Barsine**

Philip Arrhidaeus = = **Eurydice**

Alexander IV = ?

Ptolemy I = = **Thais, Artakama, Eurydice, Berenice I**

Ptolemy II = = **Arsinoe I, Arsinoe II**

Ptolemy III = = **Berenice II**

Ptolemy IV = = **Arsinoe III**

Ptolemy V = = **Cleopatra I**

Ptolemy VI = = **Cleopatra II**

Ptolemy VIII = = **Cleopatra II** (again), **Cleopatra III**

Ptolemy IX = = **Cleopatra IV, Cleopatra Selene**

Ptolemy X = = **Berenice III**

Ptolemy IX (restored) = ?

Berenice III (again) = = Ptolemy XI

Ptolemy XII = = **Cleopatra V**

Berenice IV = = Seleucus, Archelaus

Ptolemy XII (restored) = ?

Ptolemy XIII = = **Cleopatra VII**

Arsinoe IV

Ptolemy XIV = = **Cleopatra VII** (again)

Cleopatra VII (again) and Ptolemy XV (Caesarion)

Names of queens in **bold**
= = known marriage
= ? = possible marriage
= ? queen unknown

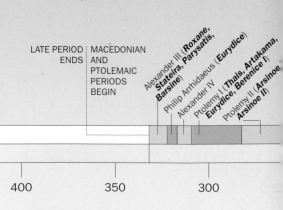

LATE PERIOD ENDS | MACEDONIAN AND PTOLEMAIC PERIODS BEGIN

Alexander III (**Roxane, Stateira, Parysatis, Barsine**)
Philip Arrhidaeus (**Eurydice**)
Alexander IV
Ptolemy I (**Thais, Artakama, Eurydice, Berenice I**)
Ptolemy II (**Arsinoe I, Arsinoe II**)

600   550   500   450   400   350   300

Arsinoe II

Cleopatra I or II

Cleopatra VII

THE LAST QUEENS OF EGYPT
The Macedonian and
Ptolemaic Periods 332–30 BC

ALEXANDER III DIED in 323 BC. The throne passed first to his brother, Philip Arrhidaeus, and then to his posthumous son, Alexander IV. The murder of the younger Alexander saw the end of the Macedonian kings of Egypt. General Ptolemy took control, ruling Egypt as Ptolemy I Soter, 'The Saviour'. Twelve Ptolemies would follow him.

Egypt's Ptolemaic kings presented their names in hieroglyphs encased within cartouches and wore the time-honoured regalia to offer to the gods. They even adopted the Egyptian custom of marrying their sisters, although polygamy was out of fashion and mistresses, rather than wives, queued to fill the royal bed. The Ptolemaic queens, strongly associated with the goddess Isis, were more powerful than Egypt's queens had ever been. But this image of an unchanged Egypt was a fiction. Rome now led the world and the Ptolemies lived, dressed and spoke as Greeks. The Greek language gave Egypt a word (*bassilisa*) that equates to our modern 'queen'.

In 30 BC, following the death of Cleopatra VII, Egypt fell to the Romans. Other conquerors had continued the practice of royal rule supported by the gods. But the Romans saw no need to pander to the locals. One thousand years of royal rule came to an abrupt end, and Egypt ceased to be an independent country.

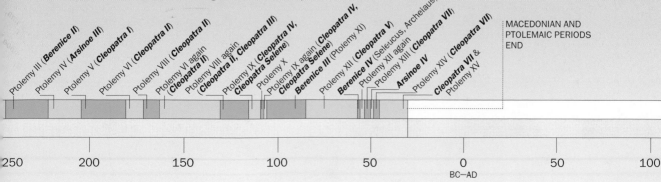

Ptolemy III (**Berenice II**)
Ptolemy IV (**Arsinoe III**)
Ptolemy V (**Cleopatra I**)
Ptolemy VI (**Cleopatra II**)
Ptolemy VIII (**Cleopatra II**)
Ptolemy VI again (**Cleopatra II**)
Ptolemy VIII again (**Cleopatra II, Cleopatra III**)
Ptolemy IX (**Cleopatra III, Cleopatra Selene**)
Ptolemy X
Ptolemy IX again (**Cleopatra IV, Cleopatra Selene**)
Berenice III (Ptolemy XI)
Ptolemy XII (**Cleopatra V**)
Berenice IV (Seleucus, Archelaus)
Ptolemy XII again
Ptolemy XIII (**Cleopatra VII**)
Arsinoe IV
Ptolemy XIV (**Cleopatra VII**)
Cleopatra VII & Ptolemy XV

MACEDONIAN AND PTOLEMAIC PERIODS END

250   200   150   100   50   0   50   100
BC—AD

Roxane

Stateira

Parysatis

Barsine

Eurydice

Thais

Artakama

Eurydice

Berenice I

Arsinoe I

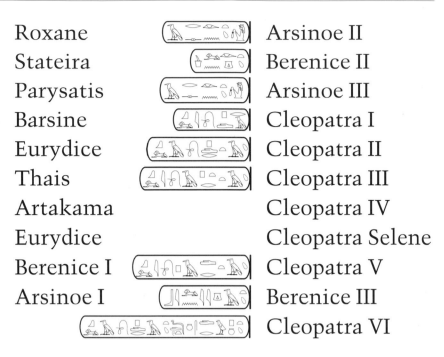

Arsinoe II

Berenice II

Arsinoe III

Cleopatra I

Cleopatra II

Cleopatra III

Cleopatra IV

Cleopatra Selene

Cleopatra V

Berenice III

Cleopatra VI

THE MACEDONIAN QUEENS OF EGYPT

The advent of Alexander heralded an unprecedented era of bloodshed within the royal family. The dramas of the Macedonian court were, however, to a large extent conducted outside Egypt's borders and had little direct effect on her people. Alexander the Great collected four wives during his various military campaigns: **Roxane** (Bactrian; daughter of Oxyartes), **Stateira** (Persian; daughter of Darius III), **Parysatis** (Persian; daughter of Artaxerxes III) and **Barsine** (Persian; great-granddaughter of Artaxerxes II). The best known of his wives, Roxane, was both the mother of his posthumous son and successor, Alexander IV, and, in 323 BC, the murderer of his second wife, Stateira. **Eurydice**, wife of Philip Arrhidaeus, was forced to commit suicide by her mother-in-law, Olympias, in 317 BC. Olympias herself would be executed in 315. Finally the unmarried Alexander IV was executed, together with his mother Roxane and half-brother Heracles, in 310 BC.

THE OBSCURE WIVES OF PTOLEMY I

Ptolemy I had at least four successive shadowy wives (**Thais**, **Artakama**, **Eurydice** and **Berenice I**), each of whom bore his children. The most important of these were the three children of Berenice I: Ptolemy II, Arsinoe II and Philotera. Berenice also had an older son, Magas, born to her first husband Philip of Macedonia, who would later become king of Cyrenaica (now Libya).

QUEENS OF THE PTOLEMAIC DYNASTY

Queen
KING
Other royal male
= marriage
? possible offspring

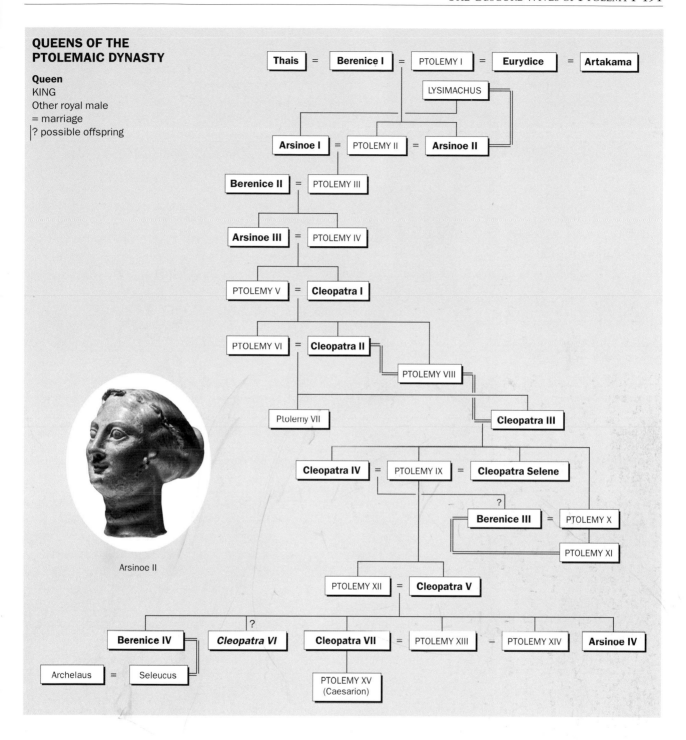

Arsinoe II

(*Opposite*) Alexander the Great plays the part of a conventional pharaoh by donning traditional kingly regalia to offer a libation to the fertility god Amun-Min in this scene from the outer wall of the sanctuary in the temple of Amun, Luxor.

ARSINOE II	
Husband Ptolemy II Philadelphus; previously married to Lysimachus and Ptolemy Ceraunus *Father* Ptolemy I Soter *Mother* Berenice I	*Children* None from her marriage to Ptolemy II *Titles* King's Sister, King's Great Wife, King's Mother

(*Right*) Restored *oinochoe* (jug) depicting Arsinoe II as a Greek woman pouring a libation. British Museum. (*Below*) Arsinoe II married Lysimachus of Thrace and Ptolemy Ceraunus before marrying her brother, Ptolemy II. In this sculpture recovered from Abu Roash she is a typical Egyptian-style queen wearing a striated tripartite wig and double uraeus. Her crown is missing. Metropolitan Museum of Art.

ARSINOE I AND II

Ptolemy II married Arsinoe, daughter of Lysimachus of Thrace, one of Alexander the Great's generals. **Arsinoe I** bore her husband three children, Ptolemy III, Lysimachus and Berenice Phernopherus, before being banished from court, accused of treason.

In need of a queen, Ptolemy II revived the Egyptian royal tradition of brother-sister unions by marrying his sister **Arsinoe II**, the widow of his former father-in-law Lysimachus. She, with no children from this, her third marriage, raised her three stepchildren as her own. Arsinoe II, queen of Egypt for a mere five to seven years, was a woman of great influence who in her images is shown wearing the double uraeus, possibly as a means of distinguishing her from her identically named predecessor. After her death Arsinoe was deified by her grieving husband and statues of the queen, now a Daughter of Amun and Daughter of Geb, were placed in all of Egypt's major temples so that she might be worshipped alongside the more traditional deities. It would perhaps be too cynical to suggest that Ptolemy II used his deified sister-wife as a means of boosting his own popularity amongst the Egyptian people, but the public's devotion to their new goddess can certainly have done him no harm. Arsinoe's cult, serviced by priestesses, flourished in Alexandria during the Roman period.

BERENICE II

Ptolemy II had successfully expanded Egypt's borders eastwards. His policy was continued by his successor, Ptolemy III, who eventually ruled an empire stretching from Syria to Libya, and as far south as northern Nubia. The Egyptian people were not, however, happy with their new ruling family, and Ptolemy III's otherwise successful reign was marred by a series of thwarted uprisings.

Queen Berenice II, sole wife of Ptolemy III, was the daughter of Magas of Cyrenaica, who was himself Ptolemy's half-uncle. She was to give her husband six children including his successor, Ptolemy IV. Berenice II was a strong and competent consort who owned both her own land and her own racing horses; a keen horsewoman, the classical authors admiringly suggest that she rode into battle alongside her husband. This, however, seems extremely unlikely, and should probably be disregarded along with another rumour, that the headstrong Berenice had murdered her first fiancé, the Macedonian prince Demetrius. When Ptolemy III left Egypt to lend his support to his sister Berenice Phernopherus, wife of Antiochus II of Syria, he looked to the old Egyptian traditions, and left his wife ruling in an absence that stretched for five years. After death Berenice II would be honoured with her own Alexandrian cult.

Alexandria, the capital city founded by Alexander the Great, and home to the Ptolemaic Dynasty. The new city allowed the Greek pharaohs to maintain close contact with the Mediterranean world. Unfortunately, much of Alexandria's archaeology, including royal palaces and tombs, has been lost beneath the sea.

(*Right*) Classical-style mosaic depicting Berenice II as the personification of the city of Alexandria. The queen wears the prow of a warship on her head. Alexandria Museum.

BERENICE II

Husband	*Daughters*
Ptolemy III	Berenice, Arsinoe III
Euergetes	*Titles*
Father	King's Mother,
Magas of Cyrenaica	Sister-Wife of the
Sons	Son of Re
Ptolemy IV	
Philopator,	
Alexander, Magas	

FAMILY AND TITLES	
ARSINOE III	Cleopatra Selene,
Husband	Cleopatra
Ptolemy IV	Tryphaena
Philopator	*Title*
Father	Lady of the Two
Ptolemy III	Lands
Euergetes	
Mother	**BERENICE III**
Berenice II	*Full name*
Son	Berenice III
Ptolemy V	Cleopatra
Epiphanes	Philopator
Titles	*Husbands*
King's Daughter,	Ptolemy X
King's Sister, King's	Alexander, Ptolemy
Great Wife, Sister-	XI Alexander
Wife of the Son of	*Father*
Re	Ptolemy IX Soter
	Mother
CLEOPATRA I	Unknown
Husband	*Children*
Ptolemy V	None known
Epiphanes	*Titles*
Father	King's Sister, King's
Antiochus III of Syria	Wife, Lady of the
Sons	Two Lands
Ptolemy VI	
Philometor and	**CLEOPATRA V**
Ptolemy VIII	*Full name*
Euergetes	Cleopatra V
Daughter	Tryphaena
Cleopatra II	*Husband*
Titles	Ptolemy XII Neos
Sister-Wife of the	Dionysos (Auletes)
Son of Re, Lady of	*Father*
the Two Lands,	Ptolemy IX Soter
God's Mother	*Mother*
	Unknown
CLEOPATRA II	*Sons*
Husband	Ptolemy XIII and
Ptolemy VI	Ptolemy XIV
Philometor, Ptolemy	*Daughters*
VIII Euergetes	Berenice IV,
Sons	Cleopatra VI
Ptolemy Eupator,	Tryphaena?,
Ptolemy VII Neos	Cleopatra VII Thea
Philopator, Ptolemy	Philopator, Arsinoe IV
Memphites	*Titles*
Daughters	Lady of the Two
Cleopatra Thea,	Lands? Co-regent
Cleopatra III	with Berenice IV?
Titles	
Sister-Wife of the	**BERENICE IV**
Son of Re, Lady of	*Full name*
the Two Lands	Berenice IV
	Cleopatra
CLEOPATRA III	Epiphaneia
Husband	*Husbands*
Ptolemy VIII	Archelaus, Seleucus
Euergetes	*Father*
Father	Ptolemy XII Neos
Ptolemy VI	Dionysos (Auletes)
Philometor	*Mother*
Mother	Cleopatra V
Cleopatra II	Tryphaena
Sons	*Children*
Ptolemy IX Soter,	None known
Ptolemy X Alexander	*Titles*
Daughters	Co-ruler of Egypt
Cleopatra IV,	

ARSINOE III

Ptolemy III had been a successful, hard-working king with a loving wife; as such the royal couple had won the respect, if not the love, of their people. His son and heir, Ptolemy IV, was a very different king. Within a year of his accession he had ordered the murder of both his mother, Berenice II, and his brother, Magas. After several anxious years his long-suffering sister-wife, Arsinoe III, bore his son and successor Ptolemy V, becoming the first Ptolemaic queen to bear a child by her brother. His marital duty done, Ptolemy IV immediately turned his affections to his mistress Agathoclea, who bore him at least one child, and who almost certainly poisoned both king and queen.

CLEOPATRA I

Following the murder of his parents, the six-year-old Ptolemy V ascended the throne with the deeply unpopular Agathoclea and her brother Agathocles acting as his guardians – until, that is, brother and sister were lynched by an angry Egyptian mob determined to avenge their murdered king and queen. With the incipient rebellion quelled, the 12-year-old king was eventually crowned at Memphis, and details of his coronation were recorded in three scripts (hieroglyphic, demotic and Greek) on the bilingual Rosetta Stone.

In 194/3 BC the teenage Ptolemy V made a sensible diplomatic alliance, marrying the 10-year-old Cleopatra I, one of the three daughters of Antiochus III 'the Great' of Syria. In so doing, he weakened Rome's involvement in both Egyptian and Syrian affairs. The Syrian queen, recognized as a living goddess in Egypt, bore her husband two sons, Ptolemy VI and Ptolemy VIII, and a daughter, Cleopatra II. Cleopatra I's name was consistently associated with that of her husband – together they were 'King Ptolemy, son of Ptolemy and Arsinoe, the father-loving gods, with his sister, his wife Queen Cleopatra, the manifest gods' – and it seems that, in spite of her foreign birth, she occupied a position of both importance and respect within the royal family. When, in 180 BC, Ptolemy V was poisoned by his generals, Cleopatra's influence grew even stronger as she acted as both co-regent and guardian for her five-year-old son, Ptolemy VI (Philometor, or 'mother loving', being an element added to the young Ptolemy's name after his father's death). Now the official titulary recorded 'the kings Cleopatra the mother, the manifest goddess, and Ptolemy son of Ptolemy, the manifest king'.

CLEOPATRA II

Cleopatra I was a skilled and experienced diplomat. While she lived, Egypt sensibly showed little interest in foreign affairs. But when the queen died just four years after her husband, the nine-year-old Ptolemy VI came under the control of a most unsuitable pair of courtiers, the eunuch Eulaeus and the ex-slave and palace accountant Lenaeus. In 176 BC the pair decreed that Ptolemy VI should marry his slightly older sister Cleopatra II. The couple were to have four children: Ptolemy Eupator, Cleopatra Thea, Ptolemy VII and Cleopatra III. At the same time Eulaeus and Lenaeus declared that the kingship was to be a triumvirate, with the two young Ptolemies (VI and VIII) plus their sister named as joint kings.

Eulaeus' and Lenaeus' next move was – most unwisely – to provoke the Syrians into war. The inevitable happened. The Sixth Syrian War (170–168 BC) saw the capture of Ptolemy VI by his uncle, Antiochus IV. Egypt suffered a humiliating invasion, and only direct Roman intervention prevented Alexandria from falling to the Syrians. Antiochus had been happy to support his elder nephew as sole puppet king, ruling Egypt from Memphis. This was not, however, acceptable to the people of Alexandria, who declared Ptolemy VIII and Cleopatra II their king and queen. For a time Egypt had two rival royal courts, but the situation was untenable and, with Cleopatra mediating between her brothers, the triumvirate was resumed.

Three kings were, however, at least one too many. Both Ptolemies were determined individuals, and neither was happy to yield to the other. With his less popular brother distracted by civil unrest, Ptolemy VIII succeeded in reclaiming the throne and, as Ptolemy VI fled to Rome, ruled from his former stronghold of Alexandria alongside his sister. Such close contact allowed the people of Alexandria to see their former favourite in his true colours. Ptolemy VIII (titled Euergetes or 'Benefactor') was unflatteringly nicknamed 'Physcon' ('pot-belly'; even as a relatively young man, Ptolemy was already obese). Although intelligent and politically astute, he was perceived as cruel, vindictive and self-indulgent, and the people of Alexandria were no longer prepared to tolerate such deficiencies in their king. The mob rose against Ptolemy VIII, and Ptolemy VI was invited home to rule alongside Cleopatra II. Exiled from Egypt, Ptolemy VIII became king of Libya.

In 145 BC the popular Ptolemy VI died in battle in Syria. With her elder son Ptolemy Eupator already dead, Cleopatra II was left to raise the infant Ptolemy VII alone. This gave the ambitious Ptolemy VIII the opportunity he had been waiting for. Returning from Libya he married his widowed sister – Cleopatra II is reported to have agreed to the match to protect her son – and almost immediately murdered his young nephew. A year later Cleopatra II was mother to another heir to the Egyptian throne, Ptolemy Memphites, son of Ptolemy VIII.

Limestone head of either Cleopatra I or, more likely, Cleopatra II as *Thea Philometor Soteira*, recovered from Alexandria. The queen wears an Egyptian-style crown, but has a classical face and hairstyle. Alexandria Museum.

CLEOPATRA III

Ptolemy VIII had married Cleopatra II to reinforce his claim to the Egyptian throne and, we may suspect, as a means of exerting some control over his headstrong sister. Belatedly realizing that the birth of Memphites might encourage Cleopatra II to seek power as regent on her young son's behalf, he then chose a second wife. His young stepdaughter Cleopatra III was the obvious choice, a lady whose own Ptolemaic blood made her an acceptable queen regent and future king's mother in place of Cleopatra II. Furthermore, Cleopatra III had already proved her fertility by bearing her uncle a son, Ptolemy IX, born most fortuitously on the same day as the sacred Apis bull (18 February 142 BC). Cleopatra II, however, still had the support of the people of Alexandria. She did not accept a divorce, did not relinquish her position, and mother and daughter shared the queenship as Cleopatra the Sister and Cleopatra the Wife until the highly unpopular Ptolemy VIII was once again forced to flee Egypt, taking Cleopatra III, her two sons and three daughters with him. Once safely settled in Cyprus, he sent for his eldest son, Ptolemy Memphites.

Back in Alexandria, with the native rebellion temporarily squashed, Cleopatra II ruled alone as Cleopatra Thea Philometor Soteira ('the Mother-Loving goddess, the Saviour'). Incensed by this not entirely unexpected turn of events, Ptolemy VIII had the 12-year-old Ptolemy Memphites murdered. In a gruesome parody of the myth of Isis and Osiris, the boy's dismembered body was reportedly sent back to his mother in a precious chest.

Meanwhile, the loyal Cleopatra III, already a priestess in the hitherto entirely male cult of the deified Alexander, was rewarded with her own personal divinity. Closely connected with the ancient cult of Isis, a cult

(*Right*) On the wall of the Ptolemaic Edfu Temple of Horus, Ptolemy VIII, Cleopatra II and their son, Ptolemy Memphites, receive jubilee symbols from the ibis-headed god Thoth. Ptolemy VIII would subsequently murder his young son.

(*Opposite*) Entirely Egyptian in appearance, a conventionally svelte Ptolemy VIII Euergetes stands before one of his two wives named Cleopatra. From the East Temple at Karnak. Berlin Museum.

Ptolemy VIII stands in front of his two wives: Cleopatra II 'the sister' and her daughter, Cleopatra III 'the wife'. Temple of Sobek and Harouris (Horus the Elder), Kom Ombo.

that now extended across the Roman world, the cult of the living Cleopatra was to be served by a priest rather than a priestess. Throughout her life Cleopatra III would consistently emphasize her links with both the cult of Isis mother of Horus, and the cult of Isis mother of the Apis bull. Her own divinity, plus her association with Isis, justified her right to rule. She was not the first Ptolemy to stress the relationship between the queen and the goddess (Berenice I, Arsinoe II and Cleopatra I had each been associated with Isis), but she was the first to effectively become the living Isis in all her many forms.

In 130 BC Ptolemy VIII returned to Egypt, forcing Cleopatra II to flee to safety in Syria. Curiously, she returned to Egypt in 124, and brother and sister were reconciled. For a brief time Cleopatra II, her daughter Cleopatra III and their husband Ptolemy VIII again ruled Egypt in an uncomfortable *ménage à trois*, with Cleopatra II taking precedence over her increasingly divine daughter.

Ptolemy VIII died in 116 BC, and Cleopatra II died a few months later. This left Cleopatra III to act as regent for two sons, Ptolemy IX and Ptolemy X. By the curious – and to modern eyes inexplicable – terms of her late husband's will, she was to choose which son ultimately became king of Egypt. Now the three ruled together in complete disharmony, with first one brother then the other being forced to take refuge in Cyprus. Finally, in 107 BC, Ptolemy IX fled, accused of plotting to murder his mother – a charge which, as the younger son had always been his mother's favourite, may well have been trumped up. Cleopatra III and Ptolemy X ruled Egypt together until the 60-year-old Cleopatra III died in 101, almost certainly murdered by her favourite son.

CLEOPATRA IV AND CLEOPATRA SELENE

Ptolemy X ruled alone for a decade until the people of Alexandria, disgusted by his louche lifestyle, turned against him. He was forced to flee, leaving the throne vacant for his brother Ptolemy IX. Ptolemy IX is known to have had at least two wives, his sister Cleopatra IV followed by another sister Cleopatra Selene. Both ladies would outlive their husband, and both would meet violent deaths: Cleopatra IV brutally murdered as she clung on to the statue in the sanctuary of Apollo at Daphne, and Cleopatra Selene – who was to marry four times – executed at Seleucia. It has been suggested that Ptolemy IX was towards the end of his life also married to his daughter Berenice III, but there is little evidence to support this claim; father-daughter incest is otherwise unknown amongst the Ptolemies.

(*Below*) Berenice III shown on the rear wall of the Edfu temple. Unlike the native Egyptian queens regnant, Berenice needed a husband to confirm her right to rule.

BERENICE III

Berenice III had married Ptolemy X in 101 BC. Their joint titulary 'King Ptolemy known as Alexander, the mother loving god, and Queen Berenice his sister, his wife...' has led to some confusion; Berenice was the niece of Ptolemy X, not his sister. After the death of Ptolemy IX in 62 BC, the widowed Berenice III took her father's throne.

The native Egyptian female kings had deliberately avoided marriage – the conflict between the role of the wife and the king was simply too great. Instead, regarding the kingship as a dual entity, they had served as the 'male' element and appointed a daughter to serve as their female counterpart. The Ptolemaic kings took a different approach. They too regarded the kingship as a dual entity, but an entity that required a true male and female element. Ideally both male and female should be of Ptolemaic descent. The widowed Berenice was therefore obliged to seek a husband in order to reinforce her right to rule. Encouraged by Rome, she solved her dilemma by marrying her young stepson Ptolemy XI and making him co-regent. This proved to be a very bad move. Within three weeks of their marriage Berenice had been murdered by her husband, who was in turn lynched by the people of Alexandria 19 days later. As Egypt was left without an obvious Ptolemaic heir, the elder of the two illegitimate sons of Ptolemy IX took the throne as Ptolemy XII. To emphasize his royalty, he married his sister, Cleopatra V. Meanwhile the younger son, also named Ptolemy, became King of Cyprus.

Broken granite statue of a late Ptolemaic queen dressed in Egyptian-style clothing and a heavy tripartite wig. The single uraeus (now broken away) suggests that this may not be Cleopatra VII but is perhaps one of her immediate predecessors.

CLEOPATRA V

Ptolemy XII was widely known to his people as Auletes, 'the flute player'. The new king knew that Egypt could not hope to stand up to the military might of Rome. Only by increasing his co-operation with the enemy did he have any hope of keeping his crown. And so 8,000 members of the Egyptian cavalry fought alongside Roman troops in Palestine while, far away in Rome, the senate coffers filled with Egyptian gold. Auletes, now officially 'an ally and friend of the Roman people', and more specifically a friend of Julius Caesar, had bought Egypt a few more years of independence. But continuing independence carried a heavy price. The people of Egypt, the Alexandrians in particular, were deeply unhappy with their weak king.

Cleopatra V, sister-wife of Auletes, bore five or six children: three or four daughters – Berenice IV, the ephemeral Cleopatra VI Tryphaena, whom many experts identify with her identically named mother, Cleopatra VII and Arsinoe – followed by two sons, Ptolemy XIII and Ptolemy XIV.

BERENICE IV

In 58 BC the Romans annexed the former Egyptian province of Cyprus, driving its ruler King Ptolemy, brother of Auletes, to commit suicide. A wave of panic swept Egypt and, as the people of Alexandria once again took to the streets, Auletes fled to Rome to appeal for military aid. Throughout this drama, the younger Cleopatra remained in Alexandria under the care of her elder sister Berenice IV, who now ruled Egypt in her father's absence. Berenice was associated in her kingship with a Cleopatra Tryphaena; whether this was her ephemeral sister or her mother is not clear. Whoever she was, Queen Cleopatra soon vanished and is presumed to have died.

Berenice was a sole female ruler in need of a male consort. Ideally she would have married one of her brothers, but both were less than five years of age. Instead she married an insignificant cousin, Seleucus, only to have him strangled within a week of their wedding. Her second husband, Archelaus, lasted longer, and the couple ruled for two years with the full support of the people of Alexandria. Meanwhile Auletes, unable to convince the Romans to back him against his daughter, borrowed vast sums of money and left Rome for Ephesus, where he bribed the governor of Syria to support him. A Roman army took Alexandria in 55 BC, Archelaus was killed, and Auletes, returning home in triumph, had Berenice executed. He was to last a mere four years on his newly reclaimed throne before dying a natural death in early 51 BC. The throne then passed to his eldest surviving son and daughter – the ten-year-old Ptolemy XIII and his 17-year-old sister-wife Cleopatra VII.

Arsinoe IV
Cleopatra VII

Partially restored marble portrait head of the Greek-style Cleopatra VII, provenance unknown but likely to be from Italy. The head was probably made to be inserted into a composite, full-length statue. Berlin Museum.

CLEOPATRA VII	
Full name	*Sons*
Cleopatra VII Thea	Ptolemy Caesar,
Philopator	Alexander Helios,
Husbands	Ptolemy
Ptolemy XIII,	Philadelphus
Ptolemy XIV	*Daughter*
Lovers	Cleopatra Selene
Julius Caesar, Mark	*Titles*
Antony	Great of Sceptre,
Father	Executive at the
Ptolemy XII Neos	Head of the Two
Dionysos (Auletes)	Lands, Mistress of
Mother	Upper and Lower
Cleopatra V	Egypt
Tryphaena	

CLEOPATRA VII

Ptolemy XIII and Cleopatra VII came to the throne in 51 BC with the blessing of their people and the qualified support of the Romans who, still debating the advantages of annexing Egypt, had troops stationed within the country. The two rulers inherited a land deep in debt, and their father's extensive borrowings had yet to be repaid. Ptolemy XIII, as king, should have been the dominant partner, but the seven-year difference in their ages meant that Cleopatra naturally became the effective ruler. Her decision to give military support to the Roman general Pompey angered the Egyptians and may in part explain why Ptolemy XIII plotted to have his sister-wife killed. Warned in time, Cleopatra fled eastwards. Here she set to work raising an army to reclaim her throne from her brother. By the summer of 48 BC, armies loyal to Ptolemy and Cleopatra stood poised to fight in the Delta.

Julius Caesar

That same year Ptolemy XIII, now 15 years old, had agreed to the murder of Pompey, rival of Julius Caesar. In so doing, he hoped to win the support of the Romans for his sole claim to the throne of Egypt. When Caesar himself came to Alexandria he was presented with the pickled head of his rival. Ptolemy had, however, miscalculated. Caesar summoned both Ptolemy and Cleopatra to Alexandria, and declared his support for the queen. Meanwhile the people of Alexandria had another queen in mind. In November 48 BC, with Caesar and Cleopatra trapped in the royal palace, they proclaimed the youngest royal sister, **Arsinoe IV**, queen of Egypt.

Cleopatra and Julius Caesar spent a long winter besieged in the palace of Alexandria. Roman reinforcements did not arrive until March 47 BC, by which time the couple were both political allies and lovers. As Caesar was liberated, Ptolemy XIII fled and drowned in the Nile while Arsinoe IV, short-lived queen of Alexandria, was captured and taken to Rome. The newly widowed Cleopatra was restored to her throne with full Roman support, taking as her husband her 11-year-old brother Ptolemy XIV. The bride was already pregnant. In June 47 BC Cleopatra gave birth to a son whom she named Ptolemy Caesar (known as Caesarion) after his father. Caesar, already married to a Roman wife, was unable to recognize his Egyptian son formally. But just before his assassination he would attempt to pass legislation in Rome that would allow him the right to a second wife and a legitimate child in a foreign land.

There was certainly far more to the relationship between Caesar and Cleopatra than careless, unthinking passion. Both were experienced politicians and neither could, by any stretch of the imagination, be considered naive. Their physical union cemented their political alliance and made perfect political sense. Egypt would remain independent, yet fall under the protection of Rome. Rome would benefit from Egypt's generosity as the most fertile country in the world. Their shared interests – ambition and, of course, their child – linked them together; both could see the benefits of keeping Egypt independent for Caesarion to inherit. Confident of her loyalty to her son if not her loyalty to himself, Caesar continued to promote Cleopatra as the true ruler of Egypt, even when he himself had left the country.

In 46 BC Caesar held a triumph in Rome, a triumph that saw the deposed Arsinoe exhibited to the Roman people in chains. Cleopatra and Ptolemy XIV followed Caesar to Rome, staying for over a year on Caesar's private estate. They were therefore present to witness Caesar's dedication of a golden statue of Cleopatra in the Temple of Venus Genetrix. Only when Caesar was assassinated on the Ides of March in 44 BC did they return to Egypt. The young Ptolemy XIV conveniently died soon after their return – whether by accident or design is not now clear. With no other male heir to the throne, the three-year-old Caesarion became Ptolemy XV Theos Philopator Philomator, 'the Father- and Mother-Loving god', and Cleopatra VII remained the effective sole ruler of Egypt.

With Caesar dead, a triumvirate of Mark Antony, Octavian and Marcus Lepidus set out to capture his assassins, Brutus and Cassius. Rome was intent on public revenge, and Egypt was called upon to lend assistance. This was a matter of all-consuming importance to Cleopatra. Already the governor of Cyprus had defected to the side of the assassins and was determined to make her sister Arsinoe, now freed and living in Ephesus, queen of Egypt once again. While she lived, Arsinoe would be a constant threat to Cleopatra; it therefore comes as little surprise that she was murdered, at her sister's command, in 40 BC.

Cleopatra wisely allied herself with the triumvirate. She raised a fleet to sail to Octavian and Mark Antony, but her ships were destroyed by a

Coins of Cleopatra (*top*) and Mark Antony (*above*). Cleopatra's coinage reveals an uncompromisingly harsh profile, with prominent nose and chin.

WHAT DID CLEOPATRA LOOK LIKE?

Cleopatra is rumoured to have written a beauty book, passing her secrets on to other women, but what did she herself really look like? The classical authors are divided. Plutarch rates her as little more than averagely good looking. Cassius Dio, in contrast, ranks her amongst the world's most beautiful women, as 'brilliant to look upon and to listen to...'.

Many early art historians had a tendency to identify any woman shown holding a snake as Cleopatra VII. If these dubious identifications are ignored, we are left with surprisingly few images of Egypt's last queen. Her surviving portraits may be split into two distinct groups. The Egyptian style images, preserved in statuary and on temple walls at Dendera, depict as we might expect a traditional enigmatic queen of Egypt: tall, slender, bewigged, draped in the finest linen and wearing the double plumes, solar disk, cow's horns and uraeus of a traditional queen. Such images reveal little of the real Cleopatra, beyond her wish to be identified with the mother goddess Isis.

Cleopatra's non-Egyptian style portraiture is very different and, although we should not fall into the trap of assuming that all representations are true-to-life, they certainly appear more realistic to modern eyes. Here Cleopatra appears in the dress and hairstyle – the diadem and braided bun – of a classical matron. Her coinage shows a woman with an unfashionably prominent nose and chin. Marble busts, recovered from Rome, show the same features slightly softened, although again the queen is by no means an outstanding beauty; she looks determined rather than seductive. Maybe, then, Cleopatra's appeal lay in the charm of her voice. The historian Plutarch, who had been less than impressed by the queen's appearance, was certainly struck by her linguistic abilities:

It was a pleasure merely to hear the sound of her voice, with which, like an instrument of many strings, she could pass from one language to another, so that there were few of the barbarian nations that she answered by an interpreter....

(Above) A marble head identified as Cleopatra VII has been incorporated into this reconstructed statue, transforming the queen of Egypt into a Roman matron.

(Left) Cleopatra VII and her son, Caesarion (not pictured), are shown on the rear wall of the temple of Hathor at Dendera.

storm. While she waited for her second fleet to be made ready, news came that the assassins had been defeated. Two men now held power – Octavian (Caesar's legal heir) controlled the western empire, while Antony controlled the east. Cleopatra, extremely vulnerable in Egypt, needed a protector. For the first time her instincts failed her and she made the wrong choice: Cleopatra allied herself with Mark Antony.

CLEOPATRA AS ISIS

Cleopatra wrote her own mythology, following the lead set by Cleopatra III in exploiting the cult of the mother goddess Isis as a means of reinforcing her own role as living goddess.

This theological blurring was acceptable in Egypt, where royalty had always been associated with the divine, and where the ordinary people were effectively excluded from the worship of the state gods. If Cleopatra wanted to declare herself a living goddess, 'The New Isis' (a title which she presumably chose to distinguish her from her predecessor Cleopatra III), few Egyptians would either know or care overmuch. But in Rome, where the cult of Isis was taken very seriously, and the temples were open to everyone, Cleopatra's role as intermediary between the goddess and her people was simply unacceptable. The queen found herself in the curious position of being semi-, or maybe even fully, divine in her own country, but a mere mortal in Rome.

Gold ring engraved with a portrait of Cleopatra VII. The queen wears a tripartite wig, vulture headdress, modius with multiple uraei, sun disk and horns, and is intended to be identified with the goddess Isis. Her profile is reminiscent of the image featured on Cleopatra's coinage.

Mark Antony

Seducing – or allowing herself to be seduced by – a Roman leader had worked in the past. Cleopatra was still young, and she had no reason to assume that her tactics would not work again. She set about replicating history. Antony, less intelligent and less experienced than Caesar, soon succumbed to her charms. In 40 BC Cleopatra gave birth to his twins, Cleopatra Selene and Alexander Helios. Antony was, by the time of their birth, back in Rome, where he was about to marry Octavia, sister of his ally and arch-rival Octavian.

Rome could only have one ruler. The relationship between Octavian and Antony, and by default the relationship between Octavia and her new husband, quickly deteriorated. In 37 BC Antony left Rome for Antioch in Syria, where he sent for Cleopatra. Together they hatched a grand plan for an eastern alliance that would see Egypt restored to some of her former glory. Thanks to Antony, Egypt now re-acquired some of her lost eastern territories.

Unfortunately Antony's 36 BC Parthian campaign – the first step towards consolidating the eastern alliance – was a total disaster. Instead of capturing new lands, Antony was forced, via his estranged wife, to beg for more troops from Octavian. A derisory 2,000 soldiers were offered, and declined, and relations between the two Romans plummeted. Antony's subsequent triumph in Armenia went some way towards

Black basalt statue showing a Ptolemaic queen carrying the double cornucopia. Originally this statue was identified as Arsinoe II, but Arsinoe, in her Egyptian-style statues, favours the double uraeus first worn by Ahmose-Nefertari at the beginning of the 18th Dynasty. The triple uraeus, often interpreted as a double uraeus plus central vulture head, also appeared during the 18th Dynasty, and is favoured by Cleopatra VII. Hermitage Museum, St Petersburg.

salvaging his wounded pride. There were extensive celebrations in Alexandria, where Antony sat on a throne and paraded his sons by Cleopatra – he now had two – as kings of Rome/Egypt's conquered lands. Nothing could have been calculated to displease Octavian, and Octavia, more.

In 32 BC Octavia was repudiated. Antony and Cleopatra were now officially a couple. But as the lovers enjoyed an extended tour of the eastern Mediterranean, Octavian prepared for war. The battle of Actium was a triumph for Octavian. Antony was forced to flee while Cleopatra returned to Alexandria and started to gather her troops. When Antony joined her a few weeks later, the two were effectively trapped.

Cleopatra's offer to abdicate in favour of her children was ignored. As Antony set off to fight his last battle, the queen barricaded herself in the mausoleum that also served as her treasury. When he received news of Cleopatra's suicide, Antony fell on his sword. The news of Cleopatra's death was, however, incorrect. The dying Antony was taken back to Alexandria and hauled up the walls of the mausoleum so that he might die in Cleopatra's arms.

Cleopatra VII, last queen of Egypt, committed suicide on 12 August 30 BC. The Greek historian Cassius Dio records her passing:

No one knew for certain how she had died. They only found small pricks on her arm. Some said she brought an asp to her....[41]

Her body has never been found.

Cleopatra's children

Cleopatra's four children all survived their mother. Her eldest son, Caesarion, was now theoretically sole king of Egypt. But Caesar's son posed too great a danger to the Romans. He was caught fleeing from Egypt and executed by Octavian. The remaining children were taken to Rome where they were first displayed in a humiliating public triumph, and then given to Octavia, fourth wife of Mark Antony, to raise. In 20 BC Cleopatra Selene was married to the Numidian prince Juba II; she was to bear him a son named, of course, Ptolemy, before dying a natural death in relative obscurity. Her full brothers, Alexander and Ptolemy Philadelphus (born 36 BC), had been sent to live out of harm's way with their married sister. In Mauretania they achieved what no other member of their family had managed: dull lives far removed from the political spotlight. The young prince Ptolemy, was not so lucky. After inheriting his father's throne, he was executed by the Roman emperor Caligula in AD 40.

Basalt statue of a young-looking late Ptolemaic pharaoh, most probably Caesarion. The king wears traditional Egyptian regalia, but the hair visible beneath the *nemes* headcloth is Greek in style. Probably recovered from Karnak; now housed in Cairo Museum.

CLEOPATRA THROUGH THE AGES

Her beauty, so we are told, was not so incomparable that no one could behold her without being struck by it. But the charm of her presence was irresistible....[42]

Cleopatra VII was an intelligent woman, a competent Hellenistic ruler and a devoted mother to her four children. Today much of this is forgotten as, thanks to her many appearances on canvas, stage and screen, Cleopatra is widely recognized as the archetypal femme fatale, whose unrivalled beauty and exotic sensuality allowed her to melt the hearts of two of Rome's greatest men.

Cleopatra's parents are almost certainly brother and sister. Her grandfather, Ptolemy IX, was a man of known Greek descent. Her grandmother is described as a 'concubine', but with no further clue to her parentage or race, we cannot be certain how she, or her granddaughter Cleopatra VII, looked.

(Above) This medieval Cleopatra dies dramatically from the bites of two snakes, while beside her Mark Antony plunges a sword into his chest. The background appears entirely French. 15th-century French manuscript.

(Right) Giambattista Tiepolo in 1757 shows Cleopatra as a fair-skinned, blonde queen. Note the steep pyramid in the background. Palazzo Labia, Venice.

(Below) Elizabeth Taylor, a modern Cleopatra.

(Left) Theda Bara in the 1917 film Cleopatra, based on a novel by Rider Haggard. The film's publicity announced that Miss Bara had been born in Egypt. In fact she hailed from Cincinnati.

(Below) Lawrence Alma-Tadema (1883) shows Cleopatra reclining on her barge as she waits for her lover. The hieroglyphs accurately identify the queen. Private collection.

CHRONOLOGY AND ROYAL COUPLES LIST

This chronology is taken from that put forward by Dr Bill Manley and used by him in *The Seventy Great Mysteries of Ancient Egypt* (2003), which he edited. All dates are BC.

THE EARLY DYNASTIC PERIOD (*c.* 3100–2650 BC)

Naqada 3/Dynasty 0 (*c.* 3100)
Various simultaneous local kings; no recorded queens

Dynasty 1 (*c.* 2950–2775)
Narmer = ? = **Neithhotep**
Aha = ? = **Benerib, Khenthap**
Djer = ? = **Herneith**
Djet = ? = **Meritneith**
Den = ? = **Seshemetka, Semat, Serethor**
Anedjib = ? = **Batirytes**
Semerkhet = ?
Qaa = ?

Dynasty 2 (*c.* 2750–2650)
Hotepsekhemwy = ?
Reneb/Nebre = ?
Nynetjer = ?
Weneg = ?
Sened = ?
Peribsen = ?
Khasekhemwy == **Nimaathap**

THE OLD KINGDOM (*c.* 2650–2125)

Dynasty 3 (*c.* 2650–2575)
Djoser = = **Hetephernebty**
Sekhemkhet = ?
Khaba = ?
Huni = ?

Dynasty 4 (*c.* 2575–2450)
Snefru = = **Hetepheres I**
Khufu = = **Henutsen, Meritetes**
Djedefre = = **Khentetka, Hetepheres II**?
Khafre = = **Meresankh III, Khamerernebty I? Persenet? Hekenuhedjet?**

Menkaure = = **Khamerernebty II**
Shepseskaf = ? = **Bunefer**

Dynasty 5 (*c.* 2450–2325)
Userkaf = ? = **Khentkawes I**
Sahure = = **Neferethanebty**
Neferirkare = = **Khentkawes II**
Shepseskare = ?
Neferefre = ?
Nyuserre = = **Reptynub**
Menkauhor = = **Meresankh IV**
Djedkare = ?
Unas = = **Nebet, Khenut**

Dynasty 6 (*c.* 2325–2175)
Teti = = **Iput I, Khuit**
Userkare = ?
Pepi I = = **'Weret-Yamtes', Nebwenet, Inenek-Inti, Meritetes, Ankhnespepi I, Ankhnespepi II, Nedjeftet**
Pepi II = = **Neith, Wedjebten, Iput II, Ankhnespepi III, Ankhnespepi IV**
Merenre I = ?
Nitocris

Dynasties 7 & 8 (*c.* 2175–2125)
A confused series of kings named Neferkare

THE FIRST INTERMEDIATE PERIOD (*c.* 2125–2010)

Dynasties 9 & 10 (*c.* 2125–1975)
A series of local rulers based at Herakleopolis

Dynasty 11 (Theban rule) (*c.* 2080–2010)
A series of local kings including Mentuhotep I, Intef I, Intef II and Intef III, based at Thebes

THE MIDDLE KINGDOM (*c.* 2010–1630)

Dynasty 11 (National rule) (*c.* 2010–1938)
Mentuhotep II = = **Nefru II, Tem, Henhenet, Sadeh, Ashayt, Kawit? Kemsit?**
Mentuhotep III = ? = **Imi**
Mentuhotep IV = ?

Dynasty 12 (*c.* 1938–1755)
Amenemhat 1 = = **Neferitatjenen**

Senusret I = = **Nefru III**
Amenemhat II = ?
Senusret II = = **Khnemetneferhedjet I, Nefret, Itaweret, Khnemet**
Senusret III = = **Sithathoriunet, Mertseger, Khnemetneferhedjet II**
Amenemhat III = = **Aat, Hetepti?**
Amenemhat IV = ? = **Sobeknefru**
Sobeknefru

Dynasties 13 & 14 (*c.* 1755–1630)
A confused series of local rulers

THE SECOND INTERMEDIATE PERIOD (*c.* 1630–1539)

Dynasty 15 (*c.* 1630–1520)
Foreign Hyksos rulers based in the Delta, amongst whom:
Apepi = ? = **Tany** (the only recorded queen)

Dynasty 16
Numerous ephemeral kings

Dynasty 17 (*c.* 1630–1539)
A series of Theban rulers culminating with:
Senakhtenre Taa I = = **Tetisheri**
Seqenenre Taa II = = **Ahhotep I, Inhapy, Sitdjehuty**
Kamose = ? = **Ahhotep II**

THE NEW KINGDOM (*c.* 1539–1069)

Dynasty 18 (*c.* 1539–1292)
Ahmose = = **Ahmose-Nefertari, Ahmose-Nebta**
Amenhotep I = = **Meritamun**
Thutmose I = = **Ahmose**
Thutmose II = = **Hatshepsut**
Hatshepsut
Thutmose III = = **Sitiah, Meritre-Hatshepsut, Nebtu, Manuwai, Manhata, Maruta**
Amenhotep II = = **Tia**
Thutmose IV = = **Nefertari, 'Iaret', Mutemwia**
Amenhotep III = = **Tiy, Sitamun, Isis? Henuttaneb? Gilukhepa, Tadukhepa**
Amenhotep IV/Akhenaten = = **Nefertiti, Kiya**
Smenkhkare = = **Meritaten**
Tutankhamun = = **Ankhesenamun**
Ay = = **Tiy**
Horemheb = = **Mutnodjmet**

Dynasty 19 (c. 1292–1190)

Ramesses I = = **Sitre**
Seti I = = **Tuya**
Ramesses II = = **Henutmire, Nefertari,**
 Isetnofret I, Bintanath I,
 Meritamun, Nebettawi,
 Maathornefrure
Merenptah = = **Isetnofret II,**
 Bintanath II
Amenmesse = ? = **Baketwernel I**
Seti II = = **Takhat, Tawosret**
Siptah = ?
Tawosret

Dynasty 20 (c. 1190–1069)

Sethnakhte = = **Tiy-Merenese**
Ramesses III = = **Iset Ta-Hemdjert, Tiy**
Ramesses IV = ? = **Tentopet**
Ramesses V = = **Henuttawi,**
 Tawerettenru
Ramesses VI = = **Nubkhesbed, Isis**
Ramesses VII = ?
Ramesses VIII = ?
Ramesses IX = ? = **Baketwernel**
Ramesses X = ? = **Titi**
Ramesses XI = = **Tentamun**

THE THIRD INTERMEDIATE PERIOD (c. 1069–657)

High Priests of Amun (Thebes)
Piankh = = **Nodjmet**
Herihor = = **Nodjmet** (again)
Pinedjem I = = **Henttawy**
Pinedjem II = = **Nesikhonsu,**
 Isetemkheb III
Psusennes 'III' = ?

Dynasty 21 (Tanis) (c. 1069–945)

Smendes = = **Tentamun**
Amenemnisu = ?
Psusennes I = = **Mutnodjmet, Wiay**
Amenemope = ?
Osorkon the Elder (Osochor) = ?
Siamun = ?
Psusennes II = ?

Dynasty 22 (c. 945–715)

Shoshenq I = = **Karomama I,**
 Penreshnes
Osorkon I = = **Maatkare,**
 Tashedkhonsu
Shoshenq II = = **Nesitanebetashru**
Takelot I = = **Kapes**
Osorkon II = = **Isetemkheb IV,**
 Djedmutesankh, Karomama II

Shoshenq III = = **Tadibast,**
 Tentamenopet, Djedbastiusankh
Shoshenq IV = ?
Pimay = ?
Shoshenq V = ?
Pedubast II = ?
Osorkon IV = ?

Dynasty 23 (c. 830–715)

*A line of Libyan kings ruling parallel
to the 22nd Dynasty*

Dynasty 24 (730–715)

Tefnakht = ?
Bakenrenef (Bocchoris) = ?

Dynasty 25 (Nubia) (c. 800–657)

Piye = = **Tabiry, Abar, Khensa,**
 Peksater
Shabaka = = **Qalhata**
Shebitku = = **Arty**
Taharqa = = **Atakhebasken,**
 Tabekenamun, Naparaye,
 Takahatamun
Tantamani = = **Piankharty**

THE LATE PERIOD (664–332)

Dynasty 26 (Sais) (664–525)

Psamtik I = = **Mehytenweskhet**
Necho II = = **Khedebneithirbinet I**
Psamtik II = = **Takhuit**
Apries = ?
Amasis = = **Nakhtubasterau,**
 Tentkheta
Psamtik III = ?

Dynasty 27 (Persia) (525–404)

*Egypt, ruled by Persian kings, is
effectively without a queen*

Dynasty 28 (404–399)

Amyrtaeus = ?

Dynasty 29 (399–380)

Nefarud (Nepherites) I = ?
Psammuthis = ?
Hakor = ?
Nefarud (Nepherites) II = ?

Dynasty 30 (380–343)

Nectanebo I = ?
Teos = ?
Nectanebo II = = **Khedebneithirbinet II**

Dynasty 31 (Persia) (343–332)

*Egypt, ruled by Persian kings, is again
effectively without a queen*

THE MACEDONIAN AND PTOLEMAIC PERIODS (332–30)

Alexander III (the Great) = = **Roxane,**
 Stateira, Parysatis, Barsine
Philip Arrhidaeus = = **Eurydice**
Alexander IV = ?
Ptolemy I = = **Thais, Artakama,**
 Eurydice, Berenice I
Ptolemy II = = **Arsinoe I, Arsinoe II**
Ptolemy III = = **Berenice II**
Ptolemy IV = = **Arsinoe III**
Ptolemy V = = **Cleopatra I**
Ptolemy VI = = **Cleopatra II**
Ptolemy VIII = = **Cleopatra II** (again),
 Cleopatra III
Ptolemy IX = = **Cleopatra IV,**
 Cleopatra Selene
Ptolemy X = = **Berenice III**
Ptolemy IX (restored) = ?
Berenice III (again) = = Ptolemy XI
Ptolemy XII = = **Cleopatra V**
Berenice IV = = Seleucus, Archelaus
Ptolemy XII (restored)
Ptolemy XIII = = **Cleopatra VII**
Arsinoe IV
Ptolemy XIV = = **Cleopatra VII** (again)
Cleopatra VII (again) and Ptolemy XV
 (Caesarion)

(pp. 210–211) Photograph showing the
Sacred Lake at Karnak, with
Hatshepsut's obelisk in the centre.

NOTES

1 Herodotus, *Histories* Book II: 35. Translated by A. de Selincourt, revised with Introduction and Notes by A. R. Burn, London, 1983.

2 Petrie, W. M. F., 1931. *Seventy Years in Archaeology* 175.

3 Recipes included in the 18th Dynasty 'Ebers Medical Papyrus'.

4 Verner, M., 2002. *The Pyramids: Their Archaeology and History*. London: 370.

5 Herodotus, *Histories* Book II: 100. Translated by A. de Selincourt, revised with Introduction and Notes by A. R. Burn, London, 1983.

6 From the Middle Kingdom 'Satire of the Trades'. The scribe is here attempting to dissuade his young readers from becoming hairdressers.

7 Recipe included in the 'Ebers Medical Papyrus'.

8 From the Instruction of King Amenemhat I for his son Senusret I; for a full translation of this text consult Lichtheim, M., 1975. *Ancient Egyptian Literature* 135–39.

9 Petrie, W. M. F., 1931. *Seventy Years in Archaeology* 232–33.

10 Adapted from Tyldesley, J., 2004. *Tales from Ancient Egypt* 99.

11 Advice offered to schoolboys by the Old Kingdom scribe Ptahhotep. For a full translation of this Wisdom Text see Lichtheim, M., 1973. *Ancient Egyptian Literature*. Berkeley: 61–80.

12 After Peden, A. J., 1994. *Egyptian Historical Documents of the 20th Dynasty* 245–57. Jonsered: Astrom.

13 Davies, W. V., 1984. *The Statuette of Queen Tetisheri: A Reconsideration*. British Museum Occasional Papers 36.

14 Private correspondence quoted in Winlock, H. E., 1924. 'Tombs of the Kings of the Seventeenth Dynasty at Thebes', *Journal of Egyptian Archaeology* 10: 217–77: 253.

15 From the story of Horus and Seth, *Papyrus Chester Beatty I*, translation after Lichtheim, M., 1976. *Ancient Egyptian Literature II: The New Kingdom*. Berkeley: 216.

16 From the tomb of Ineni (TT 81).

17 Naville, E., 1896. *The Temple of Deir el-Bahari, Vol. 2*. London: 17.

18 Gardiner, A., 1946. 'The Great Speos Artemidos Inscription', *Journal of Egyptian Archaeology* 32: 43–56; 47–48.

19 Amarna Letter EA 26.

20 Smith, G. E., 1912. *The Royal Mummies*. Cairo: 38.

21 The *Benben* stone was a pyramid-shaped cult object associated with sun worship.

22 Filer, J. M., 2002. 'Anatomy of a Mummy', *Archaeology*. March/April 2002, 26–29.

23 From the Old Kingdom 'Instruction Addressed to Kagemni'.

24 Translation based on H. G. Guterbock, as quoted in Schulman, A. R., 1978. 'Ankhesenamen, Nofretity and the Amka Affair', *Journal of the American Research Center in Egypt*. 15: 43–48.

25 Kitchen, K. A., 1996. *Ramesside Inscriptions Translated and Annotated, Vol. 2: Ramesses II, Royal Inscriptions*. Oxford: 99–110.

26 Inscription carved in Seti's Abydos temple. For a full translation and discussion of this text consult Murnane, W. J., 1977. *Ancient Egyptian Coregencies*. Chicago: 58.

27 For details of the letters sent from the Egyptian royal family to Hatti, see Edel, E., 1994. *Die Ägyptisch Hethitische Korrespondenz aus Boghazkoi I–III*. Opladen.

28 Thomas, E., 1977. 'Cairo Ostracon J.72460', *Studies in Ancient Oriental Civilization* 39: 209–16.

29 *Papyrus Salt 124*; quoted in Tyldesley, J. A., 2001. *Egypt's Golden Empire*. London: 252.

30 Suggested in Dodson, A. & Hilton, D., 2004. *The Complete Royal Families of Ancient Egypt*. London & New York: 191.

31 Leading Dodson & Hilton to suggest that this statue was originally carved for Seti II, then usurped by Amenmesse who altered the king's inscription but did not bother to change his mother's, then finally reclaimed by Seti II: Dodson, A. &

Hilton, D., 2004. *The Complete Royal Families of Ancient Egypt*. London & New York: 180.

32 Smith, G. E., 1912. *The Royal Mummies*. Cairo: 82.

33 Translation based on that given in Goedicke, H., 1963. 'Was magic used in the harem conspiracy against Ramesses III?', *Journal of Egyptian Archaeology* 49: 71–92.

34 Advice offered to schoolboys by the Old Kingdom scribe Ptahhotep, the New Kingdom scribe Ani and the Late Period scribe Ankhsheshonq. All three Wisdom Texts are to be found in full translation in Lichtheim, M., 1973–80. *Ancient Egyptian Literature* 3 Vols. Berkeley.

35 Smith, G. E., 1912. *The Royal Mummies*. Cairo: 100–01.

36 Tyldesley, J. A., 2004. *Tales from Ancient Egypt*. Bolton: 156.

37 I Kings 11:3.

38 Translation after Mysliwiec, K., 2000. *The Twilight of Egypt*. New York: 113–14.

39 Details of Nitocris' death recorded on a stela now housed in Cairo Museum.

40 Herodotus, *Histories* Book II: 181. Translated by A. de Selincourt, revised with Introduction and Notes by A. R. Burn, 1983.

41 Cassius Dio, *Roman History*. Translated by Earnest Cary, based on the version by Herbert Baldwin Foster, Cambridge, Mass., 1968.

42 Plutarch, *Life of Antony*, chap. 27.

SELECT BIBLIOGRAPHY AND ACKNOWLEDGMENTS

I have attempted to include all the important source material, but this bibliography should be regarded as a starting point only. All the works cited include their own, more extensive bibliographies which the reader is urged to consult.

The books listed below are a mixture of the old and the new. The older publications are mainly site reports and syntheses; they are important, sometimes groundbreaking, and are often charming to read, but they do contain many of the errors and assumptions of their times. The more recent publications contain the more up-to-date understandings and analyses, and include extensive bibliographies.

Aldred, C., 1974. *Akhenaten and Nefertiti*. London: Thames & Hudson

Aldred, C., 1980. *Egyptian Art*. London & New York: Thames & Hudson

Aldred, C., 1988. *Akhenaten, King of Egypt*. London & New York: Thames & Hudson

Allen, J. P., 1994. 'Nefertiti and Smenkh-ka-re', *Göttinger Miszellen* 141: 7–17

Arnold, D., 1979. *The Temple of Mentuhotep at Deir el-Bahari*. New York: Metropolitan Museum of Art

Arnold, D., 1996. *The Royal Women of Amarna: Images of Beauty from Ancient Egypt*. New York: Metropolitan Museum of Art

Arnold, D. & Ziegler, C. (eds), 1999. *Egyptian Art in the Age of the Pyramids*. New York: Metropolitan Museum of Art

Ashton, S.-A., 2003. *The Last Queens of Egypt*. London & New York: Longman

Baines, J. & Malek, J., 2000. *Atlas of Ancient Egypt*. Oxford & New York: Facts on File

Bianchi, R. S., 1992. *In the Tomb of Nefertari: Conservation of the Wall Paintings, 43–45*. Santa Monica: J. Paul Getty Museum Publications

Bryan, B. M.,1997 (A. K. Capel & G. E. Markoe eds). *Mistress of the House, Mistress of Heaven: Women in Ancient Egypt*. New York: Hudson Hills Press

De Buck, A., 1937. 'The Judicial Papyrus of Turin', *Journal of Egyptian Archaeology* 23: 2: 152–64

Christophe, L. A.,1965. 'Les temples d'Abou Simbel et la famille de Rameses II', *Bulletin de l'Institut d'Egypte* 38: 118

Clayton, P. A., 1994. *Chronicle of the Pharaohs*. London & New York: Thames & Hudson

Corzo, M. A. & Afshar, M. (eds), 1993. *Art and Eternity: The Nefertari Wall Paintings Conservation Project 1986–92*. Los Angeles: Getty Conservation Institute

Corzo, M. A. (ed.), 1987. *Wall Paintings of the Tomb of Nefertari: Scientific Studies for their Conservation, 54–57*. Joint Project of the Egyptian Antiquities Organization & Getty Conservation Institute

Cruz-Uribe, E., 1977. 'On the wife of Merenptah', *Göttinger Miszellen* 24: 23–29

Davies, N. de G., 1905. *The Rock Tombs of el-Amarna*. London: Egypt Exploration Society

Davies, W. V., 1984. 'The statuette of Queen Tetisheri: a reconsideration', *British Museum Occasional Papers* 36

Davis, T. M. *et al.*, 1910. *The Tomb of Queen Tiyi* (reprinted 2001, London: Duckworth)

Desroches Noblecourt, C., 1963. *Tutankhamen: Life and Death of a Pharaoh*. London: Michael Joseph

Desroches Noblecourt, C., 1985. *The Great Pharaoh Ramesses II and his Time*, translated by E. Mialon. Montreal: Ville de Montreal.

Desroches Noblecourt, C., 1991. 'Abou Simbel, Ramses, et les dames de la couronne', in Bleiberg and R. Freed (eds), *Fragments of a Shattered Visage: the Proceedings of the International Symposium on Ramesses the Great, 127–48*. Memphis: Memphis State University

Desroches Noblecourt, C. & Kuentz, C., 1968. *Le Petit Temple d'Abou Simbel: 'Nofretari pour qui se leve le Dieu-Soleil'*, 2 Vols. Cairo: CDEAE

Diodorus Siculus. *Bibliotheca Historica* (translated by C. H. Oldfather & C. L. Sherman), 1933–67. Cambridge MA: Loeb Classical Library

Dodson, A. M., 1997/8. 'The so-called Tomb of Osiris at Abydos', *KMT* 8: 4, 37–47

Dodson, A. M. & Hilton, D., 2004. *The Complete Royal Families of Ancient Egypt*. London & New York: Thames & Hudson

Dorman, P. F., 1991. *The Tombs of Senenmut*. New York: Metropolitan Museum of Art

Emery, W. B., 1961. *Archaic Egypt*. London: Penguin

Ertman, E. L., 1992. 'Is there visual evidence for a "king" Nefertiti?', *Amarna Letters* 2: 50–55

Fay, B., 1998. 'Royal women as represented in sculpture', in N. Grimal (ed.), *Les Critères de Datation Stylistiques à l'Ancien Empire, 159–69*. Cairo: IFAO

Freed, R. E., 1987. *Ramesses the Great: His Life and World*. Memphis: St Lukes Press

Freed, R. E. *et al.*, 1999. *Pharaohs of the Sun: Akhenaten, Nefertiti, Tutankhamen*. London: Thames & Hudson; Boston: Bulfinch Press

Gardiner, A. H., 1961. *Egypt of the Pharaohs*. Oxford: Clarendon Press

Gitton, M., 1975. *L'épouse du Dieu Ahmes Néfertary*. Paris: Belles Lettres (Annales Littéraires de l'Université de Besançon)

Goedicke, H., 1963. 'Was magic used in the harem conspiracy against Ramesses III?', *Journal of Egyptian Archaeology*, 49: 71–92

Grajetzki, W., 2005. *Ancient Egyptian Queens: a Hieroglyphic Dictionary*. London: Golden House Publications

Grandet, P., 1993. *Ramses III: Histoire*

d'un Règne. Paris: Pygmalion

Green, L., 1992. 'Queen as goddess: the religious role of royal women in the late-eighteenth dynasty', *Amarna Letters* I: 28–41

Habachi, L., 1969. 'La Reine Touy, femme de Sethi I, et ses proches parents inconnus', *Revue d'Egyptologie* 21: 27–47

Hari, R., 1965. *Horemheb et la Reine Moutnedjemet*. Geneva: Imprimerie la Sirène

Hari, R., 1976. 'La reine d'Horemheb était-elle la sœur de Nefertiti?', *Chronique d'Egypte* 51: 39–46

Hari, R., 1979. 'Mout-Nofretari épouse de Ramses II: une descendent de l'heretique Ai?', *Aegyptus* 59: 3–7

Harris, J. R., 1973a. 'Nefernefruaten', *Göttinger Miszellen* 4: 15–17

Harris, J. R., 1973b. 'Nefertiti Rediviva', *Acta Orientalia* 35: 5–13

Harris, J. R., 1974. 'Nefernefruaten Regnans', *Acta Orientalia* 36: 11–21

Harris, J. E. *et al.*, 1978. 'Mummy of the "Elder Lady" in the tomb of Amunhotep II', *Science* 200: 9: 1149–51

Hawass, Z., 2006. *The Royal Tombs of Egypt: the Art of Thebes Revealed*. London & New York: Thames & Hudson

Herodotus, *The Histories*, translated by A. de Selincourt, revised with Introduction and Notes by A. R. Burn, 1983. London: Penguin

Hoffman, M., 1980. *Egypt Before the Pharaohs*. London: Routledge

Ikram, S. & Dodson, A., 1998. *The Mummy in Ancient Egypt*. London & New York: Thames & Hudson

James, T. G. H. (ed.), 2000. *Tutankhamun: The Eternal Splendour of the Boy Pharaoh*. London: I. B. Tauris

Janssen, J. J., 1988. 'Marriage problems and public reactions', in J. Baines *et al.* (eds), *Pyramid Studies and Other Essays Presented to I. E. S. Edwards*, 134–37. London: Egypt Exploration Society

Janssen, J. J., 1963. 'La Reine Nefertari et la succession de Rameses II par Merenptah', *Chronique d'Egypte* 38: 75: 30–36

Kemp, B. J., 1967. 'The Egyptian 1st Dynasty royal cemetery', *Antiquity* 41: 22–32

Kemp, B. J., 2005. *Ancient Egypt: Anatomy of a Civilization*. 2nd ed. London: Routledge

El-Khouly, A. & Martin, G. T., 1984. *Excavations in the Royal Necropolis at El-Amarna*. Cairo: IFAO (L'Institut Français d'Archéologie Orientale)

Kitchen, K. A., 1983. *Pharaoh Triumphant: the Life and Times of Ramesses II*. Warminster: Aris & Phillips

Kitchen, K. A., 1996. *The Third Intermediate Period in Egypt (1100–650 BC)*. 3rd ed. Warminster: Aris & Phillips

Kitchen, K. A. & Gaballa, G. A., 1968. 'Ramesside Varia', *Chronique d'Egypte* 43: 251–70

Kozloff, A. P. & Bryan, B. M., 1992. *Egypt's Dazzling Sun: Amenhotep III and his World*. Cleveland: Cleveland Museum of Art

Labrousse, A., 1999. *Les Pyramides des Reines: une Nouvelle Nécropole à Saqqara*. Paris: Hazan

Lauer, J.-P., 1976. *Saqqara: the Royal Cemetery of Memphis. Excavations and Discoveries since 1850*. London & New York: Thames & Hudson

Leblanc, C., 1986. 'Henout-Taouy et la tombe no. 73 de la Vallee des Reines', *Bulletin de l'Institut Français d'Archéologie Orientale* 86: 203–26

Leblanc, C., 1988. 'L'identification de la tombe de Honout-mi-Re, fille de Ramses II et Grande Épouse royale', *Bulletin de l'Institut Français d'Archéologie Orientale* 88: 131–46

Leblanc, C., 1993. 'Isis-Nofret, Grande Épouse de Ramses II, la reine, sa famille', *Bulletin de l'Institut Français d'Archéologie Orientale* 93: 313–33

Lehner, M., 1985. *The Pyramid Tomb of Hetepheres and the Satellite Pyramid of Khufu*. Mainz: von Zabern

Lehner, M., 1997. *The Complete Pyramids*. London & New York: Thames & Hudson.

Lichtheim, M., 1973–80. *Ancient Egyptian Literature*, 3 Vols.

Berkeley: University of California Press

Lilyquist, C., 2003. *The Tomb of Three Foreign Wives of Tuthmosis III*. New York: Metropolitan Museum of Art

Loeben, C. E., 1986. 'Eine Bestrattung der grossen Königlichen Gemahlin Nofretete in Amarna,' *Mitteilungen des Deutschen Archäologischen Instituts Abteilung Kairo* 42: 99–107

Luban, M., 1999. *Do We Have The Mummy of Nefertiti?* www.geocities.com/scribelist/do_we_have.htm

Manniche, L., 1987. *Sexual Life in Ancient Egypt*. London & New York: Kegan Paul

Martin, G. T., 1905. *The Royal Tomb at el-Amarna I: the Objects*. London: Egypt Exploration Society

Mertz, B., 1978. *Red Land, Black Land: Daily Life in Ancient Egypt*. New York: Dodd, Mead & Co.

Moran, W. L., 1992. *The Amarna Letters*. Baltimore & London: Johns Hopkins University Press

Mysliwiec, K., 2000. *The Twilight of Ancient Egypt: First Millennium BCE*. New York: Cornell University Press

Naville, E., 1895–1908. *The Temple of Deir el-Bahari*, 7 Vols. London: Egypt Exploration Society

O'Connor, D. & Silverman, D. (eds), 1995. *Ancient Egyptian Kingship*. Leiden: Brill

Partridge, R. B., 1994. *Faces of Pharaohs: Royal Mummies and Coffins from Ancient Thebes*. London: Rubicon

Peden, A. J., 1994. *Egyptian Historical Documents of the 20th Dynasty* 245–57. Jonsered: Astrom

Petrie, W. M. F., 1900. *The Royal Tombs of the First Dynasty I*. London: Egypt Exploration Society

Petrie, W. M. F., 1901. *The Royal Tombs of the First Dynasty II*. London: Egypt Exploration Society

Piacentini, P., 1990. *L'autobiografia di Uni, principe e governatore dell'alto Egitto*. Pisa: Giardini Editori e Stampatori

Ratie, S., 1979. *La Reine Hatchepsout:*

Sources et Problèmes. Leiden: Brill

Ray, J., 1975. 'The parentage of Tutankhamun', *Antiquity* 49: 45–47

Redford, D. B., 1968. *History and Chronology of the Eighteenth Dynasty: Seven Studies*. Toronto: University of Toronto Press

Redford, D. B., 1984. *Akhenaten: the Heretic King*. Princeton: Princeton University Press

Redford, D. B., (ed.), 2000. *The Oxford Encyclopedia of Ancient Egypt*. Oxford & New York: Oxford University Press

Redford, S., 2002. *The Harem Conspiracy: the Murder of Ramesses III*. Illinois: Northern Illinois University Press

Reeves, C. N., 1988. 'New light on Kiya from texts in the British Museum', *Journal of Egyptian Archaeology* 74: 91–101

Reeves, C. N., 1990. *The Complete Tutankhamun: the King, the Tomb, the Royal Treasure*. London & New York: Thames & Hudson

Reeves, C. N., 2000. *Ancient Egypt: the Great Discoveries*. London & New York: Thames & Hudson

Reeves, C. N., 2001. *Akhenaten: Egypt's False Prophet*. London & New York: Thames & Hudson

Reeves, C. N., & Wilkinson, R. H., 1996. *The Complete Valley of the Kings*. London & New York: Thames & Hudson.

Reisner, G. A. & Smith, W. S., 1955. *A History of the Giza Necropolis II: the Tomb of Hetepheres the Mother of Cheops*. Cambridge MA: Harvard University Press

Reisner, G. A., 1927. 'Hetepheres, mother of Cheops', *Boston Museum Bulletin*, supplement to Vol. 30

Roberts, A.,1995. *Hathor Rising: the Serpent Power of Ancient Egypt*. Totnes: Northgate Publishers

Robins, G., 1983. 'A critical examination of the theory that the right to the throne of Egypt passed through the female line in the 18th Dynasty', *Göttinger Miszellen* 62: 68–69

Robins, G., 1984. 'Isis, Nephthys, Selket and Neith represented on the sarcophagus of Tutankhamun and in four free-standing statues found in KV 62', *Göttinger Miszellen* 72: 21–25

Robins, G., 1993. *Women in Ancient Egypt*. London: British Museum Press

Samson, J., 1987. *Nefertiti and Cleopatra: Queen-Monarchs of Ancient Egypt*. London: Rubicon

Schaden, O. J., 1992. 'The God's Father Ay', *Amarna Letters* 2: 92–115

Schulman, A. R., 1978. 'Ankhesenamun, Notretity and the Amka Affair', *Journal of the American Research Center in Egypt* 15: 43–48

Smith, G. E., 1912. *The Royal Mummies* (reprinted 2000, London: Duckworth)

Smith, W. S., revised by W. K. Simpson 1999. *The Art and Architecture of Ancient Egypt*. London & New Haven, CT: Yale University Press

Snape, S. R., 1985. 'Ramose restored: a royal prince and his mortuary cult', *Journal of Egyptian Archaeology* 71: 180–83

Sourouzian, H., 1989. *Les Monuments de Roi Merenptah*. Mainz: von Zabern

Sourouzian, H., 1983. 'Henout-mi-Re, fille de Rameses II et grande épouse de roi', *Annales du Service des Antiquités d'Egypte* 69: 365–71

Trigger, B. G. *et al.*, 1983. *Ancient Egypt: a Social History*. Cambridge: Cambridge University Press

Troy, L., 1979. 'Ahhotep: a source evaluation', *Göttinger Miszellen* 35: 81–91

Troy, L., 1986. *Patterns of Queenship in Ancient Egyptian Myth and History*. Uppsala: Acta Universitatis Upsaliensis

Tyldesley, J. A., 1994. *Daughters of Isis: Women of Ancient Egypt*. London: Penguin

Tyldesley, J. A., 1996. *Hatchepsut: the Female Pharaoh*. London: Penguin

Tyldesley, J. A., 2005. *Nefertiti: Egypt's Sun Queen*. 2nd ed. London: Penguin

Verner, M., 1985. *Abusir III: the Pyramid Complex of Khentkaus*. Prague: Academia

Verner, M., 2002. *The Pyramids: their Archaeology and History*. London: Atlantic Books; New York: Grove Press

Waddell, W. G., 1948. *Manetho*. Cambridge MA: Loeb Classical Library

Walker, S. & Ashton, S.-A. (eds), 2003. *Cleopatra Reassessed*. London: British Museum Press

Watterson, B., 1994. *Women in Ancient Egypt*. Stroud: Sutton Publishing; New York: Palgrave Macmillan

Weeks, K. R., 2001. *Valley of the Kings: the Tombs and the Funerary Temples of Thebes West*. Vercelli, Italy: White Star

Whitehorne, J., 1994. *Cleopatras*. London & New York: Routledge

Wilkinson, T. A. H., 1999. *Early Dynastic Egypt*, London: Routledge

Winlock, H. E., 1924. 'Tombs of the Kings of the Seventeenth Dynasty at Thebes', *Journal of Egyptian Archaeology* 10: 217–77

Acknowledgments

My thanks go to Steven Snape, Richard H. Wilkinson for information concerning recent work at the temple of Tawosret, Aidan Dodson and Wolfram Grajetzki for their invaluable help and advice, and Colin Ridler, Melissa Danny, Rowena Alsey, Celia Falconer and Sally Nicholls at Thames & Hudson. All hieroglyphs created with VisualGlyph by Wolfram Grajetzki.

ILLUSTRATION CREDITS

INDEX

Page numbers in *italic* refer to illustrations

(gd) god; (gds) goddess; (k) king; (fk) female king; (q) queen